365
Ways to Cook

FIREFLY BOOKS

A FIREFLY BOOK

Published by Firefly Books Ltd. 2011

First printing

Publisher Cataloging-in-Publication Data (U.S.)
     365 ways to cook : delicious variations on favorite foods /
Elanor Maxfield, editor.
[256] p. : col. photos. ; cm.
Includes index.
Summary: Everyday ingredients are organized into seven chapters
that cover: poultry; meat; fish and seafood; vegetables; pizza,
pasta and noodles; rice, dried beans and grains; and desserts.
ISBN-13: 978-1-55407-916-2
1. Cooking. I. Maxfield, Elanor. II. Title.
641.5 dc22   TX714.T574   2011

Library and Archives Canada Cataloguing in Publication
     365 ways to cook : delicious variations on favorite foods /
Eleanor Maxfield, editor.
Includes index.
ISBN 978-1-55407-916-2
     1. Cooking. 2. Cookbooks. I. Maxfield, Eleanor II. Title:
Three hundred and sixty-five ways to cook.
TX714.T47 2011   641.5   C2011-903191-4

Published in the United States by
Firefly Books (U.S.) Inc.
P.O. Box 1338, Ellicott Station
Buffalo, New York 14205

Published in Canada by
Firefly Books Ltd.
66 Leek Crescent
Richmond Hill, Ontario L4B 1H1

Printed in China

CONTENTS

COOK IT YOUR WAY...

We have changed the way we order food. You only need to walk into your local coffee shop to witness a whole new language of customization: you can order a basic filtered coffee a hundred different ways based on perimeters such as time, taste and dietary needs. We've even adopted the same habits at home. We'd all love to sit down for a family meal or dinner party where everyone wants exactly the same thing, but, in reality, life sometimes isn't that simple.

365 Ways to Cook not only offers you hundreds of enticing, delicious recipes, but it also helps you to customize your food, creating dishes just the way you like them.

If you're used to catering for everyone (someone who's vegetarian, someone who's on a diet, someone who wants an impressive sit-down meal and someone who saunters in long after dinner's been served to raid the refrigerator for leftovers), then this is the cookbook to make life easier. Alternatively, if you want to cook a special dinner just for yourself then you'll find the perfect dish to match your mood.

This book is based on a realistic everyday way of cooking so there's no need to feel intimidated or overwhelmed in the kitchen again. Simply open your refrigerator, see what's in there, gauge what type of meal you fancy and look up the recipe. Start with a core ingredient, such as a chicken breast or a package of noodles, master a basic way to cook it and then choose from nine more recipes, using the handy symbols to fit the occasion.

For example, you may have salmon fillets in the freezer, but only half an hour to spare. Or perhaps you've suddenly remembered you've got friends coming round for dinner and need to create something impressive. Maybe you need to know how to create a healthy supper that the kids will actually eat and enjoy or you want something that

will double up for lunch the next day. It may be that you're sick of the sight of salmon fillets and would love to discover a brand-new recipe you've never cooked before. You never know, you may find an inspirational recipe that's so delicious and practical that it will cater to everyone.

With over 365 recipes to choose from, you'll be able to create a variety of simple, nutritious meals whatever the occasion.

WHICH WAY TO GO FOR...

Throughout the book you'll find hundreds of recipes to fit any scenario. Picture the scene... You've bought some diced lamb from the local supermarket and you need a recipe that the whole family will enjoy. You've come home from work and there's only a package of lasagna in the cupboard. You're preparing a dinner party and want to cook a stunning, show-stopping dessert that must involve chocolate. Follow the symbols throughout the book to find the right way for you.

 BASIC Here's a very straightforward recipe that will help get the most out of your ingredient. Sometimes unadulterated is best, and these extra-easy recipes focus on good-quality, simple ingredients that are cooked well.

 GIVE IT A TWIST Add regional flavor with herbs or spices from around the world, or cook the ingredient slightly differently to give it an immediate new lease on life.

 SAVE ME TIME Cheats, quick fixes, shortcuts and speedy solutions. If you're pushed for time these recipes help you make healthy, filling, substantial meals in minutes.

 SAVE ME MONEY Cheaper alternatives that won't break the bank. Cook huge one-pot meals that will last the week or whip up a standard classic using pantry basics.

 KIDS WILL LOVE THESE Child-friendly, nutritious recipes that will be considered a treat. If you're trying to get your kids to try new ingredients you may find the perfect recipe to entice them.

 LEFTOVER TO LUNCH Use up ingredients for a portable meal the next day. Whether a hearty soup or an inspirational sandwich these light bites will satisfy any hunger fix.

 BUT I DON'T LIKE ... Creative alternatives for fussy eaters. If one person doesn't like your key ingredient create a variation with a simple substitute and avoid starting from scratch.

 FRIENDS FOR DINNER Push the boat out with impressive recipes for special occasions. Spoil a friend with a decadent meal or try a new dish you've always wanted to perfect.

 WATCHING MY WEIGHT Healthy, low-fat, low-calorie versions. Take your basic ingredient and add a wide range of nutritional extras to help follow a well-balanced diet.

 INSPIRE ME Something a little bit different... We've all got favorite foods, but sometimes it feels like we've cooked them a thousand times. These truly unique, fresh recipes will inspire you to cook something you've never thought of before.

WAYS TO BE PREPARED...

THINKING AHEAD

It's never been easier to shop for and prepare great food. Fresh herbs, high-quality ingredients and a good combination of flavors and textures mean that easy cooking does not mean boring meals. For example, a fantastic olive oil or organic beef fillet can make the difference between a dish that is merely acceptable and one that tastes wonderful.

If you know you have a busy week ahead, try to find the time to sit down the week before to plan your meals and write a shopping list. The majority of the recipes in this book make four servings for a main course, but many of the salads, soups and vegetarian options would also make great starters and will comfortably make up to eight servings. If you are cooking for two people, simply halve the quantities. Using the recipes as a base, feel free to alter the quantities or experiment with the choice of ingredients. Cooking should be fun, so make sure you follow your instincts and cook to fit your mood.

PANTRY ESSENTIALS

There are certain basics that you will always need; these include staple carbohydrates, such as rice and pasta, couscous, noodles and oatmeal. You may not always have fresh meat, but keep a bag of cashews; cans of tuna, salmon and beans in the cupboard; some eggs in the refrigerator; and a supply of frozen shrimp in the freezer and you'll have everything you need to create a nutritious, protein-rich dinner in a matter of minutes. To add flavor and to help the cooking process, ensure you have chicken and vegetable stock cubes and soy sauce in the cupboard, along with olive, sesame and canola oils, salt and pepper, tomato and sun-dried tomato paste, and key herbs and spices such as mixed herbs, pumpkin pie spice, Chinese 5-spice, ground cinnamon, coriander, cumin, nutmeg and hot pepper sauce or flakes.

Other ingredients that will enable you to whip up tasty sauces include flour, cornstarch, canned tomatoes, tomato sauce, olives, aged Cheddar and powdered milk. For last-minute desserts keep sugar, honey, maple syrup, a couple of cans of tinned fruit and some digestive cookies in the cupboard, plus some vanilla ice cream, fruit sorbet and waffles in the freezer. Cartons of crème fraîche or sour cream and plain yogurt never go amiss in the refrigerator for both savory and sweet dishes, but, as these ingredients have a short shelf life, ideally they should be bought as part of your meal-planning process.

Don't feel guilty about making life a little easier for yourself by using ready-made items, so stock up on cooked rice, lentils and beans, deli-style roast vegetables and jars of pesto and tapenades. Look out for jars of ready-minced garlic and ginger too (widely available in supermarkets), which means that you can add these wonderful flavors without having to spend time peeling, crushing and grating. Don't forget that you can also buy precut strips of meat, such as beef or pork, which are perfect for stir-fries. Frozen pastry is essential for anyone wanting to cook easy pies or tarts — just remember to take it out of the freezer in good time to thaw before you start cooking.

GET COOKING!

A successful meal takes a little planning and time, good ingredients, a dash of inspiration and some gentle encouragement. If cooking for your family has been a disappointing or time-consuming experience in the past, this book should provide you with plenty of inspiration to turn the tide on those mealtime blues.

BASE RECIPES...

Basic pasta dough

The pasta recipes in this book call for a 1-, 2- or 3-egg quantity of pasta. Make sure that you check the quantity needed before you start.

1-EGG PASTA DOUGH
Makes about 5 ounces (150 g)

⅔ cup (150 ml) all-purpose flour, plus extra for dusting
3 tablespoons (45 ml) fine semolina or durum flour, plus extra for dusting
1 egg

2-EGG PASTA DOUGH
Makes about 10 ounces (300 g)

1¼ cups (300 ml) all-purpose flour, plus extra for dusting
⅓ cup + 1 tablespoon (90 ml) fine semolina or durum flour, plus extra for dusting
2 eggs

3-EGG PASTA DOUGH
Makes about 14 ounces (400 g)

1¾ cups (425 ml) cups all-purpose flour, plus extra for dusting
⅔ cup (150 ml) fine semolina or durum flour, plus extra for dusting
3 eggs

Combine the all-purpose and semolina or durum flour in a large bowl. Make a well in the center and break in the eggs. Mix in the eggs with your fingers, slowly drawing in the flour as you go. Once the central mixture becomes too thick to handle, use the heel of your hand and knead to bring the mixture together. Alternatively, put all the ingredients in a food processor and pulse until combined.

Tip the dough onto a clean work surface that has been dusted with all-purpose flour and knead for 3–4 minutes, until it becomes smooth and elastic. Wrap in plastic wrap and chill for at least 30 minutes, or up to 4 hours.

Rolling out

Dust your work surface with all-purpose flour. Set up a pasta machine at the largest opening. Cut the pasta dough into lemon-sized pieces and pick up one piece, keeping the remaining dough covered with plastic wrap. Shape the dough you're holding roughly into a rectangle and run it through the machine. Fold the dough in half widthwise and then run it through the machine again.

Lower the setting on the machine by one notch and run the dough through it again.

Continue running the dough once through each setting until you have gone through all the settings. If while you're working you find that the pasta sheet is getting too long to handle, cut it in half and run one half through at a time. If it becomes sticky and catches in the pasta machine, dust with a little all-purpose flour.

Lay the pasta sheet on a surface dusted with semolina flour, then cover with a tea towel while you roll out the remaining dough.

Don't waste any time when shaping your rolled-out pasta — the dough will dry incredibly quickly, so work with speed while it's still moist and pliable.

Basic pizza dough

Makes 4
Preparation time: 15 minutes, plus rising

¼ ounce (5 g) fresh yeast or 1 teaspoon (5 ml) instant dried yeast
1 pinch of granulated sugar
4 cups (1 L) all-purpose flour, plus extra for dusting
1⅓ cups (325 ml) lukewarm water
1½ teaspoons (7 ml) salt

Dissolve the yeast in a bowl with the sugar, 2 tablespoons (30 ml) of the flour and ¼ cup (60 ml) of water. Leave to stand for 5 minutes, until the mixture starts to form bubbles, then add the remaining water. Add the salt and half the remaining flour and stir with one hand until you have a paste-like mixture. Gradually add all the remaining flour, working the mixture until you have a moist dough.

Shape the dough into a ball, cover with a moist cloth and leave to rest in a warm place for 5 minutes.

Lightly dust a work surface with flour and knead the dough for 10 minutes, until smooth and elastic. Shape into 4 equal-sized balls and place, spaced apart, on a lightly oiled baking sheet. Cover with a moist cloth and leave to rise in a warm place for 1 hour. Use according to the particular recipe.

HOMEMADE STOCK

The best soups are those made with homemade stocks. Traditionally soup was made from the bones of the Sunday roast and flavored with a few vegetable trimmings and herbs, as a way of making use of every part of a roast and using those scraps of leftover meat to make a hearty and filling meal. In today's age of recycling, it still makes excellent sense to use that scrappy-looking chicken carcass as the base for a delicious lunch or supper. And don't throw out those odd vegetable remnants from the refrigerator either. That slightly wrinkled carrot, those last few slightly bendy celery sticks and the stalks from that bunch of parsley or coriander can all be put into the stock. Add the odd bay leaf from the garden or the green leek or spring onion tops that are rather strong tasting and a sprinkling of peppercorns for extra flavor. The more you add, the better it will be.

The secret is to add all the ingredients and then to bring the stock to a boil; reduce the heat to a very gentle simmer so that the water barely shudders and then cook with the lid half on, half off the pan for 2 hours, or longer if you have the time. Keep the heat very low, if it is too high you will produce a thick, muddy-looking stock.

At the end of the cooking time, taste the stock. If it seems a little thin, remove the lid and simmer for another hour or two to reduce the liquid and concentrate the flavors. Strain and leave to cool. Skim any fat off the surface of meat stocks and refrigerate the stock until needed, for up to 3 days.

Alternatively, you can freeze the stock in a plastic box or loaf pan lined with a large plastic bag, for use later. Seal, label and freeze for up to 3 months. Defrost at room temperature or in the microwave.

Vegetable stock

Makes about 4 cups (1 L)
Preparation time: 10 minutes, plus cooling and chilling
Cooking time: 1 hour 5 minutes

> 1 tablespoon (15 ml) olive oil
> 2 onions, roughly chopped
> 2 leek tops, roughly chopped
> 4 carrots, roughly chopped
> 2 stalks celery, thickly sliced
> 3½ ounces (100 g) mushrooms, sliced
> 4 tomatoes, roughly chopped
> 1 small bunch of mixed herbs
> ½ teaspoon (2 ml) black peppercorns, roughly crushed
> ¼ teaspoon (1 ml) salt
> 7 cups (1.75 L) cold water

Heat the oil in a large saucepan, add the vegetables and fry for 5 minutes, until softened and just beginning to turn golden around the edges.

Add the tomatoes, herbs, peppercorns and salt. Pour in the water, slowly bring to a boil, then half cover and simmer gently for 1 hour. Pour through a sieve into a jug. Cool, then chill in the refrigerator for up to 3 days.

If you have some opened white wine or dry cider then you can add ⅔ cup (150 ml) wine in place of the same amount of water. You can mix and match vegetables depending on what you have.

Fish stock

Makes about 4 cups (1 L)
Preparation time: 10 minutes, plus cooling and chilling
Cooking time: 45 minutes

> 2 pounds (1 kg) fish trimmings, such as heads, backbones, tails, skins and shrimp shells
> 1 onion, quartered
> 2 leek tops, sliced
> 2 carrots, thickly sliced
> 2 stalks celery, thickly sliced
> sprigs thyme
> 1 bay leaf
> few stalks parsley
> ½ teaspoon (2 ml) white peppercorns, roughly crushed
> ¼ teaspoon (1 ml) salt
> 6 cups (1.5 L) cold water
> 1 cup (250 ml) dry white wine or water

Put the fish trimmings in a large sieve, rinse with cold water, drain and then put them in a large saucepan together with all the remaining ingredients.

Bring slowly to the boil. Skim off any scum with a slotted spoon. Cover and simmer for 30 minutes.

Strain the stock through a fine sieve, return it to the saucepan and then simmer it, uncovered, for about 15 minutes, until reduced by half. Cool, then chill in the refrigerator for up to 3 days.

If you are adding fish heads, don't cook them for longer than 30 minutes before straining, or they will begin to add a bitter taste.

Chicken stock

Makes about 4 cups (1 L)
Preparation time: 10 minutes, plus cooling and chilling
Cooking time: 2–2½ hours

> 1 leftover cooked chicken carcass
> 1 onion, quartered
> 2 carrots, thickly sliced
> 2 stalks celery, thickly sliced
> 1 bay leaf or small bunch of mixed herbs
> ¼ teaspoon (1 ml) salt
> ½ teaspoon (2 ml) black peppercorns, roughly crushed
> 10 cups (2.5 L) cold water

Put the chicken carcass and vegetables in a large saucepan. Add the herbs, salt and peppercorns.

Pour in the water and bring slowly to a boil. Skim off any scum with a slotted spoon. Reduce the heat to a gentle simmer, then half cover with a lid and cook for 2–2½ hours, until reduced by about half.

Strain the stock through a large sieve into a jug. Remove any chicken pieces still on the carcass, pick out the meat from the sieve and reserve for the soup, but discard the vegetables. Cool, then chill in the refrigerator for several hours or overnight.

Skim off the thin layer of fat on the top of the chilled and now jellied stock with a large metal spoon. Chill and store in the refrigerator for up to 3 days.

Beef (or lamb) stock

Makes about 4 cups (1 L)
Preparation time: 10 minutes, plus cooling and chilling
Cooking time: 4 hours 20 minutes–5 hours 20 minutes

> 4 pounds (2 kg) beef bones, such as ribs or shin
> 2 slices smoked bacon, diced
> 2 onions, quartered but with the inner brown layer still on
> 2 carrots, thickly sliced
> 2 stalks celery, thickly sliced
> 1 turnip, diced (optional)
> 2 bay leaves, rosemary sprigs or sage stems
> ¼ teaspoon (1 ml) salt
> ½ teaspoon (2 ml) black peppercorns, roughly crushed
> 14 cups (3.5 L) cold water

Put the bones and bacon in a large saucepan and heat gently for 10 minutes, until the marrow begins to run from the center of the bones. Turn the bones occasionally.

Add the vegetables and fry for 10 more minutes, stirring the vegetables and turning the bones until browned.

Add the herbs, salt and peppercorns, then pour in the water and bring slowly to a boil. Skim off any scum with a slotted spoon, then reduce the heat, half cover with a lid and simmer gently for 4–5 hours, until the liquid has reduced by half.

Strain through a large sieve into a jug. Cool, then chill in the refrigerator overnight. Skim off any fat and store in the refrigerator for up to 3 days.

Lamb stock can be made in the same way from lamb bones.

STOCK CUBES & READY-MADE STOCK

In our grandmothers' day, it would have been unheard of to make soup with a stock cube; nowadays, juggling work with family life means that time-saving shortcuts are a must. Very few people make enough stock for all their cooking needs, and while it is great to have a few handy-sized bags of stock in the freezer, most of us cheat and use store-bought products.

While there is nothing wrong with using stock cubes, there are some soups for which homemade stock is crucial, such as light, delicate-tasting soups. The strength of flavor varies hugely in store-bought stock cubes, so choose cubes or powder that are low in salt and make them up with a little extra water so that their flavor is not overpowering. More and more supermarkets now sell tubs of chilled ready-made stocks for a more authentic taste. They are more expensive, but much closer to the taste of homemade stock.

POULTRY

If you're stuck in a rut using the same chicken recipe and need some new inspiration, these winning recipes using chicken thighs, chicken breasts and a whole roast chicken, as well as duck and turkey, are sure to become new family favorites.

POULTRY

 1 **BASIC**

 2 **GIVE IT A TWIST**

 3 **SAVE ME TIME**

 4 **SAVE ME MONEY**

 5 **KIDS WILL LOVE THESE**

CHICKEN THIGHS PAGE 14

Deviled chicken

Catalan chicken

Chicken & vegetable skewers

Chicken stew & dumplings

Chicken thatch

CHICKEN BREASTS PAGE 20

Grilled salsa chicken

Grilled tandoori chicken

Rolled chicken breasts

Creamy chicken gnocchi

Chicken Kiev

ROAST CHICKEN PAGE 26

Roast chicken with herbs & garlic

Roast chicken with spice rub

Thai barbecued chicken

Chicken with vermouth

Italian chicken cushion

DUCK PAGE 32

Duck with hoisin sauce

Jungle curry with duck

Duck slices with cashews

Duck, hazelnut & peach salad

Hot duck & coconut noodles

TURKEY PAGE 38

Turkey & avocado salad

Turkey chili poblano

Turkey & bulgur salad

Baked turkey burritos

Turkey & wild mushroom turnovers

6 LEFTOVER TO LUNCH

Chicken hotpot

Grilled summer chicken salad

Chicken & spinach chowder

Peking wraps

Turkey tacos

7 BUT I DON'T LIKE...

Cashew chicken

Chicken fingers with salsa

Spiced chicken with yogurt crust

Spring braised duck

Cheesy turkey & cranberry melt

8 FRIENDS FOR DINNER

Coq au vin

Chicken cacciatore

Chicken with preserved lemons

Duck, clementine & tatsoi salad

Roast turkey

9 WATCHING MY WEIGHT

Chicken with red kidney beans

Teriyaki chicken with three seeds

Chicken & avocado salad

Aromatic braised duck

Turkey burgers & sweet potatoes

10 INSPIRE ME

Peppered chicken & eggplant

Lemon-infused chicken & spaghetti

Chicken in a salt crust

Duck with kumquat honey sauce

Wild rice & turkey salad

10 WAYS WITH CHICKEN THIGHS

1

Deviled chicken

Serves 4
Preparation time: 10 minutes
Cooking time: 16–20 minutes

8 boneless chicken thighs
salad, to serve

FOR THE DEVIL SAUCE
2 tablespoons (30 ml) Dijon mustard
6 drops hot pepper sauce
2 cloves garlic, crushed
1 tablespoon (15 ml) soy sauce

Heat a large grill pan (or ordinary frying pan). Remove the skin from the chicken thighs, open them and trim away any fat.

To make the devil sauce, mix together the mustard, hot pepper sauce, garlic and soy sauce in a shallow dish.

Dip the trimmed chicken thighs in the devil sauce and coat each piece well. Place the chicken pieces flat on the pan and cook for 8–10 minutes on each side or until fully cooked.

Serve hot or cold with salad leaves.

2

GIVE IT A TWIST

Catalan chicken

Serves 4
Preparation time: 15 minutes
Cooking time: 25 minutes

2 tablespoons (30 ml) olive oil
⅓ cup (75 ml) flaked almonds
2 onions, roughly chopped
8 chicken thighs, deboned, skinned, cubed
2 cloves garlic, finely chopped
⅔ cup (150 ml) raisins
¾ cup (175 ml) dry sherry
1 cup (250 ml) chicken stock (see page 9)
1 small bunch flat-leaf parsley, roughly chopped
salt and pepper

Heat a little of the oil in a large frying pan, add the almonds and fry, stirring for a few minutes, until golden. Scoop out of the pan and set aside.

Add the remaining oil to the pan, then add the onions, chicken and garlic and fry over medium heat for 10 minutes stirring continuously until deep golden. Mix in the raisins, sherry, stock and
a little salt and pepper.

Simmer for 10 minutes, until the sauce has reduced slightly and the chicken is cooked through. Sprinkle with the parsley and serve with rice and salad.

SAVE ME TIME

Chicken & vegetable skewers

Serves 4
Preparation time: 10 minutes
Cooking time: 15 minutes

> **4 boneless skinless chicken thighs**
> **2 tablespoons (30 ml) honey**
> **2 tablespoons (30 ml) mild whole-grain mustard**
> **1 zucchini, cut into 8 large pieces**
> **1 carrot, cut into 8 large pieces**

Cut the chicken thighs into bite-sized pieces and toss in the honey and mustard. Arrange the chicken pieces on a baking sheet and bake in a preheated 350°F (180°C) oven for 15 minutes, until cooked through and lightly golden. Set aside and leave to cool.

Take 8 bamboo skewers and thread with the cooked chicken pieces and the raw vegetables.

Serve with the honey and mustard mixture for dipping. The skewers can also be refrigerated for the following day's lunchbox.

SAVE ME MONEY

Chicken stew & dumplings

Serves 4
Preparation time: 30 minutes
Cooking time: 1 hour 25 minutes

> **8 boneless skinless chicken thighs**
> **1 tablespoon (15 ml) sunflower oil**
> **1 onion, roughly chopped**
> **2 parsnips, cut into chunks**
> **2 carrots, cut into chunks**
> **6 ounces (175g) rutabaga, cut into chunks**
> **⅓ cup (75 ml) pearl barley**
> **1 bottle (12 ounces/341 ml) pale ale**
> **1¼ cups (300 ml) chicken stock (see page 9)**
> **2 teaspoons (10 ml) prepared English mustard**
> **salt and pepper**
>
> **FOR THE DUMPLINGS**
> **1⅓ cups (325 ml) self-rising flour**
> **3 ounces (75 g) suet, light shredded**
> **4 tablespoons (60 ml) chopped chives**
> **7–8 tablespoons (105–125 ml) cold water**
> **salt and pepper**

Cut each chicken thigh in half. Heat the oil in an ovenproof casserole dish, add the chicken and onion and fry over high heat until golden. Stir in the remaining vegetables and cook for 2 minutes, then mix in the barley, ale, stock and mustard. Season and bring to a boil. Cover and transfer to a preheated 350°F (180°C) oven for 1 hour.

When the chicken has finished cooking, make the dumplings by mixing the flour, suet, chives and some seasoning in a bowl. Stir in enough water to mix a soft, slightly sticky dough, then shape large tablespoonfuls of the mixture into balls.

Stir the chicken stew and transfer to the stove. When the stock is boiling, add the dumplings, cover and simmer for about 15 minutes or until the dumplings are light and fluffy. Spoon into shallow bowls to serve.

5 😎

KIDS WILL LOVE THIS
Chicken thatch

Serves 4
Preparation time: 25 minutes
Cooking time: 45 minutes

1 tablespoon (15 ml) sunflower oil
4 boneless skinless chicken thighs, diced
1 onion, chopped
2 tablespoons (30 ml) all-purpose flour
1¾ cups (425 ml) chicken stock (see page 9)
2 teaspoons (10 ml) Dijon mustard
1 large carrot, diced
1½ pound (750 g) potatoes, quartered
5 ounces (150 g) zucchinis, diced
3 ounces (75 g) sugar snap peas, halved
3 ounces (75 g) frozen peas
2½ tablespoons (37 ml) butter
3 tablespoons (45 ml) 1% or 2% milk
3 ounces (75 g) aged (sharp) Cheddar cheese, grated
salt and pepper

Heat the oil in a saucepan, add the chicken and onion and fry for 5 minutes, stirring continuously until browned and fully cooked. Stir in the flour, then gradually mix in the stock. Bring to a boil, then add the mustard, carrot and a little seasoning. Cover and simmer for 30 minutes.

Meanwhile, cook the potatoes in a saucepan of boiling water until tender. Add the zucchinis, sugar snap peas and frozen peas to a smaller saucepan of boiling water and cook for 3 minutes. Drain and set aside.

Drain the potatoes and mash with two-thirds of the butter and all of the milk. Season and stir in two-thirds of the cheese.

Spoon the chicken mixture into a 9-inch (23 cm) deep-dish pie plate or 4 individual dishes, add the just-cooked green vegetables, then spoon the mashed potatoes on top. Dot with the remaining butter and sprinkle with the remaining cheese. Broil until golden, then serve immediately.

CHICKEN THIGHS ARE MORE ECONOMICAL THAN CHICKEN BREASTS AND ARE PACKED WITH FLAVOR. THEY ARE ALSO LOW IN FAT AND HIGHLY VERSATILE.

6 ⊕

LEFTOVER TO LUNCH
Chicken hotpot

Serves 4
Preparation time: 15 minutes
Cooking time: 50 minutes

1 tablespoon (15 ml) sunflower oil
1 onion, roughly chopped
2 small potatoes, diced
2 carrots, diced
2 small parsnips, diced
1 teaspoon (5 ml) turmeric
1 tablespoon (15 ml) mild curry paste
½ cup (125 ml) red lentils
5 cups (1.25 L) chicken stock (see page 9)
3½ ounces (100 g) cooked chicken, diced
salt and pepper
1 small bunch fresh coriander, to garnish

Heat the oil in a saucepan, add the onion and fry, stirring, until pale golden. Mix in the remaining vegetables and fry for 2–3 minutes. Stir in the turmeric and curry paste, then add the lentils and stock.

Add the chicken and seasoning, then bring to a boil. Cover and simmer for 40 minutes, stirring occasionally until the vegetables and lentils are softened.

Ladle into bowls and sprinkle with torn coriander leaves. Serve with warm naan bread.

7

BUT I DON'T LIKE ...
CHICKEN THIGHS
Cashew chicken

Serves 4
Preparation time: 10 minutes
Cooking time: 13–15 minutes

1 onion, roughly chopped
4 tablespoons (60 ml) tomato paste
½ cup (125 ml) cashews
2 teaspoons (10 ml) garam masala
2 cloves garlic, crushed
1 tablespoon (15 ml) lemon juice
¼ teaspoon (1 ml) turmeric
2 teaspoons (10 ml) sea salt
1 tablespoon (15 ml) natural yogurt
2 tablespoons (30 ml) vegetable oil
3 tablespoons (45 ml) chopped fresh coriander leaves, plus extra
    to garnish
2 ounces (50 g) ready-to-eat dried apricots, chopped
1 pound (500 g) chicken thighs, skinned, deboned, cubed
1 cup (250 ml) chicken stock (see page 9)
toasted cashews, to garnish

TO SERVE
rice
poppadums

Put the onion, tomato paste, cashews, garam masala, garlic, lemon juice, turmeric, salt and yogurt into a food processor or blender and process until fairly smooth. Set aside.

Heat the oil in a large, nonstick frying pan and, when hot, pour in the spice mixture. Fry, stirring, for 2 minutes over medium heat. Add half the coriander, the apricots and the chicken to the pan and stir-fry for 1 minute.

Pour in the stock, cover and simmer for 10–12 minutes or until the chicken is cooked through and tender. Stir in the remaining coriander and serve with rice and poppadums, garnished with toasted cashews and extra coriander.

WHY NOT TRY... SHRIMP WITH CASHEWS & SNOW PEAS

Make the spice mixture as in the recipe above and fry over low heat for 2 minutes. Omit the chicken and apricots, but add half the fresh coriander as above together with 10 ounces (300 g) shrimp and 6 ounces (175g) halved snow peas. Stir-fry for 1–2 minutes, then add the stock. Cover and cook as above. Garnish with the remaining coriander and the cashews and serve immediately.

8

FRIENDS FOR DINNER
Coq au vin

Serves 4
Preparation time: 25 minutes
Cooking time: 1½ hours

3 tablespoons (45ml) all-purpose flour
8 mixed chicken thigh and drumstick pieces
2 tablespoons (30 ml) olive oil
12 ounces (375 g) shallots, halved if large
4 ounces (125 g) smoked bacon
2 cloves garlic, finely chopped
4 tablespoons (60 ml) brandy or cognac
1¼ cups (175 ml) cheap burgundy wine
¾ cup (200 ml) chicken stock (see page 9)
2 teaspoons (10 ml) tomato paste
1 fresh or dried bouquet garni
salt and pepper
large croutons, to serve

Mix the flour on a plate with a little seasoning, then use to coat the chicken pieces. Heat the oil in a large shallow ovenproof casserole dish (or frying pan, and transfer chicken to a casserole dish later), add the chicken and cook over high heat until golden on all sides. Lift out onto a plate.

Fry the shallots and bacon until golden, then stir in the garlic and return the chicken to the casserole dish. Pour in the brandy or cognac and, when bubbling, flame with a long taper. As soon as the flames subside, pour in the red wine and stock, then mix in the tomato paste and bouquet garni. Season, then cover the casserole dish and transfer to a preheated 350°F (180°C) oven and cook for 1¼ hours, until tender.

When the chicken is fully cooked, pour the liquid from the casserole dish into a saucepan and boil for 5 minutes to reduce and thicken slightly, if desired. Return the liquid to the casserole dish.

Serve in shallow bowls topped with croûtons.

9

WATCHING MY WEIGHT
Chicken with red kidney beans

Serves 4
Preparation time: 15 minutes
Cooking time: 20–25 minutes

> sunflower oil spray
> 1 onion, roughly chopped
> 1 red pepper, cored, seeded and roughly chopped
> 1 clove garlic, halved
> 8 ounces (250 g) boneless skinless chicken thighs, cut into
> 1¼-inch (3 cm) pieces
> 2 teaspoons (10 ml) mild chili powder
> 1¼ cups (300 ml) converted long-grain rice
> 1 can (15 ounces/410 g) red kidney beans, rinsed and drained
> 1 can (15 ounces/410 g) cherry tomatoes in natural juice
> ¾ cup (175 ml) chicken stock (see page 9)
> salt and pepper
>
> **TO SERVE**
> fresh coriander leaves, roughly chopped
> lime wedges

Heat a large frying pan with an ovenproof handle and lightly spray with oil. Add the onion, red pepper, garlic and chicken and cook, stirring continuously over medium heat for 3 minutes.

Add the chili powder, rice, beans, tomatoes and stock to the pan, season to taste, bring to a boil and simmer for 15 minutes.

When the rice and chicken are fully cooked, spoon as much of the chicken on top of the rice as you can and cook under a preheated hot broiler until golden.

Serve with chopped coriander and lime wedges.

10

INSPIRE ME
Peppered chicken & eggplant

Serves 4
Preparation time: 15 minutes
Cooking time: 15 minutes

> 2 tablespoons (30 ml) sunflower oil
> 6 boneless skinless chicken thighs, cut into cubes
> 1 large eggplant, diced
> 1 red onion, sliced
> 2 cloves garlic, finely chopped
> 2 tablespoons (30 ml) medium hot curry paste
> ½ teaspoon (2 ml) black peppercorns, roughly crushed
> 1 small bunch fresh coriander, to garnish

Heat the oil in a large frying pan, add the chicken and eggplant and fry, stirring continuously for 5 minutes, until the eggplant is just beginning to soften. Stir in the onion and garlic and fry for 5 more minutes, stirring continuously until the onion and chicken are just beginning to brown.

Mix in the curry paste and peppercorns and fry for 5 minutes, until the chicken is a rich golden brown and cooked through. Tear the coriander into pieces and sprinkle over the top. Serve immediately with tomato salad, yogurt and rice.

10 WAYS WITH CHICKEN BREASTS

1

BASIC
Grilled salsa chicken

Serves 4
Preparation time: 10 minutes
Cooking time: 6 minutes

> 4 boneless skinless chicken breasts
> 3 tablespoons (45 ml) olive oil
> salt and pepper
>
> **FOR THE CUCUMBER AND TOMATO SALSA**
> 1 red onion, finely chopped
> 2 tomatoes, seeded and diced
> 1 cucumber, finely diced
> 1 red chili, finely chopped
> 1 small handful of fresh coriander leaves, chopped
> juice of 1 lime

Using kitchen scissors, cut each breast in half lengthwise but without cutting the whole way through. Open each breast out flat. Brush with the oil and season well with salt and pepper. Heat a grill pan until very hot. Add the chicken breasts and cook for 3 minutes on each side or until cooked through and grill-marked.

Meanwhile, to make the salsa, mix together the onion, tomatoes, cucumber, red chili, coriander and lime juice. Season well with salt and pepper.

Serve the chicken hot with the spicy salsa spooned over.

2

GIVE IT A TWIST
Grilled tandoori chicken

Serves 4
Preparation time: 10 minutes, plus marinating
Cooking time: 16–20 minutes

> 4 boneless skinless chicken breasts, about 4 ounces (125 g) each
> 4 tablespoons (60 ml) tandoori paste or powder
>
> **FOR THE SALAD**
> 2 red onions, finely sliced
> 4 tomatoes, finely sliced
> 1 bunch fresh coriander, roughly chopped
> 4 tablespoons (60 ml) lemon juice
> 4 tablespoons (60 ml) olive oil
> lemon wedges, grilled (optional), to serve
> salt and pepper

Using a sharp knife, make a series of small slashes in the flesh of the chicken breasts and rub in the tandoori paste or powder. Leave to marinate in the refrigerator overnight.

Heat a grill pan (or ordinary frying pan). Cook the marinated chicken breasts for 8–10 minutes on each side, allowing the authentic tandoori charred color to appear, or until cooked through.

Mix the red onions, tomatoes and coriander together with the lemon juice, olive oil and seasoning in a small bowl. Serve the salad with the tandoori chicken, accompanied by lemon wedges, grilled if prefered.

3 🕐

SAVE ME TIME
Rolled chicken breasts

Serves 4
Preparation time: 10 minutes
Cooking time: 20 minutes

 4 boneless skinless chicken breasts, 15 ounces (150 g) each
 4 slices prosciutto
 4 thin slices buffalo mozzarella cheese
 4 asparagus tips, plus extra to serve
 ⅔ cup (150 ml) all-purpose flour
 1 tablespoon (15 ml) olive oil
 ¼ cup (60 ml) butter
 ¼ cup (60 ml) dry white wine
 ⅓ cup (75 ml) chicken stock (see page 9)
 7 ounces (200 g) baby spinach
 7 ounces (200 g) chilled pack sun-blushed tomatoes in oil, drained
 salt and pepper

Place each chicken breast between 2 sheets of waxed paper and flatten to about 2½ times its original size by pounding with a rolling pin.

Season the chicken with salt and pepper, place a slice of prosciutto, a slice of mozzarella and an asparagus tip on top and tightly roll up the chicken breasts. Tie with a piece of strong thread or spear with wooden cocktail sticks.

Season the flour with salt and pepper. Dip the prepared chicken rolls into the flour to coat evenly.

Heat the oil and half the butter in a frying pan, add the chicken rolls and sauté over low heat for 15 minutes or until golden all over and cooked through, turning frequently to brown the chicken evenly.

Remove the chicken, place in a warmed serving dish and keep warm. Pour the wine and stock into the pan, bring to a boil and simmer for 3 minutes.

Remove the thread or cocktail sticks just before serving the chicken. Add the remaining butter to the pan, mix quickly with a small whisk to emulsify the sauce, add the spinach and tomatoes and cook for 2 minutes, until the spinach has just wilted. Spoon onto plates, slice the chicken and arrange in a line down the center.

4 🐷

SAVE ME MONEY
Creamy chicken gnocchi

Serves 4
Preparation time: 15 minutes
Cooking time: 14–16 minutes

 2 tablespoons (30 ml) olive oil
 1 onion, thinly sliced
 1 pound (500 g) butternut squash, peeled, seeded, diced
 4 slices smoked bacon, diced
 14½ ounces (450 g) mini chicken breast fillets, diced
 12 fresh sage leaves
 1¼ cups (300 ml) chicken stock (see page 9)
 1 package (1 pound/500 g) chilled gnocchi
 6 tablespoons (90 ml) crème fraîche or sour cream
 4 tablespoons (60 ml) freshly grated Parmesan cheese
 salt and pepper

Heat the oil in a frying pan, add the onion, butternut squash and bacon and fry for 5 minutes, until just beginning to brown. Stir in the chicken and sage and fry for 5 minutes, stirring continuously until golden.

Add the stock and a little seasoning and cook for 2–3 minutes, until the chicken and squash are cooked through.

Bring a large saucepan of water to the boil, add the gnocchi and cook for 2–3 minutes, until the gnocchi rise to the surface. Drain and add to the frying pan with the crème fraîche. Gently toss together, then spoon into shallow bowls and sprinkle with the Parmesan.

5

KIDS WILL LOVE THIS
Chicken Kiev

Serves 4
Preparation time: 40 minutes, plus freezing and chilling
Cooking time: 20 minutes

- ½ cup (125 ml) butter, at room temperature
- 2 tablespoons (30 ml) chopped fresh chives
- 1 tablespoon (15 ml) chopped frech parsley
- 2 teaspoons (10 ml) chopped fresh tarragon (optional)
- 1 clove garlic, finely chopped
- 2 teaspoons (10 ml) lemon juice
- 4 boneless skinless chicken breasts, each about 5 ounces (150 g)
- 2 tablespoons (30 ml) all-purpose flour
- 2 cups (500 ml) fresh breadcrumbs
- 2 eggs
- 3 tablespoons (45 ml) sunflower oil
- pepper

Beat the butter with the herbs, garlic, lemon juice and a little pepper. Spoon into a line about 10 inches (25 cm) long on a sheet of plastic wrap or foil, then roll up into a neat log shape. Freeze for 15 minutes.

Meanwhile, put one of the chicken breasts between two large sheets of plastic wrap and beat with a rolling pin until it forms a rectangle about ⅛ inch (3 mm) thick, being careful not to make any holes in the chicken. Repeat with the other chicken breasts.

Cut the herb butter into 4 pieces and put one in the middle of each chicken breast. Fold in the sides, then the top and bottom, to make a tight parcel.

Put the flour on a plate and the breadcrumbs on a second plate, and beat the eggs in a shallow dish. Roll the Kiev in the flour, then coat in the egg and roll in the breadcrumbs. Put back on the empty flour plate and chill in the refrigerator for 1 hour (or longer if you have time).

Heat the oil in a large frying pan, add the Kiev and cook over a medium heat for 5 minutes, turning until evenly browned.

Transfer to a baking sheet, then complete cooking in a preheated 400°F (200°C) oven for 15 minutes or until the chicken is cooked through. Serve with new potatoes and braised red cabbage.

CHICKEN BREASTS ARE LOW IN FAT AND QUICK TO COOK. THEY ARE ALSO SOMETIMES CALLED CHICKEN SUPREMES.

6

LEFTOVER TO LUNCH
Grilled summer chicken salad

Serves 4
Preparation time: 15 minutes
Cooking time: 45 minutes

- 4 boneless skinless chicken breasts, about 4 ounces (125 g) each
- 2 small red onions
- 2 red peppers, cored, seeded, cut into flat pieces
- 1 bunch asparagus, trimmed
- 7 ounces (200 g) new potatoes, boiled, cut in half
- 1 bunch fresh basil
- 5 tablespoons (75 ml) olive oil
- 2 tablespoons (30 ml) balsamic vinegar
- salt and pepper

Heat a grill pan (or ordinary frying pan). Place the chicken breasts in the pan and cook for 8–10 minutes on each side. When fully cooked, remove from the pan and cut roughly into chunks.

Cut the red onions into wedges, keeping the root ends intact to hold the wedges together. Place in the pan and cook for 5 minutes on each side. Remove from the pan and set aside.

Place the flat pieces of red pepper in the pan and cook for 8 minutes on the skin side only, so that the skins are charred and blistered. Remove and set aside, then cook the asparagus in the pan for 6 minutes, turning frequently.

Put the boiled potatoes in a large bowl. Tear the basil, reserving a few leaves intact to garnish, and add to the bowl, together with the chicken and all of the vegetables. Add the olive oil, balsamic vinegar and seasoning. Toss the salad and garnish with the reserved basil leaves.

7

**BUT I DON'T LIKE...
CHICKEN BREASTS**

Chicken fingers with salsa

Serves 4
Preparation time: 20 minutes
Cooking time: 6–8 minutes

> 2 eggs
> 2 tablespoons (30 ml) 1% or 2% milk
> 1½ cups (375 ml) fresh breadcrumbs
> 4 tablespoons (60 ml) freshly grated Parmesan cheese
> 3 boneless skinless chicken breasts, about 1 pound (500 g) in total, cut into long, finger-like strips
> 2 tablespoons (30 ml) butter
> 2 tablespoons (30 ml) vegetable oil
> salt and pepper
>
> **FOR THE SALSA**
> 2 tomatoes, diced
> ¼ cucumber, diced
> ⅔ cup (150 ml) corn, defrosted if frozen
> 1 tablespoon (15 ml) fresh coriander leaves, chopped

Put the salsa ingredients in a bowl and mix together. Beat the eggs, milk and a little salt and pepper together in a bowl. Mix the breadcrumbs with the Parmesan.

Dip one chicken strip into the egg, then roll in the breadcrumbs. Carry on doing this until all the chicken strips are well covered.

Heat the butter and oil in a large frying pan and add the chicken strips. Cook for 6–8 minutes, turning a few times until they are brown all over and fully cooked. Serve with the salsa as dip.

WHY NOT TRY... SALMON GOUJONS

Alternatively, try cooking this recipe with salmon and serve with a minty dip instead: Cut 1 pound (500 g) raw salmon fillets into strips. Mix 2 tablespoons (30 ml) chopped parsley with 1½ cups (375 ml) breadcrumbs and coat each piece of salmon in the mixture. Cook the fish in butter and oil as above for 2–3 minutes, until it is fully cooked and the breadcrumbs are golden, taking care not to break the fish when turning. Mix 1¼ cups (300 ml) plain yogurt with 4 tablespoons (60 ml) chopped mint leaves and 3 tablespoons (45 ml) finely diced cucumber. Serve the salmon with the dip in a separate bowl.

8

FRIENDS FOR DINNER

Chicken cacciatore

Serves 4
Preparation time: 10 minutes
Cooking time: 20 minutes

> 4 boneless skinless chicken breasts, about 4 ounces (125 g) each
> 1 pound (500 g) cherry or mini plum tomatoes, halved
> 1 red onion, cut into wedges
> 2 cloves garlic, finely chopped
> 2–3 stems fresh rosemary, torn into pieces
> 6 tablespoons (90 ml) red wine
> 2 tablespoons (30 ml) balsamic vinegar
> 8 ounces (250 g) dried linguine or fettuccine
> 2 tablespoons (30 ml) low-fat aged Cheddar cheese (optional), grated
> pepper

Arrange the chicken in a large roasting pan or baking dish so that it lies in a single layer. Add the tomatoes and onion, then sprinkle over the garlic and rosemary. Drizzle with the wine and vinegar and add a little pepper.

Bake in a preheated 425°F (220°C) oven for 20 minutes or until the onions and chicken are browned and the juices run clear when the chicken is pierced with a skewer.

Halfway through cooking, bring a large saucepan of water to a boil, add the pasta and cook for 8–10 minutes, until just tender.

Drain the pasta and return to the empty pan. Slice the chicken breasts and add to the pasta with the onions, tomatoes and pan juices. Toss together and spoon into bowls. Sprinkle with a little rosemary and top with grated cheese, if desired.

9

Teriyaki chicken with three seeds

Serves 4
Preparation time: 20 minutes, plus marinating
Cooking time: 20–25 minutes

- 4 boneless skinless chicken breasts, about 4 ounces (125 g) each
- 2 tablespoons (30 ml) sunflower oil
- 4 tablespoons (60 ml) soy sauce
- 2 cloves garlic, finely chopped
- 1-inch (2.5 cm) piece gingerroot, finely grated
- 2 tablespoons (30 ml) sesame seeds
- 2 tablespoons (30 ml) sunflower seeds
- 2 tablespoons (30 ml) pumpkin seeds
- juice of 2 limes
- 3½ ounces (100 g) herb salad
- ½ small iceberg lettuce, torn into bite-sized pieces
- 2 ounces (50 g) alfalfa or brocco sprouts

Put the chicken breasts into a shallow dish. Spoon ¾ of the oil over the chicken, then add half the soy sauce, garlic and ginger.

Turn the chicken to coat in the mixture, then leave to marinate for 30 minutes.

Heat a nonstick frying pan, lift the chicken out of the marinade and add to the pan. Fry for 8–10 minutes each side, until dark brown and cooked all the way through. Lift out and set aside.

Heat the remaining oil in the pan, add the seeds and fry for 2–3 minutes, until lightly toasted. Add the remaining marinade and remaining soy sauce, bring to a boil, then take off the heat and mix in the lime juice.

Mix the herb salad, lettuce and sprouts, then spoon over 4 serving plates. Thinly slice the chicken and arrange on top, then spoon the seed and lime dressing over the top. Serve immediately.

10

Lemon-infused chicken & spaghetti

Serves 4
Preparation time: 15 minutes
Cooking time: 16–20 minutes

- 4 lemons
- 4 boneless skinless chicken breasts, about 4 ounces (125 g) each
- 1 bunch fresh oregano, chopped
- 10 ounces (300 g) dried spaghetti
- 1 bunch fresh parsley, chopped
- 2 tablespoons (30 ml) olive oil
- salt and pepper

Thinly slice 3 of the lemons, setting aside 8 large slices. Grate the zest and squeeze the juice from the fourth lemon and set aside.

Using a sharp knife, make a pouch in the middle of each chicken breast. Fill each chicken pocket with the smaller slices of lemon, some chopped oregano leaves and salt and pepper.

Heat a grill pan (or ordinary frying pan). Sandwich each chicken breast between two of the reserved large lemon slices and a sprig of oregano. Place the chicken in the pan and cook for 8–10 minutes on each side — try to keep the lemon intact with the chicken so that all the citrus flavor infuses into the chicken — until fully cooked.

Meanwhile, bring a large saucepan of lightly salted water to a boil. When boiling, plunge the spaghetti into the water and cook for 12 minutes, or according to the instructions on the package. Drain well, then toss with the lemon zest and juice, the parsley, the olive oil and seasoning to taste. Serve with the lemon chicken.

10 WAYS WITH ROAST CHICKEN

1

Roast chicken with herbs & garlic

Serves 4
Preparation time: 10 minutes
Cooking time: 1 hour

>   8 cloves garlic, unpeeled
>   4 large sprigs fresh thyme
>   3 large sprigs fresh rosemary
>   3½-pound (1.75 kg) whole chicken
>   1 tablespoon (15 ml) olive oil
>   salt and pepper

Put the garlic cloves and half the herb sprigs in the body cavity of the chicken. Pat the chicken dry with paper towels and rub the oil all over the outside of the bird. Strip the leaves off the remaining herb sprigs and rub over the bird, with a little salt and pepper.

Place the chicken, breast side up, in a roasting pan. Roast in a preheated 425°F (220°C) oven for 10 minutes. Turn the chicken over, breast side down, reduce the oven temperature to 350°F (180°C) and cook for a further 20 minutes. Finally, turn the chicken back to its original position and roast for another 25 minutes, until the skin is crisp and golden. Check that the chicken is cooked by piercing the thigh with a knife. The juices should run clear, with no sign of pink. If not, cook for a further 10 minutes.

Transfer to a warmed serving plate and leave the chicken to rest for 5 minutes before serving it with the pan juices.

2 ◎

Roast chicken with spice rub

Serves 4
Preparation time: 20 minutes
Cooking time: 1 hour 20 minutes–1 hour 30 minutes

>   3-pound (1.5 kg) whole chicken
>   3 tablespoons (45 ml) olive oil
>   1 teaspoon (5 ml) fennel seeds, roughly crushed
>   1 teaspoon (5 ml) cumin seeds, roughly crushed
>   1 teaspoon (5 ml) crushed dried red pepper flakes
>   1 teaspoon (5 ml) dried oregano
>   ½ teaspoon (2 ml) ground cinnamon
>   1¼ pounds (625 g) baby new potatoes
>   2 shallots, finely chopped
>   2 cloves garlic, finely chopped (optional)
>   5 ounces (150 g) slender green beans
>   juice of 1 lemon
>   ¾ cup (175 ml) chicken stock (see page 9)
>   1 small bunch fresh coriander or flat-leaf parsley, or mix of the two, roughly chopped
>   salt and pepper

Put the chicken into a large roasting pan and drizzle with 2 tablespoons (30 ml) of the oil. Mix the crushed seeds, red pepper flakes, oregano and cinnamon with some salt and pepper, then sprinkle half over the chicken.

Cover the chicken loosely with foil, then roast in a preheated 375°F (190°C) oven for 40 minutes. Remove the foil and baste with the pan juices. Add the potatoes to the pan, toss them in the juices, then cook uncovered for 40–50 minutes, basting and turning the potatoes once or twice, until golden brown. Re-cover the chicken with foil if the spice rub begins to overbrown.

Meanwhile, heat the remaining oil in a small saucepan, add the shallots and garlic, if using, and fry for 5 minutes, until softened. Stir in the remaining spice rub and cook for 1 minute. Cook the green beans in a saucepan of boiling water for 5 minutes, then drain and toss with the shallot mixture and the lemon juice.

When the chicken is cooked and a skewer inserted in one of the legs reveals clear juices, add the green bean mixture to the potatoes. Mix together, then add the stock and bring to a boil on the stove. Sprinkle with the herbs, carve the chicken and serve.

SAVE ME TIME
Thai barbecued chicken

Serves 4–6
Preparation time: 20–25 minutes, plus chilling
Cooking time: 30–40 minutes or 10–15 minutes, depending on type of chicken

> **3-pound (1.5 kg) whole chicken, spatchcocked (backbone removed, breastbone cracked so the chicken lies flat), or part-boned chicken breasts**
> **2-inch (5 cm) piece galangal, peeled, finely chopped**
> **4 cloves garlic, crushed**
> **1 large red chili, finely chopped**
> **4 shallots, finely chopped**
> **2 tablespoons (30 ml) finely chopped fresh coriander leaves**
> **⅔ cup (150 ml) thick coconut milk or sour cream**
> **chive flowers, to garnish**
> **lime wedges, to serve**
> **salt and pepper**

Rub the chicken all over with salt and pepper and place it in a shallow container.

Put the galangal, garlic, red chili, shallots and coriander in a food processor and blend to a paste, or use a pestle and mortar. Add the coconut milk and mix until well blended. Pour over the chicken, cover and leave to marinate overnight in the refrigerator.

Remove the chicken from the marinade, place it on a hot barbecue and cook for 30–40 minutes for spatchcocked chicken and 10–15 minutes for chicken breasts, turning and basting regularly with the remaining marinade. The whole chicken is cooked when a skewer inserted in one of the legs reveals clear juices.

Leave the chicken to stand for 5 minutes, then chop it into small pieces with a cleaver. Garnish with chive flowers and eat with fingers. Serve with lime wedges, as well as a dipping sauce and sticky rice, if desired.

SAVE ME MONEY
Chicken with vermouth

Serves 4
Preparation time: 20 minutes
Cooking time: about 2 hours

> **1 tablespoon (15 ml) olive oil**
> **7 ounces (200 g) shallots, peeled, halved**
> **2 slices smoked back bacon, diced**
> **2 cloves garlic, finely chopped**
> **1 pound (500 g) baby new potatoes**
> **2 tablespoons (30 ml) butter**
> **3-pound (1.5 kg) whole chicken**
> **4 stocks celery, each cut into 3 sections**
> **8 ounces (250 g) baby carrots, large ones halved**
> **3 bay leaves**
> **¾ cup + 2 tablespoons (200 ml) dry vermouth**
> **¾ cup + 2 tablespoons (200 ml) chicken stock (see page 9)**
> **2 tablespoons (30 ml) chopped fresh parsley, to garnish (optional)**
> **salt and pepper**

Heat the oil in a large ovenproof casserole dish, add the shallots and bacon and fry for 3–4 minutes over medium heat, until just beginning to brown. Add the garlic and potatoes and fry until just beginning to color. Tip onto a plate.

Add the butter to the pan and, when melted, add the chicken, breast side down. Fry each breast until golden, then turn over and fry the underside. Return the fried vegetables to the pan and tuck the celery and carrots around the sides of the chicken, adding the bay leaves and a little salt and pepper.

Pour in the vermouth and stock, then bring to a boil. Cover with a tight-fitting lid and transfer to a preheated 375°F (190°C) oven for 1¼ hours. Spoon the vermouth juices over the chicken, then cook, uncovered, for 20–30 minutes, until golden and a skewer inserted into one of the legs reveals clear juices.

Lift the chicken onto a serving plate, scoop the vegetables out with a draining spoon and nestle them around the chicken. Cover with foil and keep hot. Boil the remaining pan juices for about 5 minutes or until reduced by half, then pour into a serving dish or pitcher and sprinkle the vegetables with the parsley, if desired. Carve as for a traditional roast and serve with the gravy.

KIDS WILL LOVE THIS
Italian chicken cushion

Serves 4
Preparation time: 30 minutes
Cooking time: 1½ hours

- 3-pound (1.5 kg) whole chicken, deboned
- 13 ounces (400 g) Italian sausages or other flavored sausages (such as Parmesan and pancetta)
- 4 green onions, finely chopped
- 1 large whole red pepper, from a jar of roasted peppers in water, drained, diced
- 3 ounces (75 g) sun-dried tomatoes in oil, drained, roughly chopped
- 2 ounces (50 g) pitted olives, roughly chopped
- 3 tablespoons (45 ml) chopped fresh basil
- ¾ cup (175 ml) fresh breadcrumbs
- 1 egg yolk
- 1 tablespoon (15 ml) olive oil or oil from the sun-dried tomato jar
- salt and pepper

Put the deboned chicken on a large chopping board with the breast skin down, tidy up the edges with a knife and open out flat.

Slit the sausages lengthwise, peel off the skins and put the meat into a large bowl. Add the onions, red pepper, sun-dried tomatoes, olives, basil, breadcrumbs, egg yolk and plenty of seasoning and mix with a wooden spoon. Spoon onto the center of the chicken. Fold the legs, wings and remaining skin back into position so that the stuffing is enclosed. Tie with string like the spokes of a wheel, adjusting the string and patting into shape to form a round cushion.

Weigh the chicken, then put it breast side up in a roasting pan. Drizzle with the oil and season lightly. Cover with foil and roast in a preheated 375°F (190°C) oven for 20 minutes per pound (500 g) plus 20 minutes. Remove the foil for the last 30 minutes and baste the chicken once or twice with pan juices, until a deep golden brown and a skewer inserted in one of the legs reveals clear juices.

Allow to cool, remove the string and cut into wedge shapes. Serve with salad.

AS WELL AS BEING ONE OF EVERYONE'S FAVORITE SUNDAY ROASTS, A CHICKEN WILL GIVE YOU GREAT LEFTOVERS TO EAT DURING THE WEEK.

LEFTOVER TO LUNCH
Chicken & spinach chowder

Serves 6
Preparation time: 15 minutes
Cooking time: 35 minutes

- 1 tablespoon (15 ml) sunflower oil
- 2 tablespoons (30 ml) butter
- 4 slices smoked back bacon, chopped
- 2 small leeks, thinly sliced, green and white slices separated
- 1½ pound (750 g) potatoes, diced
- 3½ cups (875 ml) chicken stock (see page 9)
- 5–7 ounces (50–200 g) cooked chicken, diced
- 2½ cups (625 ml) 2 % milk
- ⅔ cup (150 ml) heavy cream
- 3½ ounces (100 g) spinach, rinsed, roughly chopped
- nutmeg, grated
- salt and pepper

Heat the oil and butter in a large saucepan, add the bacon, white part of leeks and diced potatoes and cook over a low heat for 5 minutes, stirring continuously until lightly golden.

Mix in the stock, then bring to a boil, cover and simmer for 20 minutes, until the potatoes are just tender. Add the chicken and boil rapidly for 3 minutes.

Stir in the green parts of the leeks, milk, cream and a little salt and pepper. Simmer gently for 5 minutes, then stir in the spinach and a little nutmeg. Cook for 2 minutes, until the spinach is just cooked. Ladle into bowls, sprinkle with a little extra nutmeg and serve with crusty bread.

7

BUT I DON'T LIKE . . .
ROAST CHICKEN

Spiced chicken with yogurt crust

Serves 4
Preparation time: 30 minutes, plus marinating
Cooking time: 1 hour 20 minutes

> 3-pound (1.5 kg) whole chicken
> 1-inch (2.5 cm) piece gingerroot, sliced
> 2 small green chilies
> 1 small bunch fresh coriander, plus extra to garnish
> 4 cloves garlic, peeled
> ¾ cup (175 ml) low-fat natural yogurt
> grated zest and juice of 1 lemon
> 1 teaspoon (5 ml) each ground garam masala and ground turmeric
> 1 teaspoon (5 ml) cumin seeds, roughly crushed
> 1 teaspoon (5 ml) salt
> ¼ cup (60 ml) butter, melted

Slash each chicken leg and breast 2–3 times with a sharp knife, then put the chicken in a large plastic bag. Finely chop the ginger, chilies, coriander and garlic in a food processor or with a large knife. Mix into the yogurt, then stir in the lemon zest and juice, spices and salt. Spoon the mixture into the plastic bag, seal well and marinate in the refrigerator for 4 hours (or overnight).

Allow the chicken to come to room temperature for 1 hour, then remove it from the bag (with a thick coating) and put it in a roasting pan.

Spoon 4 tablespoons (60 ml) of water into the base of the pan. Drizzle the chicken with butter.

Roast, uncovered, in a preheated 375°F (190°C) oven for 1 hour 20 minutes, spooning a little more of the yogurt marinade over the chicken once or twice.

When the chicken is cooked and a skewer inserted in one of the legs reveals clear juices, transfer it to a serving dish, garnish with coriander and serve with rice pilaf.

WHY NOT TRY... A NECTARINE CHUTNEY

As an accompaniment to roast chicken, and to add a different, spicy flavor, fry 1 finely chopped red onion in 1 tablespoon (15 ml) sunflower oil for 5 minutes. Add 6 roughly crushed cardamom pods, then mix in 13 ounces (400 g) nectarines and 2 tablespoons (30 ml) each of red wine vinegar, light brown sugar and water. Cover and simmer for 10 minutes.

8

FRIENDS FOR DINNER

Chicken with preserved lemons

Serves 4–5
Preparation time: 20 minutes
Cooking time: 1¾ hours

> 2 tablespoons (30 ml) olive oil
> 1 onion, finely chopped
> 3 cloves garlic
> 1 teaspoon (5 ml) ground ginger
> 1½ teaspoon (7 ml) ground cinnamon
> 1 large pinch of saffron threads, toasted, crushed
> 3½-pound (1.75 kg) whole chicken
> 3 cups (750 ml) chicken stock (see page 9) or water
> 5 ounces (150 g) large black olives (optional), rinsed, soaked
> 1 preserved lemon, chopped
> 1 large bunch fresh coriander, finely chopped
> 1 large bunch fresh parsley, finely chopped
> salt and pepper

Heat the oil in a frying pan, add the onion and fry gently, stirring frequently, until softened and golden.

Meanwhile, using a pestle and mortar, crush the garlic with a pinch of salt, then work in the ginger, cinnamon, saffron and a little pepper. Stir mixture into the onions, cook until fragrant, then remove from the pan and spread over the chicken.

Put the chicken into a heavy saucepan or ovenproof casserole dish that it just fits, heat gently and brown the chicken for about 2–3 minutes, turning often. Add the stock or water and bring to a simmer. Cover and simmer gently for about 1¼ hours, turning the chicken over 2–3 times.

Add the olives, if using, preserved lemon, coriander and parsley to the pan. Cover and cook for about 15 minutes until the chicken is very tender. Taste the sauce — if the flavor needs to be more concentrated, transfer the chicken to a warmed serving dish, cover and keep warm, and boil the cooking juices to a rich sauce. Tilt the pan and skim off any surplus fat, then pour over the chicken. Serve with couscous, if desired.

9

WATCHING MY WEIGHT
Chicken & avocado salad

Serves 4
Preparation time: 15 minutes

- ½ cup (125 ml) light mayonnaise
- 2 tablespoons (30 ml) mango chutney
- grated zest and juice of 1 lime
- 2 avocados, halved, pitted, peeled, diced
- 4 green onions, thinly sliced
- ¼ cucumber, diced
- 4–5 ounces (125–150 g) cooked chicken, diced
- 2 Little Gem lettuces or romaine hearts
- 1½ ounces (40 g) mixed salad leaves
- 1 small bunch fresh coriander, optional

Mix the mayonnaise, mango chutney and lime zest together in a large bowl. Toss the lime juice with the avocados, then add to the dressing. Add the green onions, cucumber and chicken and fold the mixture together lightly so that it is semi-mixed.

Divide the lettuce leaves between 4 serving plates and top with the other salad leaves. Spoon over the chicken salad and garnish with torn coriander leaves, if desired. Serve immediately.

10

INSPIRE ME
Chicken in a salt crust

Serves 4
Preparation time: 20 minutes
Cooking time: 2 hours

- 6 pounds (3 kg) salt
- 3-pound (1.5 kg) whole chicken
- 1 bulb garlic
- 3–4 stems fresh rosemary
- ⅔ cup (150 ml) water

FOR THE RED PEPPER KETCHUP
- 4 whole red peppers from a jar of roasted peppers in water, drained
- 1 tablespoon (15 ml) sweet Thai chili dipping sauce
- 1 tablespoon (15 ml) olive oil
- 1 tablespoon (15 ml) balsamic vinegar
- black pepper, to taste

Line a baking dish or roasting pan (large enough to hold the salt and chicken) with two large pieces of foil. Pour a thin layer of salt into the base, then sit the chicken on top. Cut the garlic in half through the center, then put both halves into the body cavity of the chicken with one of the rosemary stems. Tear the leaves from the other stems and sprinkle over the chicken.

Pour the remaining salt over the chicken, pulling up the foil to contain the salt in an even thickness around the chicken. Drizzle the water over the top, then spread the dampened salt into an even layer over the breast. Seal the edges of the foil tightly. Bake in a preheated 375°F (190°C) oven for 2 hours. Loosen the edge of the foil, then lift the package out. Open the foil and crack the salt crust away from the chicken.

To make the ketchup, remove one of the cooked garlic halves from inside the chicken cavity, discarding the papery skins, and put into a food processor with the other ketchup ingredients. Purée until smooth. Brush the salt off the chicken with a pastry brush, then carve normally and serve with the ketchup, salad and warm ciabatta bread.

10 WAYS WITH DUCK

BASIC
Duck with hoisin sauce

Serves 4
Preparation time: 15 minutes, plus marinating
Cooking time: 8 minutes

1 pound (500 g) duck breasts with skin, trimmed and cut into thin strips
2 cloves garlic, thinly sliced
3 tablespoons (45 ml) hoisin sauce
1½ tablespoons (22 ml) malt vinegar
1 tablespoon (15 ml) Chinese rice wine or dry sherry
1 tablespoon (15 ml) light soy sauce
1 teaspoon (5 ml) granulated sugar
1 red chili, seeded and finely chopped
1 teaspoon (5 ml) Chinese 5-spice powder
½ teaspoon (2 ml) salt
2 tablespoons (30 ml) peanut oil

TO GARNISH
2-inch (5 cm) piece cucumber, halved, seeded and cut into strips
3 green onions, cut into thin strips

Place the duck in a bowl with the garlic, hoisin, vinegar, rice wine, soy sauce, sugar, chili, 5-spice powder and salt. Mix well to combine, then marinate, covered, in the refrigerator for 30 minutes.

Heat half the peanut oil in a wok over high heat. Toss in half the duck with its marinade and stir-fry for 3 minutes, until cooked yet still slightly pink in the center. Use a slotted spoon to remove the duck from the pan, drain away any excess fat and wipe the wok clean with paper towels. Heat the remaining oil and stir-fry the rest of the duck in the same way. Serve the duck topped with a scattering of cucumber and green onion strips.

GIVE IT A TWIST
Jungle curry with duck

Serves 4
Preparation time: 20 minutes
Cooking time: 30 minutes

2 tablespoons (30 ml) sunflower oil
1¼ pounds (625 g) duck breast, sliced into thin strips
1⅔ cups (400 ml) chicken stock (see page 9)
1 tablespoon (15 ml) Thai fish sauce
2½ ounces (65 g) canned bamboo shoots, rinsed and drained
4 baby eggplants, quartered
1 small handful of Thai basil leaves

FOR THE CURRY PASTE
2 tablespoons (30 ml) green curry paste
2 tablespoons (30 ml) finely chopped lemongrass
3 lime leaves, finely shredded
1 teaspoon (5 ml) shrimp paste
6 cloves garlic, crushed
5 shallots, finely chopped
3 tablespoons (45 ml) finely chopped fresh coriander root
4 tablespoons (60 ml) sunflower oil

Make the curry paste by blending all the ingredients in a small food processor. (You might need to add a little water to make a smooth paste.)

Heat the oil in a large, nonstick wok over high heat and add the curry paste. Stir-fry for 1–2 minutes and then add the duck. Stir-fry for 4–5 minutes, until sealed, and then pour in the stock and fish sauce and bring to a boil. Remove the duck from the pan with a slotted spoon, set aside and keep warm.

Add the bamboo shoots and eggplant to the pan and cook for 12–15 minutes or until tender.

Return the meat to the pan and cook gently for 3–4 minutes. Stir in half the basil leaves and remove from the heat. Ladle the curry into deep plates or bowls, garnish with the remaining basil leaves and serve immediately with steamed jasmine rice.

3 🕐

SAVE ME TIME
Duck slices with cashews

Serves 4
Preparation time: 15 minutes, plus resting
Cooking time: 20 minutes

1½ teaspoons (7 ml) sunflower oil
1 teaspoon (5 ml) toasted sesame oil
½ teaspoon (2 ml) Chinese 5-spice powder
1 pinch of sea salt
1 pinch of ground black pepper
2 duck breasts, scored with a sharp knife 3–4 times, dried
5 ounces (150 g) small green mangoes or 1 green apple
4-inch (10 cm) piece cucumber, cut in half, finely sliced
2 tomatoes, cut into pieces
2 shallots, finely sliced
1-inch (2.5 cm) piece fresh gingerroot, peeled, finely shredded
2½ tablespoons (37 ml) light soy sauce
2½ tablespoons (37 ml) lime juice
2 small bird's-eye red chilies, finely chopped
½ cup (125 ml) roasted cashews
mixed salad leaves, to serve

Rub both oils, Chinese 5-spice powder and salt and pepper over the duck breasts. Put the breasts skin side down in a cold wok, then bring it slowly up to medium-low so the white fat turns into wonderful thin, crispy, golden crackling. Cook for 10–12 minutes, then turn the breasts over and cook for a further 5 minutes. Let it rest for 5 minutes before slicing.

Peel and finely shred the mangoes or apple just before mixing (to prevent their color darkening) and mix with the duck slices, cucumber, tomatoes, shallots, ginger, soy sauce, lime juice, chilies and cashews. Taste and adjust the seasoning.

Pile mixed salad leaves onto each serving plate. Spoon the duck and cashews on top and serve as a salad, side dish or starter.

4

SAVE ME MONEY
Duck, hazelnut & peach salad

Serves 4
Preparation time: 15 minutes
Cooking time: 20 minutes

3 duck breasts, about 7 ounces (200 g) each
4 peaches
½ cup (125 ml) toasted hazelnuts, roughly chopped
4 ounces (125 g) arugula

FOR THE DRESSING
1 teaspoon (5 ml) Dijon mustard
2 tablespoons (30 ml) balsamic vinegar
4 tablespoons (60 ml) hazelnut oil
salt and pepper

Heat a grill pan until it is very hot and fry the duck breasts, skin side down, for 4 minutes or until golden brown. Turn the duck over and cook for 2 minutes, then transfer it to a preheated 375°F (190°C) oven and cook for 6–8 minutes, until cooked through. Remove from the oven, cover with foil and leave to rest.

Meanwhile, halve the peaches and remove the pits. Heat a grill pan to medium heat, add the peach halves, cut side down, and cook until they are golden yellow. Cut the peaches into wedges and mix them in a bowl with the hazelnuts and arugula.

Make the dressing by whisking together the mustard, vinegar and oil. Season to taste with salt and pepper.

Thinly slice the duck meat and add it to the salad. Drizzle over the dressing, combine gently and serve.

5

Hot duck & coconut noodles

Serves 4–6
Preparation time: 10 minutes
Cooking time: 15 minutes

> 4 confit duck legs
> 1 cup (250 ml) coconut milk
> ¾ cups + 2 tablespoons (200 ml) chicken stock (see page 9)
> 2 tablespoons (30 ml) Thai fish sauce
> 3 whole star anise
> 1 teaspoon (5 ml) hot pepper flakes
> 1 ounce (25 g) gingerroot, thinly sliced
> 1 small bunch coriander, chopped
> juice of 2 limes
> 8 ounces (250 g) flat rice noodles
> 4 tablespoons (60 ml) coconut shavings, toasted
> ½ cup (125 ml) cashews, toasted

Heat a large frying pan and put the duck legs and their fat, skin side down, in the pan. Cook over medium heat for 10 minutes, until the skins turn golden and crispy. Turn and cook for a further 2–3 minutes, until the legs are heated through. Drain on paper towels, then tear the meat into small pieces and discard the bones.

Meanwhile, pour the coconut milk into a pan with the stock, fish sauce, star anise, hot pepper flakes, ginger and half the chopped coriander and bring to a simmer. Leave to simmer gently for 10 minutes to allow the flavors to infuse. Stir in the lime juice.

Cook the noodles in unsalted boiling water for about 3 minutes or according to the instructions on the package, then drain and heap into serving bowls.

Scatter on the duck meat and pour in the hot coconut broth. Sprinkle with the coconut shavings, cashews and remaining coriander. Serve immediately.

DUCK CONTAINS PLENTY OF FAT. YOU WILL NOT USUALLY NEED TO ADD ANY MORE — AND REMEMBER TO USE THE FAT LEFT IN THE PAN TO COOK ROAST POTATOES LATER.

6

Peking wraps

Serves 2
Preparation time: 10 minutes, plus chilling
Cooking time: 6 minutes

> 1 duck breast, about 6 ounces (175g), with skin, cut across into very thin slices
> ½ teaspoon (2 ml) Chinese 5-spice powder
> 1 tablespoon (15 ml) vegetable oil
> 2 large soft flour tortillas
> 2 tablespoons (30 ml) hoisin sauce
> 2 iceberg lettuce leaves, thinly shredded
> 2-inch (5 cm) piece cucumber, sliced into matchstick-sized pieces
> 2 green onions, thinly sliced diagonally

Put the slices of duck on a plate and sprinkle with the 5-spice powder. Turn the slices in the spice until coated all over. Heat the oil in a small frying pan for 1 minute. Add the duck and fry gently for 5 minutes, turning the pieces with a spatula. Using the spatula, transfer the duck to a plate and leave to cool while you prepare the filling.

Heat the tortillas one at a time in the microwave on high for 8 seconds. Alternatively, warm them under a hot broiler or in a frying pan for approximately 10 seconds.

Spread the hoisin sauce over one side of each tortilla. Scatter a line of lettuce, then the cucumber, green onions and duck down the center of each tortilla, keeping the ingredients away from the ends.

Fold two sides of each tortilla over the ends of the filling, then roll them up tightly from an unfolded side so that the filling is completely enclosed. Cut the wraps in half, wrap in parchment paper and chill in the refrigerator until ready to go.

BUT I DON'T LIKE ...
DUCK
Spring braised duck

Serves 4
Preparation time: 20 minutes
Cooking time: 1¾ hours

4 duck legs
2 teaspoons (10 ml) all-purpose flour
2 tablespoons (30 ml) butter
1 tablespoon (15 ml) olive oil
2 onions, sliced
2 slices bacon, finely chopped
2 cloves garlic, crushed
⅔ cup (150 ml) white wine
1¼ cups (300 ml) chicken stock (see page 9)
3 bay leaves
1 pound (500 g) small new potatoes, e.g., Jersey Royals
1½ cups (375 ml) fresh peas
1¼ cups (300 ml) asparagus tips
2 tablespoons (30 ml) chopped fresh mint
salt and pepper

Halve the duck legs through the joints. Mix the flour with a little seasoning and use to coat the duck pieces.

Melt the butter with the oil in a sturdy roasting pan or ovenproof casserole dish and gently fry the duck pieces for about 10 minutes, until browned. Move the cooked duck to a plate and pour off all but 1 tablespoon (15 ml) of the fat that is left in the pan.

Add the onions and bacon to the pan and fry gently for 5 minutes. Add the garlic and fry for a further 1 minute. Add the wine, stock and bay leaves and bring to a boil, stirring continuously. Return the duck pieces and cover with a lid or foil. Place in a preheated 325°F (160°C) oven for 45 minutes.

Add the potatoes to the pan, stirring them into the juices. Sprinkle with salt and return to the oven for 30 minutes.

Add the peas, asparagus and mint to the pan and return to the oven for a further 15 minutes or until all the vegetables are tender. Check the seasoning and serve.

WHY NOT TRY...
SPRING BRAISED CHICKEN

You can replace the duck with 4 chicken thighs and omit the bacon. When adding the peas, asparagus and mint, add the following spring vegetables: 7 ounces (200 g) baby turnips, 3½ ounces (100 g) baby carrots and 2 small sliced zucchinis. Cook as above.

FRIENDS FOR DINNER
Duck, clementine & tatsoi salad

Serves 4–6
Preparation time: 20 minutes
Cooking time: 15 minutes

3 duck breasts, about 7½ ounces (225 g) each
10 ounces (300 g) green beans, trimmed
3 clementines, peeled, segmented
7 ounces (200 g) tatsoi or spinach

FOR THE DRESSING
juice of 2 clementines
1 tablespoon (15 ml) white wine vinegar
4 tablespoons (60 ml) olive oil
salt and pepper

Put the duck breasts, skin side down, in a cold ovenproof dish and cook over medium heat for 6 minutes or until the skin has turned crisp and brown. Turn them over and cook for a further 2 minutes. Transfer the duck to a preheated 350°F (180°C) oven and cook for 5 minutes, until cooked through. Remove the duck breasts from the oven, cover with foil and leave to rest.

Meanwhile, blanch the green beans in lightly salted boiling water for 2 minutes, until cooked but still firm and bright green. Drain and refresh in cold water. Transfer the beans to a large salad bowl with the clementine segments.

Make the dressing by whisking together the clementine juice, vinegar and oil in a small bowl. Season to taste with salt and pepper.

Add the tatsoi or spinach to the beans and clementines, drizzle on the dressing and combine well. Slice the duck meat and combine it with the salad and. Serve immediately.

9

WATCHING MY WEIGHT
Aromatic braised duck

Serves 4
Preparation time: 25 minutes
Cooking time: 2 hours

4 duck portions
2 teaspoons (10 ml) Chinese 5-spice powder
2 stalks lemongrass, bruised
5 cloves garlic, crushed
4 red shallots, chopped
4 ounces (125 g) dried shiitake mushrooms, soaked for 30 minutes
2-inch (5 cm) piece gingerroot, peeled and cut into thick julienne strips
2½ cups (625 ml) chicken stock (see page 9)
1 ounce (25 g) dried medlar berries or Chinese red dates
½ ounce (15 g) dried black fungus, broken into pieces
1 tablespoon (15 ml) Thai fish sauce
2 teaspoons (10 ml) cornflour
4 green onions, quartered
salt and pepper
1 handful fresh coriander, to garnish

Season the duck portions with the 5-spice powder. Place them skin side down in a very hot frying pan or casserole dish to brown the skin. Turn the pieces over. Add the lemongrass, garlic, shallots, mushrooms and ginger to the pan, then cover the duck with the stock. Cover the pan with a lid and simmer gently for 1½ hours.

Remove the duck from the pan and add the medlar berries or Chinese red dates, black fungus and fish sauce. Season with salt and pepper to taste. Mix the cornstarch to a smooth paste with a little water and add to the pan. Bring the sauce to a boil, stirring continuously, and cook until thickened. Return the duck to the pan and simmer gently for 30 minutes.

Add the green onions to the sauce and garnish the duck with the coriander.

10

INSPIRE ME
Duck with kumquat honey sauce

Serves 4
Preparation time: 15 minutes
Cooking time: 45 minutes

4 duck leg portions
½ teaspoon (2 ml) Chinese 5-spice powder
1½ cups (300 ml) freshly squeezed orange juice
2 tablespoons (30 ml) liquid honey
2 cloves
1 tablespoon (15 ml) Cointreau or brandy
10 kumquats, sliced
1 tablespoon (15 ml) chopped flat-leaf parsley
salt and pepper

Place the duck legs on a rack standing inside a roasting pan, season well with salt, pepper and the Chinese 5-spice powder and roast in a preheated 425°F (220°C) oven for 10 minutes.

Put the orange juice, honey, cloves, Cointreau or brandy and kumquats in the roasting pan under the rack. Return the pan to the oven for a further 25 minutes.

Remove the duck from the oven and add to the roasting pan with the kumquat sauce. Simmer gently together on the stovetop for 10 minutes.

Add the chopped parsley to the sauce. Thickly slice the duck and serve piping hot with boiled potatoes and green beans.

10 WAYS WITH TURKEY

1

BASIC
Turkey & avocado salad

Serves 4
Preparation time: 20 minutes

12 ounces (375 g) cooked turkey
1 large avocado
1 container of mustard and cress sprouts
5 ounces 1(50 g) mixed salad leaves
2 ounces (50 g) mixed toasted seeds, such as pumpkin and
    sunflower

FOR THE DRESSING
2 tablespoons (30 ml) apple juice
2 tablespoons (30 ml) natural yogurt
1 teaspoon (5 ml) liquid honey
1 teaspoon (5 ml) whole-grain mustard
salt and pepper

Thinly slice the turkey. Peel, pit and dice the avocado and mix it with the mustard and cress and salad leaves in a large bowl. Add the turkey and toasted seeds and stir to combine.

Make the dressing by whisking together the apple juice, yogurt, honey and mustard. Season to taste with salt and pepper.

Pour the dressing over the salad and toss to coat. Serve the salad with toasted whole-grain rye bread or rolled up in flatbreads.

2

GIVE IT A TWIST
Turkey chili poblano

Serves 6
Preparation time: 25 minutes
Cooking time: 1 hour

1 cup (250 ml) flaked almonds
½ cup (125 ml) peanuts
½ tablespoon (7ml) coriander seeds
1 teaspoon (5 ml) ground cloves
3 tablespoons (45 ml) sesame seeds
½ cinnamon stick
1 teaspoon (5 ml) fennel seeds or aniseed
4 large dried chilies
1 green jalapeño chili, chopped
1 can (13 ounces/298 ml) chopped tomatoes
⅔ cup (150 ml) raisins
6 tablespoons (90 ml) vegetable oil
2 onions, finely chopped
3 cloves garlic, crushed
1¼ pounds (625 g) turkey fillets, finely sliced or cubed
1¼ cups (300 ml) vegetable stock (see page 8)
2 ounces (50 g) plain dark chocolate, roughly chopped
red and green chilies, finely chopped, to garnish

Spread the almonds, peanuts, coriander seeds, cloves, sesame seeds, cinnamon, fennel or aniseed and dried chilies over a baking sheet and roast in a preheated 400°F (200°C) oven for 10 minutes, stirring once or twice.

Remove from the oven and put the nuts and spices in a food processor or blender and process until well combined. Add the chopped jalapeño and process once more until well mixed.

Spoon the spice mixture into a bowl and mix in the tomatoes and raisins. Heat the oil in a large saucepan and fry the onions and garlic with the turkey on all sides until browned. Remove the turkey and set aside.

Add the spice mixture to the oil remaining in the saucepan and cook, stirring frequently, for 5–6 minutes or until the spice paste has heated through and is bubbling. Add the stock and chocolate and simmer gently until the chocolate has melted.

Reduce the heat, return the turkey to the pan and mix well. Cover the pan and simmer gently for 30 minutes, adding extra water if the sauce begins to dry out. Garnish with the chopped red and green chilies.

3

Turkey & bulgur salad

Serves 4
Preparation time: 10 minutes, plus marinating
Cooking time: 10 minutes

2 tablespoons (30 ml) sunflower oil
2 tablespoons (30 ml) lemon juice
1 teaspoon (5 ml) paprika
3 tablespoons (45 ml) chopped flat-leaf parsley, plus extra to garnish
13 ounces (400 g) turkey breast, diced
salt and pepper

FOR THE BULGUR SALAD
1⅔ cups (400 ml) chicken stock (see page 9)
1⅔ cups (400 ml) bulgur
1 can (15 ounces/410 ml) green lentils, rinsed and drained
½ cucumber
10 cherry tomatoes
¾ ounce (20 g) fresh mint, chopped
lemon wedges, to garnish

FOR THE HUMMUS DRESSING
4 tablespoons (60 ml) hummus
1 tablespoon (15 ml) lemon juice
1 tablespoon (15 ml) water

Presoak 8 wooden skewers in warm water. Mix together the oil, lemon juice, paprika and parsley, and season to taste. Add the turkey and turn to coat thoroughly. Set aside to marinate for at least 20 minutes.

Drain the turkey (discard any marinade) and thread the pieces onto the skewers. Cook under a preheated hot broiler, turning once or twice, for 10 minutes or until cooked through.

Meanwhile, bring the stock to a boil and cook the bulgur according to the instructions on the package. Drain and spread out to cool. Stir in the green lentils, cucumber, tomatoes and mint.

Make the dressing by combining the hummus with the lemon juice and water.

Serve the turkey skewers with the bulgur salad, garnished with lemon wedges and flat-leaf parsley. Serve the dressing separately.

TURKEY IS HIGH IN PROTEIN AND LOW IN FAT, MAKING IT THE PERFECT EVERYDAY FOOD — DON'T SAVE IT FOR THE HOLIDAYS!

4

Baked turkey burrito

Serves 4
Preparation time: 12 minutes
Cooking time: 30 minutes

4 tablespoons (60 ml) vegetable oil
1 pound (500 g) turkey breast, thinly sliced
1 large onion, sliced
1 red pepper, cored, seeded and sliced
1 yellow pepper, cored, seeded and sliced
1 can (5 ounces/150 g) red kidney beans, rinsed and drained
1 cup (250 ml) cooked rice
juice of 1 lime
8 medium-sized all-purpose flour tortillas
6 tablespoons (90 ml) medium-hot ready-made salsa
2 tablespoons (30 ml) preserved jalapeño peppers (optional), sliced
8 ounces (250 g) Cheddar cheese, grated
salt and pepper

TO SERVE
guacamole
½ iceberg lettuce, shredded

Heat 2 tablespoons (30 ml) of the oil in a large frying pan and stir-fry the sliced turkey for 3–4 minutes until it is beginning to color, then remove it with a slotted spoon. Increase the heat, add the remaining oil and fry the onion and peppers for 5–6 minutes, stirring only occasionally so that they color quickly without softening too much.

Reduce the heat, return the turkey to the pan and stir in the beans and cooked rice. Season well, squeeze over the lime juice and remove from the heat. Spoon the filling on to the tortillas, roll them up and arrange them in a rectangular ovenproof dish.

Pour the salsa over the tortillas and scatter over the jalapeño peppers (if used) and Cheddar. Cook in a preheated 200°C (400°F) oven for about 20 minutes, until hot and the cheese has melted. Serve immediately with guacamole and shredded lettuce.

5

KIDS WILL LOVE THIS
Turkey & wild mushroom turnovers

Serves 4
Preparation time: 8 minutes, plus soaking
Cooking time: 40 minutes

    1 ounce (25 g) dried wild mushrooms
    4 tablespoons (60 ml) olive oil
    14½ ounces (450 g) turkey breast, sliced
    3½ ounces (100 g) prosciutto, torn into pieces
    7 ounces (200 g) white or portobello mushrooms, sliced
    ⅓ cup + 2 tablespoons (100ml) red wine
    1 teaspoon (5 ml) chopped fresh thyme
    8 ounces (250 g) mascarpone cheese
    1 pound (500 g) puff pastry (thawed if frozen)
    1 egg, beaten
    salt and pepper
    watercress, to garnish

Soak the mushrooms in 4 tablespoons (60 ml) boiling water for 5–10 minutes. Heat 2 tablespoons (30 ml) of the oil in a frying pan and fry the turkey for 2–3 minutes, until golden. Add the prosciutto and cook for 2 minutes before adding the fresh and dried mushrooms. Fry for 3–4 minutes, until the mushrooms are soft and golden.

Pour the wine into the pan, then add the thyme. Allow the liquid to simmer for 2–3 minutes, until evaporated. Remove from the heat, stir in the mascarpone and season to taste.

Roll out the pastry into a rectangular shape until it forms a thin layer and cut into 4. Spoon one-quarter of the mixture onto the center of each quarter of pastry. Brush a little beaten egg around the edges, fold over the pastry and press firmly to seal.

Brush the remaining egg over the closed turnovers, score the tops with a knife, if desired, and bake in a preheated 400°F (200°C) oven for 20 minutes, until golden and crispy.

Serve garnished with watercress.

6

LEFTOVER TO LUNCH
Turkey tacos

Serves 4
Preparation time: 12 minutes, plus cooling
Cooking time: 5–6 minutes

    3 tablespoons (45 ml) sunflower oil
    13 ounces (400 g) ground turkey
    1 tablespoon (15 ml) pickled jalapeño peppers, sliced
    1 can (7ounces/200 g) corn, drained
    1 ripe avocado, peeled, pitted and cut into chunks
    2 ripe tomatoes, chopped
    1 small red onion, finely diced
    1 small bunch fresh coriander, chopped
    salt and pepper

    FOR THE DRESSING
    juice of 2 limes
    1 teaspoon (5 ml) liquid honey
    4 tablespoons (60 ml) pumpkin seed oil

    TO SERVE
    4 taco shells
    ½ small red cabbage, shredded
    8 ounces (250 g) buffalo mozzarella cheese, cubed
    3 tablespoons (45 ml) pumpkin seeds, to sprinkle

Make the dressing by mixing together all the ingredients in a small bowl. Season to taste and set aside.

Heat the oil in a large frying pan and fry the turkey for 5–6 minutes, until cooked and beginning to color. Scrape into a bowl, mix with half the dressing and set aside to cool.

Make a chunky salsa by combining the peppers, corn, avocado, tomatoes, red onion and coriander. Mix with the remaining dressing.

When the turkey is cool, mix it with the salsa and serve in the taco shells with the cabbage and mozzarella and scatter the pumpkin seeds on top.

7

BUT I DON'T LIKE ...
TURKEY
Cheesy turkey
& cranberry melt

Serves 4
Preparation time: 5 minutes
Cooking time: 8 minutes

4 flat rolls
2 tablespoons (30 ml) whole-grain mustard
2 tablespoons (30 ml) cranberry sauce
7 ounces (200 g) cooked turkey breast, sliced
4 ounces (125 g) Cheddar cheese, grated

Split the rolls in half and spread half with the mustard and the other half with the cranberry sauce. Top with the turkey slices and cheese and then sandwich together.

Heat a dry frying pan until hot, add the sandwich and cook over medium-high for 4 minutes on each side, until golden and the cheese has melted. Serve hot.

WHY NOT TRY... AVOCADO, BLUE
CHEESE & SPINACH MELT

Split the rolls in half and spread the bottom of each one with a little butter. Mash together 1 peeled, pitted and sliced avocado, 2 ounces (50 g) crumbled blue cheese and 2 tablespoons (30 ml) sour cream. Divide between the roll bottoms and add a few baby spinach leaves. Add the roll tops and cook as above until the filling starts to ooze.

8

FRIENDS FOR DINNER
Roast turkey

Serves 10 with leftovers
Preparation time: 30 minutes
Cooking time: 3 hours 25 minutes–3 hours 40 minutes, according to weight

1 small onion, halved
11–13 pounds (5–6 kg) oven-ready turkey, giblets removed and cavity wiped clean
2½ tablespoons (37 ml) butter, softened
2 tablespoons (30 ml) vegetable oil
3 sprigs fresh thyme, chopped
salt and pepper

Place the onion in the turkey's body cavity and season the cavity with salt and pepper. Tie the turkey legs with string at the top of the drumsticks.

Weigh the stuffed turkey to calculate the Cooking time: (allow 20 minutes per 2 pounds (1 kg), plus 70 minutes for birds under 8½ pounds (4 kg), or plus 90 minutes for birds weighing 8½ pounds (4 kg) or more), then place the bird in a large roasting pan. Rub all over with softened butter and season the outside of the turkey. Add the vegetable oil to the pan.

Cover the prepared turkey loosely with foil and roast in a preheated 375°F (190°C) oven for the required Cooking time, basting from time to time. Remove the foil for the last 40 minutes of cooking to brown the bird, and scatter over the chopped thyme. Check that the turkey is cooked by inserting a skewer into one of the legs, and if the juices are clear it is ready.

Transfer the turkey to a large dish, cover with clean foil and leave to rest for 15–20 minutes before carving.

Arrange the turkey on a warmed serving platter and serve with an assortment of vegetables.

WATCHING MY WEIGHT
Turkey burgers & sweet potatoes

Serves 4
Preparation time: 15 minutes, plus chilling
Cooking time: 55 minutes

> 1½ pounds (750 g) sweet potatoes, washed but unpeeled and cut into wedges
> 2 tablespoons (30 ml) sunflower oil
> 1 pound (500 g) ground turkey
> ½ red pepper, cored, seeded and chopped
> 1 can (11 ounces/325 ml) corn, rinsed and drained
> 1 onion, chopped
> 1 egg, beaten
> 6 whole wheat bread rolls
> salad leaves, to serve
> tomato slices, to serve
> salt and pepper

Toss the potato wedges in 1 tablespoon (15 ml) oil, season to taste and bake in a preheated 400°F (200°C) oven for 30 minutes, turning after 15 minutes.

Meanwhile, in a large bowl, mix the turkey with the red pepper, corn and onion. Season to taste and add the egg. Shape the mixture into 6 burgers and refrigerate until ready to cook.

Heat the remaining oil in a shallow frying pan over medium heat. Add the burgers, 3 at a time, and cook for 2 minutes on each side, until brown. Transfer to a baking sheet and finish cooking in the oven, below the potato wedges, for 15 minutes or until cooked.

Cut the rolls in half and toast them, cut side down, in the hot pan. Put a few salad leaves and tomato slices in each roll, add a burger and serve them with the sweet potato wedges.

INSPIRE ME
Wild rice & turkey salad

Serves 4
Preparation time: 10 minutes, plus cooling
Cooking time: 30 minutes

> 10 ounces (300 g) wild rice
> 2 green apples, finely sliced
> 3 ounces (75 g) pecans
> 2¼ ounces (60 g) cranberries
> zest and juice of 2 oranges
> 3 tablespoons (45 ml) olive oil
> 2 tablespoons (30 ml) chopped fresh parsley
> 4 turkey fillets, about 4 ounces (125 g) each
> salt and pepper

Cook the rice according to the instructions on the package and allow to cool to room temperature.

Mix the apples into the rice with the pecans, cranberries and orange zest and juice. Season to taste with salt and pepper.

Mix together the oil and parsley. Cut the turkey fillets into halves or thirds lengthwise and cover with this mixture. Heat a frying pan until it is hot but not smoking and cook the turkey for 2 minutes on each side. Slice the turkey, arrange the pieces next to the rice salad and serve immediately.

MEAT

Discover a brand-new recipe you've never cooked before with these delicious and exciting recipes for steak, sausages, bacon, ground beef and diced lamb for the whole family to enjoy.

MEAT

 1 BASIC

 2 GIVE IT A TWIST

 3 SAVE ME TIME

 4 SAVE ME MONEY

 5 KIDS WILL LOVE THESE

GROUND BEEF PAGE 48

Classic bolognese

Kheema mutter

Chili tacos

Classic meatloaf

Spicy beef burgers

STEAK PAGE 54

Deviled medallions

Red curry with beef

Chili Thai beef subs

Beef & pepper kebabs

Steak sliders

SAUSAGES PAGE 60

Sausages with mustard mashed potatoes

Penne with sausage

Morning muffins & ketchup

Sausage meatballs, peas & pasta

Homemade sausage rolls

BACON PAGE 66

BLT sandwich

Bacon & egg crispy bread tarts

Quick pasta carbonara

Tartiflette-style pizza

Bacon & pancakes with maple syrup

DICED LAMB PAGE 72

Taverna-style grilled lamb with feta

Lamb & spinach curry

Sri Lankan–style lamb curry

Lamb tenderloin with vegetables

Lamb ragu with toasted walnuts

6 LEFTOVER TO LUNCH

Mexican pie

Chili beef salad
with coriander

Picnic pie

Potato & bacon cakes

Marinated minty
lamb kebabs

7  BUT I DON'T LIKE...

Meatballs with tomato
sauce

Japanese beef
& noodle salad

Pork & cabbage bake

Vegetable soup with
bacon dumplings

Coconut lamb curry

8 FRIENDS FOR DINNER

Bobotie

Beef stroganoff

Sausage & sweet potato
hash

Braised liver & bacon
with prunes

Caribbean lamb stoba

9 WATCHING MY WEIGHT

Chili con carne

Sliced steak with
hot & sour sauce

Spicy sausage cassoulet

Spinach, avocado
& bacon salad

Lamb & flageolet
bean stew

10 INSPIRE ME

Thai chili beef subs

Individual Italian fillet
steak parcels

Chestnut & sausage
tagliatelle

Risoni, sweet potato
& bacon salad

Lamb & prune tagine
with barley

10 WAYS WITH GROUND BEEF

BASIC
Classic bolognese

Serves 4
Preparation time: 10 minutes
Cooking time: 4–6 hours

- 2 tablespoons (30 ml) unsalted butter
- 1 tablespoon (15 ml) olive oil
- 1 small onion, finely chopped
- 2 stalks celery, finely chopped
- 1 carrot, finely chopped
- 1 bay leaf
- 7 ounces (200 g) lean ground beef
- 7 ounces (200 g) lean ground pork
- ⅔ cup (150 ml) dry white wine
- ⅔ cup (150 ml) 1% or 2% milk
- 1 large pinch of freshly grated nutmeg
- 2 cans (each 14 ounces/398 ml) chopped tomatoes
- 1½–2¼ cups (375–560 ml) chicken stock (see page 9)
- 13 ounces (400 g) fettuccine
- salt and pepper
- freshly grated Parmesan cheese, to serve

Melt the butter with the oil in a large, heavy-bottomed saucepan over low heat. Add the onion, celery, carrot and bay leaf and cook, stirring occasionally, for 10 minutes, until softened but not colored. Add the meat, season with salt and pepper and cook, stirring continuously, over medium heat until no longer pink.

Pour in the wine and bring to a boil. Gently simmer for 15 minutes, until evaporated. Stir in the milk and nutmeg and simmer for a further 15 minutes, until the milk has evaporated. Stir in the tomatoes and cook, uncovered, over very low heat for 3–5 hours. The sauce is very thick, so when it begins to stick, add ⅓ cup (75 ml) of the stock at a time, as needed.

Cook the pasta in a large saucepan of salted boiling water until al dente or according to the package instructions. Drain thoroughly, reserving a ladleful of the cooking water.

Return to the pan and place over low heat. Add the pasta and stir for 30 seconds, then pour in the reserved pasta cooking water and stir until the pasta is well coated and looks silky. Serve immediately, with a scattering of grated Parmesan.

GIVE IT A TWIST
Kheema mutter

Serves 4
Preparation time: 20 minutes
Cooking time: 1¾–2 hours

- 2 tablespoons (30 ml) sunflower oil
- 1 large onion, finely chopped
- 3 cloves garlic, crushed
- 1 teaspoon (5 ml) finely grated fresh gingerroot
- 3–4 green chilies, seeded and finely sliced
- 1 tablespoon (15 ml) cumin seeds
- 3 tablespoons (45 ml) hot curry paste
- 1½ pounds (750 g) ground beef
- 1 can (14 ounces/398 ml) chopped tomatoes
- 1 teaspoon (5 ml) sugar
- 4 tablespoons (60 ml) tomato paste
- 4 tablespoons (60 ml) coconut cream
- 1¾ cups (425 ml) fresh or frozen peas
- salt and pepper
- 1 large handful of chopped fresh coriander, to garnish

Heat the oil in a heavy-bottomed saucepan and add the onion. Cook over low heat for 15–20 minutes, until softened and light brown.

Add the garlic, ginger, chilies, curry paste and cumin seeds and stir-fry over high heat for 1–2 minutes.

Add the ground beef and stir-fry for 3–4 minutes. Stir in the tomatoes, sugar and tomato paste and bring to a boil. Season, cover and reduce the heat to low. Cook for about 1½ hours, until tender. Pour in the coconut cream and add the peas 10 minutes before the end of the cooking time.

Garnish with coriander and serve.

3 🕐

SAVE ME TIME
Chili tacos

Serves 4
Preparation time: 15 minutes
Cooking time: 25 minutes

> 2 tablespoons (30 ml) olive oil
> 1 large onion, finely chopped
> 2 cloves garlic, crushed
> 1 pound (500 g) lean ground beef
> 1 jar (24 ounces/700 ml) tomato sauce
> 1 can (14 ounces/398 ml) red kidney beans, drained
> 2–3 tablespoons (30–45 ml) hot chili sauce
> 8 soft corn tortillas
> 4 ounces (125 g) Cheddar cheese, grated
> ½ cup (125 ml) sour cream
> 1 handful of fresh coriander sprigs
> salt and pepper

Heat the oil in a saucepan, add the onion and garlic and cook over high heat for 5 minutes.

Add the ground beef and cook, breaking it up with a wooden spoon, for 5 minutes, until browned. Stir in the tomato sauce, beans, chili sauce and salt and pepper to taste and bring to a boil. Reduce the heat and simmer, uncovered, for 15 minutes, until the sauce has thickened.

Meanwhile, put the corn tortillas on a large baking sheet and heat in a preheated 350°F (180°C) oven for 5 minutes.

Serve the tortillas on a platter in the center of the table. Take 2 tortillas per person and spoon some chili into each one. Top with a quarter of the cheese and sour cream and a little coriander, roll up and serve.

4

SAVE ME MONEY
Classic meatloaf

Serves 4
Preparation time: 25 minutes, plus soaking
Cooking time: 55 minutes

> 2 thick slices white bread, crusts removed, broken into chunks
> 2 tablespoons (30 ml) 1% or 2% milk
> 1 large pinch of freshly grated nutmeg
> 1 pound (500 g) ground beef
> 6 slices pancetta or bacon, finely chopped
> 1 small onion, finely chopped
> 3 cloves garlic, finely chopped
> 4 tablespoons (60 ml) freshly grated Parmesan cheese
> 1 egg, lightly beaten
> ¾ cup (175 ml) fine dry white breadcrumbs
> 2 tablespoons (30 ml) olive oil
> ⅔ cup (150 ml) dry white wine
> 1 can (14 ounces/398 ml) chopped tomatoes
> finely grated zest of 1 orange
> 2 tablespoons (30 ml) roughly chopped flat-leaf parsley
> salt and pepper

Soak the bread in a bowl with the milk and nutmeg for about 10 minutes, until the milk is absorbed. Mash with a fork. Combine the beef, pancetta or bacon, onion and half the garlic in a large bowl. Add the Parmesan, egg and bread. Season with salt and pepper. Mix gently with your hands until well combined. Form into a loaf shape. Spread the breadcrumbs out on a large plate and roll the meatloaf through to coat thoroughly.

Heat the oil in a shallow saucepan with a tight-fitting lid over medium heat. Add the meatloaf and cook, turning occasionally, until golden all over. Add the wine, boil rapidly until reduced by half, then add the tomatoes. Cover and simmer very gently, turning the meatloaf occasionally and adding a little water if necessary, for 40–45 minutes or until a knife inserted into the center comes out hot.

Lift onto a serving dish. Stir the orange zest, parsley and remaining garlic into the pan and simmer for 2 minutes. Season with salt and pepper. Spoon over the meatloaf.

5

KIDS WILL LOVE THIS
Spicy beef burgers

Serves 4
Preparation time: 10 minutes
Cooking time: 6–14 minutes

1 pound 3 ounces (575 g) lean ground beef
2 cloves garlic, crushed
1 red onion, finely chopped
1 hot red chili, finely chopped
1 bunch parsley, chopped
1 tablespoon (15 ml) Worcestershire sauce
1 egg, beaten
4 rolls, such as whole wheat or multigrain, cut in half
hot salad leaves, such as mizuna or arugula
1 beefsteak tomato, sliced
salt and pepper
snipped chives, to garnish

TO SERVE
burger relish
grilled or fried new potatoes

Put the ground beef, garlic, red onion, chili and parsley in a large bowl. Add the Worcestershire sauce, beaten egg and a little salt and pepper and mix well.

Heat a grill pan. Using your hands, divide the mixture into 4 parts and shape into burgers. Cook the burgers in the grill pan for 3 minutes on each side for rare, 5 minutes for medium or 7 minutes for well done.

Place the roll halves under a preheated hot broiler and toast on one side. Fill each bun with some hot salad leaves, some tomato slices and a grilled burger, garnish with snipped chives and serve with your favourite relish and grilled or fried new potatoes.

GROUND BEEF IS INCREDIBLY VERSATILE. USE IT TO MAKE BOTH HEARTY WINTER SUPPERS AND SUMMERY BURGERS FOR YOUR BARBECUE.

6

LEFTOVER TO LUNCH
Mexican pie

Serves 4
Preparation time: 10 minutes
Cooking time: 30 minutes

2 tablespoons (30 ml) olive oil
1 onion, finely chopped
2 cloves garlic, crushed
2 carrots, diced
8 ounces (250 g) ground beef
1 red chili, finely chopped
1 can (14 ounces/398 ml) chopped tomatoes
1 can (14 ounces/398 ml) red kidney beans, drained and rinsed
2 ounces (50 g) tortilla chips
3½ ounces (100 g) Cheddar cheese, grated
salt and pepper
chopped fresh parsley or coriander, to garnish

Heat the oil in a saucepan, add the onion, garlic and carrots and cook until softened. Add the ground beef and chili and cook, stirring and breaking up with a wooden spoon, for 5 minutes or until the meat has browned. Add the tomatoes and beans, mix well and season to taste with salt and pepper.

Transfer to an ovenproof dish, cover with the tortilla chips and sprinkle with the Cheddar. Bake in a preheated 400°F (200°C) oven for 20 minutes or until golden brown. Garnish with chopped parsley or coriander before serving.

7

BUT I DON'T LIKE ...
GROUND BEEF
Meatballs with tomato sauce

Serves 4
Preparation time: 25 minutes
Cooking time: 30 minutes

> 1 pound (500 g) lean ground beef
> 3 cloves garlic, crushed
> 2 small onions, finely chopped
> ¼ cup (60 ml) dry breadcrumbs
> ¼ cup (60 ml) freshly grated Parmesan cheese
> 6 tablespoons (90 ml) olive oil
> ⅓ cup + 2 tablespoons (100 ml) red wine
> 2 cans (each 14 ounces/398 ml) chopped tomatoes
> 1 teaspoon (5 ml) granulated sugar
> 3 tablespoons (45 ml) sun-dried tomato paste
> 3 ounces (75 g) pitted Italian black olives, roughly chopped
> 4 tablespoons (60 ml) roughly chopped fresh oregano
> 4 ounces (125 g) mozzarella cheese, thinly sliced
> salt and pepper

Put the beef in a bowl with half the crushed garlic and half the onion, the breadcrumbs and 3 tablespoons (45 ml) of the Parmesan. Season and use your hands to thoroughly blend the ingredients. Shape into small balls, about 1 inch (2.5 cm) in diameter.

Heat half the oil in a large frying pan or skillet and fry the meatballs, shaking the pan frequently, for about 10 minutes, until browned. Remove and reserve meatballs.

Add the remaining oil and onion to the pan and fry until softened. Add the wine and let the mixture simmer until the wine has almost evaporated. Stir in the remaining garlic, tomatoes, sugar, tomato paste and a little seasoning. Bring to a boil and let the mixture simmer, until slightly thickened.

Stir in the olives, all but 1 tablespoon (15 ml) of the oregano and the meatballs. Cook gently for a further 5 minutes.

Arrange the mozzarella slices over the top and scatter with the remaining oregano and Parmesan. Season with black pepper and cook under the broiler until the cheese starts to melt. Serve in shallow bowls with warmed, crusty bread.

WHY NOT TRY...
GREEK-STYLE MEATBALLS

You could use 1 pound (500 g) lean ground lamb instead of beef. Replace the olives with 2 ounces (50 g) pine nuts. Before adding these to the pan in the fourth step, dry-fry in a small frying pan over a medium heat for 3–5 minutes until lightly browned, shaking them constantly.

8

FRIENDS FOR DINNER
Bobotie

Serves 4
Preparation time: 10 minutes, plus cooling
Cooking time: 40 minutes

> 2 tablespoons (30 ml) olive oil
> 1 onion, chopped
> 2 cloves garlic, chopped
> 2 tablespoons (30 ml) medium curry paste
> 1 pound (500 g) ground beef
> 2 tablespoons (30 ml) tomato paste
> 1 tablespoon (15 ml) white wine vinegar
> ⅓ cup (75 ml) sultanas
> 1 slice white bread, soaked in 3 tablespoons (45 ml)
>   1% or 2% milk and mashed
> 4 eggs, beaten
> ⅓ cup + 2 tablespoons (100 ml) whipping (35%) cream
> salt and pepper

Heat the oil in a saucepan, add the onion and garlic and cook until soft and starting to brown. Add the curry paste and ground beef and cook, stirring and breaking up with a wooden spoon, for 5 minutes or until browned.

Add the tomato paste, vinegar, sultanas and mashed bread. Season to taste with salt and pepper and transfer to a deep, medium-sized ovenproof dish or a 8-inch (20 cm) heavy cake pan.

Mix together the eggs and cream in a bowl, season to taste with salt and pepper and pour over the meat mixture.

Bake in a preheated 350°F (180°C) oven for 30 minutes or until the topping is set and golden brown. Remove from the oven and leave to cool for 10–15 minutes before serving.

9

WATCHING MY WEIGHT
Chili con carne

Serves 2
Preparation time: 15 minutes
Cooking time: about 45 minutes

2 tablespoons (30 ml) olive oil
1 red onion, finely chopped
3 cloves garlic, finely chopped
8 ounces (250 g) lean ground beef
½ teaspoon (2 ml) ground cumin
1 small red bell pepper, seeded and diced
1 can (14 ounces/398 ml) chopped tomatoes
1 tablespoon (15 ml) tomato paste
2 teaspoons (10 ml) mild chili powder
¾ cup (175 ml) beef stock (see page 9)
1 can (14 ounces/398 ml) red kidney beans, rinsed and drained
salt and pepper

Heat the oil in a saucepan. Add the onion and garlic and cook for 5 minutes or until beginning to soften. Add the ground beef and cumin and cook for a further 5–6 minutes or until browned all over.

Stir in the red pepper, tomatoes, tomato paste, chili powder and stock and bring to a boil. Reduce the heat and simmer gently for 30 minutes.

Add the beans and cook for a further 5 minutes. Season to taste and serve with brown rice, cooked according to the package instructions.

10

INSPIRE ME
Thai chili beef subs

Serves 4
Preparation time: 10 minutes
Cooking time: 8–10 minutes

1 pound (500 g) ground beef
1 tablespoon (15 ml) Thai red curry paste
⅓ cup (75 ml) fresh white breadcrumbs
2 tablespoons (30 ml) chopped fresh coriander
1 egg, lightly beaten
1 tablespoon (15 ml) light soy sauce
black pepper

TO SERVE
1 baguette, cut into 4 and split lengthwise
shredded lettuce
sweet chili sauce

Put the ground beef in a bowl and stir in the red curry paste, breadcrumbs, coriander, egg, soy sauce and pepper. Mix together thoroughly with your hands until sticky. Shape the mixture into 8 mini burgers.

Heat a ridged grill pan until very hot, add the burgers and cook over high heat for 4–5 minutes on each side, until charred and cooked through.

Serve 2 burgers in each baguette with some shredded lettuce and sweet chili sauce.

10 WAYS WITH STEAK

1

Deviled medallions

Serves 4
Preparation time: 10 minutes
Cooking time: 10 minutes

- 2 tablespoons (30 ml) olive oil
- 4 beef medallions (fillet steaks), about 6 ounces (175 g) each
- 2 tablespoons (30 ml) balsamic vinegar
- ⅓ cup (75 ml) full-bodied red wine
- 4 tablespoons (60 ml) beef stock (see page 9)
- 2 cloves garlic, chopped
- 1 teaspoon (5 ml) crushed fennel seeds
- 1 tablespoon (15 ml) sun-dried tomato paste
- ½ teaspoon (2 ml) hot pepper flakes
- salt and pepper

TO GARNISH
chopped flat-leaf parsley
wild arugula leaves (optional)

Heat the oil in a nonstick frying pan until smoking hot. Add the steaks and cook over very high heat for about 2 minutes on each side, if you want your steaks to be medium rare. Remove to a plate, season with salt and pepper and keep warm in a low oven.

Pour the vinegar, wine and stock into the pan and boil for 30 seconds, scraping any sediment from the base of the pan. Add the garlic and fennel seeds and whisk in the sun-dried tomato paste and hot pepper flakes. Bring the sauce to a boil and then boil on high to reduce, until the mixture is syrupy.

Transfer the steaks to warmed serving plates, pouring any collected meat juices into the sauce. Return the sauce to a boil, then season with salt and pepper.

Pour the sauce over the steaks and serve immediately, garnished with chopped parsley and wild arugula leaves, if desired. Slice the steaks before serving, if desire.

2

Red curry with beef

Serves 4
Preparation time: 15 minutes
Cooking time: 10–15 minutes

- 1½ tablespoons (22 ml) sunflower oil
- 2–3 tablespoons (30–45 ml) Thai red curry paste
- 1 pound (500 g) beef tenderloin (fillet steak), finely sliced
- 7 ounces (200 g) mixed Thai eggplants, quartered
- 1 can (14 ounces/400 ml) coconut milk
- ¼ cup (60 ml) beef stock (see page 9), vegetable stock (see page 8) or water
- 2½ tablespoons (37 ml) fish sauce
- 2 tablespoons (30 ml) coconut, palm or brown sugar, or liquid honey
- 2 tomatoes, cut in half
- 2–3 kaffir lime leaves, torn in half

TO GARNISH
fresh coriander leaves
a few slices red chili

Heat the oil in a wok or saucepan and stir-fry the curry paste over medium heat for 3–4 minutes or until fragrant.

Add the beef and stir for 4–5 minutes. Add the eggplants, coconut milk, stock or water, fish sauce and sugar or honey and cook for about 4–5 minutes or until the eggplants are tender, stirring occasionally. Add the tomatoes and kaffir lime leaves during the last few seconds.

Spoon into 4 serving bowls and garnish with coriander leaves and chili slices.

3

SAVE ME TIME
Chili Thai beef subs

Serves 4
Preparation time: 5 minutes
Cooking time: 4 minutes

- 1 pound (500 g) thick sirloin steak, trimmed
- 1 tablespoon (15 ml) olive oil
- 4 submarine buns
- 4 sprigs fresh coriander
- 4 sprigs Thai or ordinary basil
- 4 sprigs mint
- salt and pepper

FOR THE DRESSING
- 2 tablespoons (30 ml) Thai fish sauce
- 2 tablespoons (30 ml) lime juice
- 2 tablespoons (30 ml) light brown sugar
- 1 large red chili, thinly sliced

Heat a ridged grill pan until very hot. Brush the steak with the oil and season liberally with salt and pepper. Add the steak to the pan and cook over high heat for 2 minutes on each side, making sure that you sear all over. Leave to rest for 5 minutes, then cut into thin slices. The steak should be rare.

Meanwhile, make the dressing. Place the fish sauce, lime juice and brown sugar in a bowl and stir in the chili until the sugar has dissolved.

Cut the buns in half and fill with the herbs, beef slices and any juices. Pour the dressing carefully over and serve.

4

SAVE ME MONEY
Beef & pepper kebabs

Serves 4
Preparation time: 15 minutes, plus chilling
Cooking time: 15 minutes

- 13 ounces (400 g) steak, such as round or ribeye
- 1 red bell pepper, cored and seeded
- 1 green bell pepper, cored and seeded
- 1 teaspoon (5 ml) crushed coriander seeds
- 3 tablespoons (45 ml) vegetable oil
- ⅓ cup (75 ml) chopped fresh coriander
- 1 red chili, seeded and chopped
- 1 garlic clove, crushed
- 2 tablespoons (30 ml) lime juice
- 4 chapatis or flour tortillas
- salt and pepper

Presoak 8 wooden skewers in warm water. Cut the beef and peppers into 1-inch (2.5 cm) cubes.

Mix together the coriander seeds, 2 tablespoons (30 ml) oil and half the chopped coriander in a bowl and season to taste. Add the beef and peppers and toss to coat.

Thread the beef and peppers onto the skewers, cover and refrigerate for up to 1 hour. Mix together the remaining coriander and oil with the chili, garlic and lime juice to make a dressing, season to taste and set aside.

Grill the skewers under a preheated hot brpoiler or on a hot barbecue grill for 15 minutes, turning often and basting with the juices. Warm the chapatis under the broiler.

Serve 2 skewers per person on a hot chapati and drizzle on the coriander dressing.

5

KIDS WILL LOVE THIS
Steak sliders

Serves 8
Preparation time: 10 minutes, plus chilling
Cooking time: 12–15 minutes

   12 ounces (375 g) finely ground steak
   2 tablespoons (30 ml) tomato ketchup
   1 tablespoon (15 ml) whole-grain mustard
   3 tablespoons (45 ml) chopped chives
   1 tablespoon (15 ml) olive oil
   4 ounces (100 g) cremini mushrooms, sliced
   8 thin slices Gruyère cheese

   TO SERVE
   4 mini burger buns, cut in half
   ketchup or sauces

Place the ground steak in a bowl with the ketchup, mustard and chives. Mix really well together, working the mixture with a fork to blend the ingredients. Shape into 8 patties and place on a plate. Cover with plastic wrap and chill for 30 minutes to firm.

Heat the oil in a large frying or grill pan and cook the mushrooms over high heat for 3–4 minutes, until golden and soft. Remove from the pan using a slotted spoon. Add the burgers and cook over moderate heat for 4–5 minutes on each side, until golden and cooked through. Sit a Gruyère slice on top of each of the burgers and cover with a baking sheet for 1 minute to allow the cheese to soften.

Top the base of each bun with a burger, then spoon over the mushrooms and spread the top half of each bun with ketchup (or a sauce of the child's choice). Place the top of each bun, and serve.

6

LEFTOVER TO LUNCH
Chili beef salad with coriander

Serves 4
Preparation time: 10 minutes, plus cooling
Cooking time: 10 minutes

   13 ounces (400 g) beef rump or round steaks
   4 whole wheat tortillas, cut into 8 wedges
   3 ounces (75 g) baby spinach leaves, washed
   salt and pepper

   FOR THE LIME AND CORIANDER DRESSING
   ⅓ cup (75 ml) fresh coriander leaves
   2 tablespoons (30 ml) lime juice
   1 tablespoon (15 ml) sunflower oil
   1 garlic clove, crushed
   1 red chili, finely chopped

Season the beef with salt and pepper. Heat a large frying pan and sear the beef over high heat until it is cooked but still pink. This will take about 2 minutes each side, depending on thickness. Set aside at room temperature.

Grill the tortillas under a preheated hot broiler for about 5 minutes, shaking the pan frequently, until they are crispy. Set aside to cool.

Meanwhile, make the dressing, combining all the ingredients.

Thinly slice the beef and arrange it on the spinach leaves. Spoon on the dressing just before serving with the tortilla wedges.

7

BUT I DON'T LIKE ...
STEAK

Japanese beef & noodle salad

Serves 4
Preparation time: 15 minutes, plus marinating
Cooking time: 15 minutes

> 2 sirloin steaks, about 8 ounces (250 g) each
> 5 ounces (150 g) soba noodles
> 1 small daikon, peeled and finely sliced
> 2 carrots, peeled and finely sliced
> ½ cucumber, peeled and finely sliced
>
> **FOR THE DRESSING**
> 1 garlic clove, finely chopped
> ¾ inch (1.5 cm) piece gingerroot, peeled and chopped
> 5 tablespoons (75 ml) soy sauce
> 4 tablespoons (60 ml) sweet chili sauce
> 5 teaspoons (20 ml) sesame oil
>
> **TO GARNISH**
> 5 green onions, finely sliced
> 2 tablespoons (30 ml) toasted sesame seeds

Make the dressing. Mix the garlic and ginger with the soy sauce, sweet chili sauce and sesame oil.

Put the steaks in a non-metallic dish and add 2 tablespoons (30 ml) of the dressing, reserving the rest. Cover and leave to marinate for at least 2 hours, or preferably overnight.

Bring a saucepan of lightly salted water to a boil and cook the noodles for about 5 minutes or until done. Refresh in cold water, drain and transfer to a bowl.

Add the vegetables to the bowl with the noodles.

Heat a grill pan on high heat and cook the steaks for 5 minutes on each side, until medium rare (longer if you prefer your meat well done). Allow to rest for 5 minutes and then finely slice. Drizzle the dressing over the noodle and vegetable mixture, add the sliced steak and combine well. Garnish with green onions and toasted sesame seeds and serve immediately.

WHY NOT TRY... SESAME-CRUSTED SALMON & SOBA NOODLE SALAD

Combine 1 tablespoon (15 ml) black sesame seeds, 1 tablespoon (15 ml) white sesame seeds and 1 tablespoon (15 ml) coriander seeds. Put 4 small fillets of salmon, about 4 ounces (125 g) each, flesh side down into the seed mix and press the seeds onto the flesh. Heat 1 tablespoon (15 ml) vegetable oil in a large frying pan over medium heat and fry the salmon, flesh side down, for 1 minute. Turn over the salmon and fry for about 4 minutes or until the salmon is just cooked through. Serve with the noodle salad above, garnished with coriander.

8

FRIENDS FOR DINNER
Beef stroganoff

Serves 4
Preparation time: 10 minutes
Cooking time: 15 minutes

> ¼ cup (60 ml) butter
> 3 onions, finely chopped
> 8 ounces (250 g) button mushrooms, thinly sliced
> 1 green bell pepper, seeded and cut into fine strips
> 1 pound (500 g) fillet steak or good rump steak, cut into strips 2 inches (5 cm) long and ¼ inch (5 mm) thick
> ⅔ cup (150 ml) soured cream
> salt and pepper
> 1 teaspoon (5 ml) chopped fresh parsley, to garnish

Melt half the butter in a large deep frying pan and fry the onions until pale golden. Add the mushrooms and green pepper to the pan and cook for 5 minutes. Remove the onions, mushrooms and green pepper from the pan.

Melt the remaining butter and heat, then fry the steak strips for about 4 minutes, turning so they are cooked evenly.

Return the onions, mushrooms and pepper to the pan and season well, then stir in the sour cream and blend well. Heat until piping hot, but do not allow to boil. Garnish with chopped parsley.

> **STEAK MIGHT SEEM LIKE A PRICEY OPTION, BUT IF YOU CHOOSE THE RIGHT CUT AND COOK IT THE RIGHT WAY, IT CAN ALSO BE AN EVERYDAY TREAT.**

9

WATCHING MY WEIGHT
Sliced steak with hot & sour sauce

Serves 4
Preparation time: 5 minutes, plus resting
Cooking time: 6–8 minutes

12 ounces (375 g) lean steak (sirloin, rump or tenderloin)
½ teaspoon (2 ml) sea salt
½ teaspoon (2 ml) ground black pepper
1½ tablespoons (22 ml) Thai fish sauce
4 tablespoons (60 ml) lime juice
3–4 shallots, finely sliced
3 green onions, finely sliced
½ handful of fresh coriander leaves, roughly chopped
¼–½ teaspoon (1–2 ml) cayenne pepper, or to taste
mixed salad leaves, to serve

TO GARNISH
fresh mint or coriander leaves
a few slices red chili

Sprinkle both sides of the beef with salt and pepper. Grill or barbecue each side for 3–4 minutes (depending on the thickness of the steak), turning occasionally. Fat should drip off the meat and the meat should cook slowly enough to remain juicy and not burn. You can pan-fry the meat if you prefer. Rest it for 4–5 minutes before thinly slicing.

Mix the beef slices with the fish sauce, lime juice, shallots, green onions, coriander and cayenne. Taste and adjust the seasoning if necessary.

Spoon over a pile of mixed salad leaves and garnish with a few mint or coriander leaves and chili slices.

10

INSPIRE ME
Individual Italian fillet steak parcels

Serves 4
Preparation time: 10 minutes, plus resting
Cooking time: 20 minutes

1 tablespoon (15 ml) olive oil
4 beef medallions (fillet steaks), about 5 ounces (50 g) each
8 large squares phyllo pastry
⅔ cup (150 ml) butter, melted
4 ounces (125 g) buffalo mozzarella cheese, cut into 4 slices
2 teaspoons (10 ml) chopped fresh marjoram
2 teaspoons (10 ml) chopped fresh oregano
4 semi-sun-dried tomatoes, shredded
2 tablespoons (30 ml) finely grated Parmesan cheese
salt and pepper

FOR THE SALAD
5 ounces (150 g) arugula
4 ounces (125 g) buffalo mozzarella cheese, cubed
½ red onion, finely sliced (optional)
2 ripe plum tomatoes, sliced

Heat the oil in a hot frying pan and sear the steaks for 2 minutes on each side (they will continue cooking in the oven). Remove and set aside.

Brush each sheet of pastry with melted butter and arrange two sheets on a work surface. Place a steak in the center of the pastry, followed by a slice of mozzarella, one-quarter of the herbs and semi-sun-dried tomato shreds. Season and bring up the sides of the pastry. Scrunch it together at the top to seal the steak into a parcel. Sprinkle on one-quarter of the grated Parmesan. Repeat with the remaining steaks.

Cook in a preheated 425°F (220°C) oven for 15 minutes, until the pastry is crisp and golden brown. Remove and leave to rest for 2–3 minutes. Toss the salad ingredients together, season and serve with the parcels.

10 WAYS WITH SAUSAGES

1

BASIC

Sausages with mustard mashed potatoes

Serves 4
Preparation time: 5 minutes
Cooking time: 20 minutes

> 8 sausages
> 2 onions, cut into wedges
> 2 apples, cored and cut into wedges
> 1 tablespoon (15 ml) all-purpose flour
> ¾ cup + 2 tablespoons (200 ml) chicken stock (see page 9)
>
> **FOR THE MUSTARD MASH**
> 2 pounds (1 kg) potatoes, quartered and scrubbed
> ⅓ cup (75 ml) butter
> 1–2 tablespoons (15–30 ml) whole-grain mustard
> 1 clove garlic, crushed
> 1 large bunch fresh parsley, chopped
> dash of olive oil
> salt and pepper

Put the potatoes into a large saucepan of cold water, bring to a boil and simmer for 15 minutes, until tender.

Meanwhile, fry or grill the sausages over medium heat for 10 minutes, turning to get an even color.

Add the onion and apple wedges and cook with the sausages for 6–7 minutes.

Drain the potatoes well. When they are cool enough to touch, peel them, then mash well so they are nice and creamy.

Add the butter, mustard, garlic and a good sprinkling of salt and pepper to the potatoes, and carry on mashing. Taste and add more mustard if you want. Finally, stir in the parsley and olive oil.

Transfer the sausages, onion and apple to a serving plate. Pour off the excess fat from the pan to leave about 1 tablespoon (15 ml), then mix in the flour. Gradually stir in the stock, bring to a boil and stir until thickened. Season and strain into a serving dish or pitcher.

Pile the mashed potatoes up on a plate and stick the sausages and onion wedges on top. Spoon over the gravy and serve.

2

GIVE IT A TWIST

Penne with sausage

Serves 4
Preparation time: 5 minutes
Cooking time: 45–50 minutes

> 2 tablespoons (30 ml) olive oil
> 1 large onion, finely chopped
> 8 ounces (250 g) Italian sausage
> ½ teaspoon (2 ml) fennel seeds
> 1 dried red chili, finely chopped
> 1 stalk celery, kept whole
> 1 bay leaf
> ¾ cup (175 ml) red wine
> 1 can (28 ounces/796 ml) chopped tomatoes
> 4 tablespoons (60 ml) 1% or 2% milk
> 13 ounces (400 g) dried penne or rigatoni
> salt
> freshly grated Parmesan or pecorino cheese, to serve

Heat the oil in a frying pan over low heat, add the onion and cook, stirring occasionally, for 6–7 minutes, until softened.

Split the sausage open and break up the sausage meat with a fork. Add the sausage meat chunks, fennel seeds and chili to the pan and increase the heat to medium. Cook, stirring continuously, for 4–5 minutes, until the sausage meat is golden brown.

Add the celery, bay leaf and wine and simmer until most of the wine has evaporated. Stir in the tomatoes, season with salt and bring to a boil. Reduce the heat and simmer for 25–30 minutes, until thick. Stir in the milk and simmer for a further 5 minutes. Remove the celery and bay leaf from the sauce.

Meanwhile, cook the pasta in a large saucepan of salted boiling water according to the package instructions until al dente.

Drain the pasta and stir into the sauce. Serve immediately with some grated Parmesan or pecorino on the side.

SAVE ME TIME
Morning muffins & ketchup

Serves 4
Preparation time: 15 minutes, plus cooling
Cooking time: 20–25 minutes

- **1 pound (500 g) good-quality sausages**
- **1 tablespoon (15 ml) chopped fresh rosemary**
- **3 tablespoons (45 ml) chopped fresh parsley**
- **1 tablespoon (15 ml) thick honey**
- **1 teaspoon (5 ml) vinegar**
- **4 eggs**
- **2 English muffins, cut in half**

FOR THE KETCHUP
- **1 can (14 ounces/398 ml) chopped tomatoes**
- **2 tablespoons (30 ml) maple syrup**
- **1 tablespoon (15 ml) brown sugar**
- **3 tablespoons (45 ml) red wine vinegar**

Place all the ketchup ingredients into a small, heavy-bottomed frying pan and bring to a boil. Reduce the heat and gently simmer for 5–7 minutes, uncovered, stirring occasionally, until the sauce is thick and pulpy. Whiz in a food processor until smooth, then place in a jar and cool. (Store in the refrigerator for up to 2 weeks.)

Cut along the length of each sausage, ease the skin off and discard it. Place the sausage meat in a bowl with the herbs and honey and mix well. Using damp hands, shape into 8 small patties, then cook under a preheated medium broiler for 10–12 minutes, turning once, until golden.

Meanwhile, bring a frying pan half-filled with water, with the vinegar added, to a boil. Reduce the heat to a simmer, then immediately break the eggs, well spaced apart, into the water and cook for 1 minute, until the white is opaque. Remove from the water using a slotted spoon and keep warm.

Toast the muffin halves until golden and lightly crisp. Place a warm muffin half on each of 4 serving plates and top with 2 sausage patties, a poached egg and a spoonful of ketchup.

SAVE ME MONEY
Sausage meatballs, peas & pasta

Serves 4
Preparation time: 20 minutes
Cooking time: 15 minutes

- **1 pound (500 g) beef or pork sausages, skins removed**
- **4 tablespoons (60 ml) extra virgin olive oil**
- **13 ounces (400 g) dried fusilli**
- **8 ounces (250 g) frozen peas, thawed**
- **2 cloves garlic, sliced**
- **2 tablespoons (30 ml) chopped fresh sage**
- **½ teaspoon (2 ml) hot pepper flakes**
- **salt and pepper**
- **freshly grated Parmesan cheese, to serve**

Cut the sausage meat into small pieces and roll into meatballs the size of walnuts.

Heat half the oil in a large nonstick frying pan, add the meatballs and cook over medium heat, stirring frequently, for 10 minutes, until cooked through. Remove from the pan with a slotted spoon.

Meanwhile, plunge the pasta into a large saucepan of lightly salted boiling water. Return to a boil and cook for 8 minutes. Add the peas, return to a boil and cook for a further 2 minutes until the peas are just tender and the pasta is al dente. Drain well, reserving 4 tablespoons (60 ml) of the cooking water.

Add the garlic, sage, hot pepper flakes and salt and pepper to taste to the meatball pan and cook over a low heat for 2–3 minutes, until the garlic is soft but not browned. Return the meatballs to the pan.

Return the pasta and peas to the pan and stir in the meatball mixture, reserved cooking water and remaining oil and heat through for 2 minutes. Serve in bowls, topped with grated Parmesan.

5

KIDS WILL LOVE THIS
Homemade sausage rolls

Makes 15
Preparation time: 15 minutes, plus chilling
Cooking time: 15 minutes

13 ounces (400 g) good-quality sausages
1⅔ cups (400 ml) all-purpose flour, plus extra for dusting
⅓ cup (75 ml) whole wheat flour
1 pinch of salt
⅔ cup (150 ml) butter, chilled and diced
3 tablespoons (45 ml) iced water
1 tablespoon (15 ml) poppy seeds
1 egg, beaten

Snip each sausage at one end and squeeze the sausage meat out on a chopping board lightly dusted with flour. Roll out into thinner sausages.

Sift both flours and the salt into a bowl. Add the butter and rub it in with your fingertips until the mixture resembles fine breadcrumbs. Add enough of the iced water to the mix to soften the dough, then stir in the poppy seeds. Turn the dough out onto a lightly floured surface and knead briefly.

Roll the pastry out on a well-floured surface to a rectangle measuring 12 x 10 inches (30 x 25 cm), then cut into three 4 x 10-inch (10 x 25 cm) strips.

Lay the sausage meat down the center of each strip. Brush one edge of each strip with beaten egg, roll over and flute the edges. Cut each strip into five 2-inch (5 cm) sausage rolls and put on a baking sheet.

Make a couple of cuts in the top of each roll and brush with the remaining egg. Refrigerate for 15 minutes before baking in a preheated 400°F (200°C) oven for 15 minutes. Remove from the oven and leave to cool before removing from sheet.

6

LEFTOVER TO LUNCH
Picnic pie

Serves 6–8
Preparation time: 35 minutes
Cooking time: 1½ hours

¾ cup (175 ml) lard
¾ cup (175 ml) 1% or 2% milk and water mixed
2 teaspoons (10 ml) prepared English mustard
3 cups (750 ml) all-purpose flour
½ teaspoon (2 ml) salt

FOR THE FILLING
1 pound (500 g) lean pork and leek or Cumberland sausages, skinned
1 pound (500 g) skinless boneless chicken thighs, chopped
4 ounces (125 g) smoked bacon, diced
5 cloves, roughly crushed
¼ teaspoon (1 ml) ground allspice
1 small bunch sage
1 Braeburn or Macintosh apple, cored and sliced
1 egg yolk, mixed with 1 tablespoon (15 ml) water
salt and pepper

First make the pastry. Heat the lard in the milk and water in a small saucepan until melted, then stir in the mustard. Mix the flour and salt in a bowl, then stir in the melted lard mixture and mix to a soft ball. Cool for 10 minutes. Mix the sausage meat, chicken, bacon, cloves, allspice and plenty of salt and pepper together in a bowl.

Remove one-third of the pastry and set aside. Press the remaining warm pastry over the base and sides of a deep 7-inch (18 cm) cake pan with removable bottom. Spoon in half the filling and level. Cover with half the sage leaves, then the apple slices, then spoon over the rest of the filling. Level and top with the remaining sage. Brush the edges of the pastry with the egg glaze.

Roll the reserved pastry to a circle a little larger than the pan, arrange on the pie and press the edges together. Trim off the excess, then crimp the edge. Make a slit in the top of the pie, then brush with egg glaze. Cook in a preheated 350°F (180°C) oven for 1½ hours, covering with foil after 40 minutes, until golden. Leave to cool, remove the pan then put the pie, still on the pan base, in the refrigerator for 3–4 hours or overnight. When ready to serve, remove the base and cut the pie into wedges.

7

BUT I DON'T LIKE ...
SAUSAGES

Pork & cabbage bake

Serves 4
Preparation time: 15 minutes
Cooking time: 40 minutes

¼ cup (60 ml) butter
1 pound (500 g) pork and apple sausages, skins removed
1 onion, chopped
2 teaspoons (10 ml) caraway seeds
1¼ pounds (625 g) Savoy cabbage, shredded
13 ounces (400 g) russet or baking potatoes, diced
¾ cup + 2 tablespoons (200 ml) chicken stock (see page 9) or
   vegetable stock (see page 8)
1 tablespoon (15 ml) cider vinegar
salt and pepper

Melt half the butter in a shallow, ovenproof casserole dish. Add the sausage meat to the pan. Fry quickly, breaking the meat up with a wooden spoon and stirring until it has browned.

Add the onion, caraway seeds and a little salt and pepper and fry for a further 5 minutes.

Stir in the cabbage and potatoes, mixing the ingredients together thoroughly. Pour the stock and cider vinegar over them and add a little more seasoning. Dot with the remaining butter and cover with a lid.

Bake in a preheated 325°F (160°C) oven for 30 minutes, until the cabbage and potatoes are very tender. Serve with chunks of whole wheat bread.

WHY NOT TRY...
CHICKEN AND CABBAGE BAKE

Replace the sausages with 13 ounces (400 g) skinned and boned chicken thighs, cut into chunks. Shallow-fry as above in the first step. Instead of the Savoy cabbage, use the same quantity of shredded red cabbage and replace the cider vinegar with 1 tablespoon (15 ml) red wine vinegar along with 2 tablespoons (30 ml) liquid honey. Cook as above.

8

FRIENDS FOR DINNER

Sausage & sweet potato hash

Serves 4–5
Preparation time: 15 minutes
Cooking time: 45 minutes

3 tablespoons (45 ml) olive oil
8 pork sausages
3 large red onions, thinly sliced
1 teaspoon (5 ml) granulated sugar
1 pound (500 g) sweet potatoes, scrubbed and cut into small
   chunks
8 fresh sage leaves
2 tablespoons (30 ml) balsamic vinegar
salt and pepper

Heat the oil in a large frying pan or ovenproof casserole dish and fry the sausages, turning frequently, for about 10 minutes, until browned. Drain to a plate.

Add the onions and sugar to the pan and cook gently, stirring frequently, until lightly browned. Return the sausages to the pan with the sweet potatoes, sage leaves and a little seasoning.

Cover the pan with a lid or foil and cook over very gentle heat for about 25 minutes, until the potatoes are tender.

Drizzle with the vinegar and check the seasoning before serving.

ALWAYS TRY TO BUY THE BEST-QUALITY SAUSAGES — IT REALLY WILL MAKE A DIFFERENCE TO THE TASTE OF YOUR RECIPES.

9

WATCHING MY WEIGHT

Spicy sausage cassoulet

Serves 2
Preparation time: 15 minutes
Cooking time: 35 minutes

    3 tablespoons (45 ml) olive oil
    1 red onion, finely chopped
    1 garlic clove, crushed
    1 red bell pepper, seeded and roughly chopped
    2 stalks celery, roughly chopped
    1 can (7 ounces/200 ml) can chopped tomatoes
    ½ cup (125 ml) chicken stock (see page 9)
    2 teaspoons (10 ml) dark soy sauce
    1 teaspoon (5 ml) Dijon mustard
    1 can (14 ounces/398 ml) black-eyed peas, rinsed and drained
    4 ounces (125 g) smoked pork sausage, roughly chopped
    ¾ cup (175 ml) fresh breadcrumbs
    3 tablespoons (45 ml) freshly grated Parmesan cheese
    2 tablespoons (30 ml) fresh chopped parsley

Heat 1 tablespoon (15 ml) of the oil in a frying pan or small skillet. Add the onion, garlic, red pepper and celery and cook over a low heat, stirring occasionally, for 3–4 minutes.

Add the tomatoes, stock and soy sauce. Bring to a boil, then reduce the heat and simmer for about 15 minutes or until the sauce begins to thicken. Add the mustard, peas and sausage and continue to cook for a further 10 minutes.

Mix the breadcrumbs, Parmesan and parsley together and sprinkle over the sausage mixture. Drizzle with the remaining oil. Place under a preheated broiler for 2–3 minutes or until golden brown.

10

INSPIRE ME

Chestnut & sausage tagliatelle

Serves 4
Preparation time: 10 minutes
Cooking time: 10–20 minutes

    7 ounces (200 g) Italian sausage
    3 ounces (75 g) canned or vacuum-packed chestnuts, drained and roughly chopped
    2 tablespoons (30 ml) roughly chopped fresh thyme
    ¾ cup + 2 tablespoons (200 ml) whipping (35%) cream
    13 ounces (400 g) tagliatelle
    ¼ cups (60 ml) Parmesan cheese, freshly grated, plus extra to serve (optional)
    5 tablespoons (75 ml) 1% or 2% milk
    salt and pepper
    1 sprig fresh thyme, to garnish

Split the sausage open and break up the sausage meat with a fork. Heat a large, heavy-based frying pan over a low heat, add the sausage meat chunks and cook, stirring continuously, until they are lightly golden. As the fat from the sausages heats, it will melt and stop the meat from sticking to the pan.

Increase the heat to high and stir in the chestnuts and thyme. Cook, stirring, for 1–2 minutes to colour the chestnuts, then pour in the cream and simmer gently for 1 minute until slightly thickened.

Cook the pasta in a large saucepan of salted boiling water until it is al dente or according to the packet instructions. Drain thoroughly, then toss into the sauce.

Place over a very low heat and add the Parmesan and milk. Season with salt and pepper. Toss gently until the sauce has thickened and the pasta is well coated with the sauce. Serve immediately with a scattering of grated Parmesan, if liked, and the thyme sprig.

10 WAYS WITH BACON

1

BASIC

BLT sandwich

Serves 1
Preparation time: 5 minutes
Cooking time: 10 minutes

> 2 slices lean bacon
> 2 slices whole wheat or multigrain bread
> 2 tablespoons (30 ml) mayonnaise
> 2 tomatoes, sliced
> about 4 baby lettuce leaves
> salt and pepper

Heat a small nonstick frying pan and cook the bacon, turning once, until it is golden brown and crisp. Remove and drain on paper towels.

Toast the bread on both sides. Spread one side of each piece of toast with mayonnaise and arrange the bacon, tomatoes and lettuce on top of one of the pieces. Season with salt and pepper and top with the other piece of toast. Cut into quarters. Serve hot or cold.

2

GIVE IT A TWIST

Bacon & egg crispy bread tarts

Serves 4
Preparation time: 10 minutes
Cooking time: 30 minutes

> olive oil spray, for oiling
> 16 slices white bread
> ⅓ cup (75 ml) butter, melted
> 5 ounces (150 g) smoked bacon, diced
> 2 eggs
> ½ cup (125 ml) whipping (35%) cream
> 2 tablespoons (30 ml) freshly grated Parmesan cheese
> 8 vine cherry tomatoes
> salt and pepper

Spray a muffin tin lightly with oil. Cut the crusts off the bread and discard. Flatten each bread slice by rolling over it firmly with a rolling pin. Brush each slice with the melted butter and place 8 of the slices diagonally on top of the others to form the bases. Carefully press each base into a cup of the prepared muffin tin, making sure that they fit evenly (they need to reach up the sides).

Bake in a preheated 400°F (200°C) oven for 12–15 minutes, until crisp and golden.

Meanwhile, heat a dry frying pan until hot, add the bacon and cook for 2–3 minutes, until crisp and golden.

Divide the bacon between the baked bread cases.

Beat together the eggs, cream, cheese and salt and pepper to taste in a bowl. Spoon into the cases and top each with a cherry tomato. Bake in the oven for 15 minutes, until set. Serve immediately.

3 🕐

SAVE ME TIME
Quick pasta carbonara

Serves 4
Preparation time: 10 minutes
Cooking time: 10 minutes

> 13 ounces (400 g) spaghetti or other long thin dried pasta
> 2 tablespoons (30 ml) olive oil
> 1 onion, finely chopped
> 7 ounces (200 g) bacon or pancetta, cut into cubes
> 2 cloves garlic, finely chopped
> 3 eggs
> 4 tablespoons (60 ml) freshly grated Parmesan cheese, plus extra to garnish
> 3 tablespoons (45 ml) chopped fresh parsley, plus extra for garnish
> 3 tablespoons (45 ml) cream
> salt and pepper

Cook the spaghetti in a saucepan of lightly salted boiling water for 8–10 minutes, or according to the package instructions, until al dente.

Meanwhile, heat the oil in a large frying pan. Add the onion and fry until soft, then add the bacon or pancetta and garlic, and fry gently for 4–5 minutes.

Beat the eggs with the Parmesan, parsley and cream. Season with salt and pepper and mix well.

Drain the spaghetti and add it to the pan with the onion and bacon or pancetta. Stir over low heat until well mixed, then pour in the egg mixture. Stir and take the pan off the heat. Carry on mixing well for a few seconds, until the eggs are lightly cooked and creamy, then serve immediately, garnished with Parmesan and parsley.

4 🐷

SAVE ME MONEY
Tartiflette-style pizza

Serves 4
Preparation time: 20 minutes, plus resting
Cooking time: 23–25 minutes

> 9½ ounces (290 g) pizza dough mix
> 2 tablespoons (30 ml) butter
> 1 tablespoon (15 ml) olive oil
> 7 ounces (200 g) smoked bacon lardons or smoky bacon bits
> 2 onions, sliced
> 1 clove garlic, chopped
> ¾ cup (175 ml) crème fraîche or sour cream
> 8 ounces (250 g) cooked potatoes, thinly sliced
> 8 ounces (250 g) Reblochon cheese, sliced

Make the pizza dough according to the instructions on the package. Form the dough into 4 balls and roll them out into ovals. Cover lightly with oiled plastic wrap and leave in a warm place.

Melt the butter and olive oil in a large frying pan and fry the bacon for 3–4 minutes or until cooked. Add the onions and garlic and fry gently for 5–6 minutes or until soft and golden.

Spread 1 tablespoon (15 ml) of the crème fraîche over each pizza. Top with slices of potato, some of the bacon and onion mixture and 2–3 slices of Reblochon. Cook in a preheated 425°F (220°C) oven for 15 minutes, until bubbling and golden.

Serve immediately with an extra dollop of the remaining crème fraîche on top, if desired.

5

KIDS WILL LOVE THIS
Bacon & pancakes with maple syrup

Serves 4
Preparation time: 5 minutes
Cooking time: 30 minutes

> 2½ cups (625 ml) all-purpose flour
> 2½ teaspoons (12 ml) baking powder
> ½ teaspoon (2 ml) salt
> 1 egg, lightly beaten
> 1¾ cup (425 ml) 1% or 2% milk
> 2 tablespoons (30 ml) butter, melted
> olive oil spray, for oiling
> 8 slices smoked back bacon
> maple syrup, to serve

Sift the flour, baking powder and salt into a bowl. Make a well in the center and gradually beat in the egg and milk. Continue to beat until the batter is smooth. Stir in the melted butter.

Heat a heavy-bottomed frying pan until hot, spray lightly with oil and spoon on about ⅓ cup (75 ml) of the pancake batter. Cook over medium heat for 1–2 minutes, until bubbles start appearing on the surface. Carefully flip the pancake over and cook for a further 1–2 minutes until browned on the underside. Remove from the pan and keep warm in a preheated 300°F (150°C) oven while you cook the remainder of the batter — it should make 8 pancakes in total.

Meanwhile, cook the bacon under a preheated broiler for 2 minutes on each side until golden.

Serve the pancakes topped with the bacon and drizzled with maple syrup.

BACON CAN BE BOUGHT EITHER SMOKED OR UNSMOKED. UNLESS YOUR RECIPE IS SPECIFIC ABOUT WHAT BACON TO USE, YOU SHOULD CHOOSE THE FLAVOR YOU LIKE BEST.

6

LEFTOVER TO LUNCH
Potato & bacon cakes

Serves 4
Preparation time: 15 minutes, plus chilling
Cooking time: about 45 minutes

> 2 pounds (1 kg) potatoes, cut into chunks
> vegetable oil, for shallow-frying
> 6 green onions, sliced
> 7 ounces (200 g) back bacon, chopped
> 2 tablespoons (30 ml) chopped flat-leaf fresh parsley
> all-purpose flour, for coating
> 2 tablespoons (30 ml) butter
> salt and pepper
>
> **FOR THE TOMATO SAUCE**
> ¾ cup (175 ml) crème fraîche or sour cream
> 2 tablespoons (30 ml) chopped fresh basil
> 2 tablespoons (30 ml) chopped tomatoes

Cook the potatoes in a large saucepan of salted boiling water for 15–20 minutes, until tender. Drain well, return to the pan and mash well.

Heat a little oil in a frying pan, add the green onions and cook for 2–3 minutes, then add the bacon and cook until browned. Add to the mashed potatoes with the parsley. Season well with salt and pepper. Form the potato mixture into 8 cakes, then cover and chill in the refrigerator until firm.

Lightly coat the cakes in flour. Melt the butter in a nonstick frying pan, add the cakes, in batches, and cook over medium heat for 4–5 minutes on each side, until they have browned and heated through.

Meanwhile, to make the sauce, put the crème fraîche in a bowl and mix in the basil and tomatoes. Season well with salt and pepper. Serve the cakes hot with the sauce.

7

BUT I DON'T LIKE . . . BACON

Vegetable soup with bacon dumplings

Serves 6
Preparation time: 30 minutes
Cooking time: 1¼–1½ hours

- ¼ cup (60 ml) butter
- 1 onion, finely chopped
- 1 leek, diced, white and green parts kept separate
- 10 ounces (300 g) rutabaga, diced
- 10 ounces (300 g) parsnip, diced
- 10 ounces (300 g) carrot, diced
- 2 stalks celery, diced
- 3–4 stems fresh sage
- 10 cups (2.5 L) chicken stock (see page 9)
- salt and pepper

FOR THE DUMPLINGS
- ¾ cup (175 ml) all-purpose flour
- ½ teaspoon (2 ml) dry mustard
- 2 teaspoons (10 ml) finely chopped fresh sage
- 2 ounces (50 g) vegetable suet or shortening
- 2 slices smoked bacon, finely chopped
- 4 tablespoons (60 ml) water

Heat the butter in a large saucepan, add the onion and white parts of diced leeks and fry for 5 minutes, until just beginning to soften. Add the rutabaga, parsnip, carrot, celery and sage, toss in the butter, then cover and fry for 10 minutes, stirring occasionally.

Pour in the stock, season with salt and pepper and bring to a boil. Cover and simmer for 45 minutes, stirring occasionally, until the vegetables are tender. Remove the sage, then taste and adjust the seasoning if needed.

Make the dumplings by mixing the flour, mustard powder, sage, suet and bacon in a bowl with a little salt and pepper. Gradually stir in the water and mix, first with a spoon, then squeeze together with your hands to make a smooth dough. Cut into 18 slices and roll each slice into a small ball.

Stir the remaining green parts of diced leek into the soup. Add the dumplings to the simmering soup, re-cover the pan and cook for 10 minutes, until the dumplings are light and fluffy. Ladle into bowls and serve immediately.

WHY NOT TRY... CREAMY WINTER VEGETABLE SOUP

Omit the dumplings and reduce the amount of stock to 7 cups (1.75 L). Simmer for 45 minutes, then purée in batches in a blender or food processor. Pour back into the saucepan, stir in 1¼ cups (300 ml) milk and reheat. Ladle into bowls, swirl 2 tablespoons (30 ml) whipping (35%) cream into each and garnish with sage and crispy bacon.

8

FRIENDS FOR DINNER

Braised liver & bacon with prunes

Serves 4
Preparation time: 15 minutes
Cooking time: 1 hour

- 13 ounces (400 g) lamb's liver, sliced
- 2 teaspoons (10 ml) all-purpose flour
- 8 thin slices smoked bacon
- 16 pitted prunes
- 3 tablespoons (45 ml) olive oil
- 2 large onions, thinly sliced
- 1½ pound (750 g) large potatoes, sliced
- 1¾ cups (425 ml) lamb or chicken stock (see page 9)
- 3 tablespoons (45 ml) roughly chopped fresh parsley, to garnish
- salt and pepper

Cut the liver into thick strips, removing any tubes. Season the flour with salt and pepper and use to coat the liver. Cut the bacon slices in half and wrap a piece around each prune.

Heat half the oil in an ovenproof casserole dish and fry the onions until lightly browned. Drain to a plate. Add the liver to the casserole dish and brown on both sides. Drain to the plate. Add the remaining oil to the pan with the bacon-wrapped prunes and fry on both sides until browned. Drain.

Arrange the potatoes in the casserole dish and put all the fried ingredients on top. Pour in the stock, season lightly and bring to a boil. Cover with a lid and transfer to a preheated 350°F (180°C) oven for 50 minutes, until the potatoes are very tender. Serve sprinkled with the parsley.

9

WATCHING MY WEIGHT
Spinach, avocado & bacon salad

Serves 4
Preparation time: 15 minutes
Cooking time: 10 minutes

- 1 ripe avocado, halved, peeled and pitted
- 2 tablespoons (30 ml) lemon juice
- 1 pound (500 g) baby spinach leaves
- 1 small bunch green onions, shredded into long thin strips
- 2 tablespoons (30 ml) vegetable oil
- 4 slices back bacon, chopped
- 1 clove garlic, crushed

FOR THE DRESSING
- 3 tablespoons (45 ml) balsamic vinegar
- 1 teaspoon (5 ml) light brown sugar
- 1 teaspoon (5 ml) Dijon mustard
- ½ cup (125 ml) olive oil
- 1 tablespoon (15 ml) finely chopped walnuts, plus extra to garnish (optional)
- 1 tablespoon (15 ml) chopped fresh parsley or basil
- salt and pepper

Make the dressing. Mix the vinegar, brown sugar and mustard in a bowl. Add a dash of salt and pepper, then slowly whisk in the olive oil. Stir the chopped walnuts and herbs into the dressing and add more salt and pepper if needed.

Chop the avocado into cubes and sprinkle with lemon juice to stop it going brown.

Put the spinach leaves in a bowl together with the green onion strips and avocado cubes.

Heat the oil in a frying pan and fry the bacon and garlic until crisp and brown, then drain on paper towels. Scatter over the spinach mixture.

Drizzle some of the dressing over the salad, toss gently and serve straight away, garnished with extra walnut pieces, if desired.

10

INSPIRE ME
Risoni, sweet potato & bacon salad

Serves 4–6
Preparation time: 20 minutes
Cooking time: 20–25 minutes

- 2 large sweet potatoes, peeled and cut into small dice
- 2 tablespoons (30 ml) olive oil, plus extra for drizzling
- 7 ounces (200 g) smoked bacon
- 8 ounces (250 g) risoni or orzo pasta
- 7 ounces (200 g) frozen peas
- 3½ ounces (100 g) feta cheese
- 1 small bunch fresh mint, chopped
- salt and pepper

Put the sweet potatoes on a large baking sheet and drizzle with olive oil and salt and pepper. Bake in a preheated 375°F (190°C) oven for 20–25 minutes or until just cooked through.

Finely slice the bacon if necessary. Heat a large frying pan over a high heat and fry the bacon for 4 minutes, until golden and crispy. Drain on kitchen paper and reserve.

Meanwhile, cook the pasta in a large saucepan of boiling water for 10 minutes or according to the instructions on the package. Add the peas, cook for 2 more minutes and drain.

Remove the sweet potatoes from the oven and mix with the pasta and peas. Add the bacon and crumble over top the feta, reserving some of both for garnish. Add 2 tablespoons (30 ml) olive oil and the chopped mint and combine well. Garnish with the bacon and feta and serve.

10 WAYS WITH DICED LAMB

1

BASIC
Taverna-style grilled lamb with feta

Serves 4
Preparation time: 8 minutes
Cooking time: 6–8 minutes

1 pound (500 g) leg or shoulder of lamb, diced

FOR THE MARINADE
2 tablespoons (30 ml) chopped fresh oregano
1 tablespoon (15 ml) chopped fresh rosemary
grated zest of 1 lemon
2 tablespoons (30 ml) olive oil
salt and pepper

FOR THE FETA SALAD
7 ounces (200 g) feta cheese, sliced
1 tablespoon (15 ml) chopped fresh oregano
2 tablespoons (30 ml) chopped fresh parsley
grated zest and juice of 1 lemon
½ small red onion, finely sliced
3 tablespoons (45 ml) olive oil

Mix the marinade ingredients in a non-metallic bowl, add the lamb and mix to coat thoroughly. Thread the meat onto 4 skewers.

Arrange the sliced feta on a large serving dish and sprinkle on the herbs, lemon zest and sliced onion. Drizzle on the lemon juice and oil and season with salt and pepper.

Cook the lamb skewers under a preheated hot broiler or in a grill pan for about 6–8 minutes, turning frequently, until browned and almost cooked through. Remove from the heat and leave to rest for 1–2 minutes.

Serve the lamb, with any pan juices poured over, with the salad and accompanied with plenty of crusty bread, if desired.

2 ◎

GIVE IT A TWIST
Lamb & spinach curry

Serves 4
Preparation time: 20 minutes
Cooking time: 2 hours

4 tablespoons (60 ml) sunflower oil
1 pound 4 ounces (600 g) boneless shoulder of lamb, cut into bite-sized pieces
1 onion, finely chopped
3 cloves garlic, crushed
1 teaspoon (5 ml) ground ginger
2 teaspoons (10 ml) ground turmeric
large pinch of grated nutmeg
4 tablespoons (60 ml) sultanas
1 teaspoon (5 ml) ground cinnamon
1 teaspoon (5 ml) paprika
1 can (14 ounces/398 ml) chopped tomatoes
1¼ cups (300 ml) lamb stock (see page 9)
13 ounces (400 g) baby spinach
salt and pepper

Heat half the oil in a large, heavy-bottomed saucepan and brown the lamb in batches for 3–4 minutes. Remove and set aside.

Heat the remaining oil in the pan and add the onion, garlic, ginger, turmeric, nutmeg, sultanas, cinnamon and paprika. Stir-fry for 1–2 minutes, then add the lamb. Stir-fry for 2–3 minutes, then add the tomatoes and stock. Season and bring to a boil. Reduce the heat, cover tightly and simmer gently for 1½ hours.

Add the spinach in batches until it is all wilted, cover and cook for a further 10–12 minutes, stirring occasionally. Remove from the heat and serve drizzled with whisked yogurt, if desired.

3

SAVE ME TIME
Sri Lankan–style lamb curry

Serves 4
Preparation time: 10 minutes
Cooking time: 35 minutes

> 1 pound (500 g) shoulder or leg of lamb, diced
> 2 potatoes, peeled and cut into large chunks
> 4 tablespoons (60 ml) olive oil
> 1 can (14 ounces/398 ml) chopped tomatoes
> ⅔ cup (150 ml) water
> salt and pepper
>
> **FOR THE CURRY PASTE**
> 1 onion, grated
> 1 tablespoon (15 ml) finely chopped gingerroot
> 1 teaspoon (5 ml) finely chopped garlic
> ½ teaspoon (2 ml) ground turmeric
> 1 teaspoon (5 ml) ground coriander
> ½ teaspoon (2 ml) ground cumin
> ½ teaspoon (2 ml) fennel seeds
> ½ teaspoon (2 ml) cumin seeds
> 3 cardamom pods, lightly crushed
> 2 green chilies, finely chopped
> 2-inch (5 cm) cinnamon stick
> 2 stalks lemongrass, finely sliced

Make the curry paste by mixing together all the ingredients in a large bowl — for a milder curry remove the seeds from the chilies before chopping them finely. Add the lamb and potatoes and combine well.

Heat the oil in a heavy-bottomed pan or casserole dish and tip in the meat and potatoes. Use a wooden spoon to stir-fry for 6–8 minutes. Pour in the chopped tomatoes and water, bring to a boil and season well with salt and pepper. Allow to simmer gently for 20–25 minutes, until the potatoes are cooked and the lamb is tender. Serve accompanied with toasted naan bread and a bowl of Greek yogurt, if desired.

4

SAVE ME MONEY
Lamb tenderloin with vegetables

Serves 4
Preparation time: 20 minutes
Cooking time: 35–45 minutes

> 1 pound (500 g) even-sized baby new potatoes
> 1 tablespoon (15 ml) chopped fresh rosemary
> 13 ounces (400 g) lamb tenderloin, diced
> 3 cloves garlic, halved
> 1 can (13 ounces/398 ml) artichokes, drained, rinsed and halved
> 1 red bell pepper, seeded and quartered
> 7 ounces (200 g) small leeks
> salt and pepper

Put the potatoes in a pan with plenty of lightly salted water and bring to a boil. Drain immediately and toss with the rosemary.

Transfer the potatoes to a roasting pan with the lamb, garlic, artichokes and peppers. Cover and cook in a preheated 350°F (180°C) oven for 30–40 minutes or until cooked through and the potato skins are golden. Meanwhile, steam the leeks.

Drain the excess fat and serve the lamb with the roasted vegetables, leeks and any pan juices.

> **TRY USING DICED LAMB IN YOUR CASSEROLES RATHER THAN ALWAYS STICKING TO CHICKEN OR BEEF. IT'S GOT SO MUCH FLAVOR AND MAKES A LOVELY CHANGE.**

5 😊

KIDS WILL LOVE THIS
Lamb ragu with toasted walnuts

Serves 4
Preparation time: 15 minutes
Cooking time: 1¾ hours
Finishing time: 10 minutes

> 1 tablespoon (15 ml) olive oil
> 1 pound (500 g) lamb, diced
> 1 onion, chopped
> 2 cloves garlic, finely chopped
> ½ cup (125 ml) walnut pieces, plus extra to garnish
> 1 tablespoon (15 ml) all-purpose flour
> 1¾ cups (425 ml) lamb stock (see page 9)
> ¾–1 cup (175–250 ml) red wine
> 2 tablespoons (30 ml) tomato paste
> 1 bouquet garni
> 8 ounces (250 g) rigatoni or penne
> 1 handful of chopped fresh flat-leaf parsley, to garnish
> salt and pepper

Heat the oil in an ovenproof casserole dish, add the lamb a few pieces at a time, then add the onion. Fry for about 5 minutes, stirring continuously until browned all over.

Add the garlic and walnuts and fry for 2 minutes more, until the nuts are lightly toasted. Stir in the flour, then add the stock, wine, tomato paste, bouquet garni and a little seasoning. Bring to a boil, stirring occasionally. Cover and cook in a preheated 325°F (160°C) oven for 1½ hours or until the lamb is tender. Allow to cool, then chill until required.

When ready to serve, cook the pasta in a large saucepan of boiling water for 8–10 minutes, until just tender. Reheat the lamb on the stovetop, stirring until piping hot. Drain the pasta, then toss with the lamb and sprinkle with chopped parsley and a few extra walnuts. Spoon into shallow bowls.

Serve with a salad of arugula, watercress and spinach dressed with lemon juice and sprinkled with Parmesan shavings.

6

LEFTOVER TO LUNCH
Marinated minty lamb kebabs

Serves 4
Preparation time: 15 minutes, plus marinating
Cooking time: 10 minutes

> 1 clove garlic, crushed
> 2 tablespoons (30 ml) chopped fresh mint
> 1 tablespoon (15 ml) prepared mint sauce
> ⅔ cup (150 ml) low-fat natural yogurt
> 12 ounces (375 g) lean lamb, cubed
> 2 small onions, cut into wedges
> 1 green bell pepper, cored, seeded and cut into wedges
> lemon wedges, to serve

Mix together the garlic, mint, mint sauce and yogurt in a medium bowl, add the lamb and stir well. Cover and leave to marinate in a cool place for 10 minutes.

Thread the lamb, onion and pepper wedges onto 8 metal skewers and cook under a preheated hot broiler for 8–10 minutes or until cooked through.

Serve the kebabs with lemon wedges and, if desired, accompany them with a green salad and couscous.

7

BUT I DON'T LIKE ...
DICED LAMB
Coconut lamb curry

Serves 4
Preparation time: 15 minutes
Cooking time: about 2 hours

2 tablespoons (30 ml) sunflower oil
1 onion, thinly sliced
2 teaspoons (10 ml) grated gingerroot
2 teaspoons (10 ml) crushed garlic
1 teaspoon (5 ml) ground cinnamon
20 curry leaves
2 tablespoons (30 ml) mild curry powder
1 tablespoon (15 ml) ground coriander
1 teaspoon (5 ml) ground turmeric
1 teaspoon (5 ml) cayenne pepper
1¼ pounds (625 g) lamb, cut into chunks
1 can (14 ounces/ 400ml) coconut milk
¾ cup (175 ml) vegetable stock (see page 8)
3½ ounces (100 g) fresh coconut, grated
6 tablespoons (90 ml) chopped fresh coriander
salt and pepper

Heat the oil in a large, heavy-bottomed saucepan. Add the onion and stir-fry over medium heat for 4–5 minutes. Stir in the ginger, garlic, cinnamon, curry leaves, curry powder, ground coriander, turmeric and cayenne. Stir-fry for 2–3 minutes, then add the lamb.

Stir-fry for 2–3 minutes, then stir in the coconut milk and stock. Bring to a boil, season well and cover tightly. Cook over very low heat (using a heat diffuser if possible), stirring occasionally, for 1½–2 hours or until the lamb is tender. Remove from the heat and sprinkle with the grated coconut and chopped fresh coriander before serving.

WHY NOT TRY...
COCONUT CHICKEN CURRY

Use 1½ pounds (750 g) skinless chicken thighs on the bone, instead of the lamb, and reduce the Cooking time: to 1–1½ hours. After 1 hours cooking, add ½ small cauliflower, cut into florets, and 8 ounces (250 g) carrots, peeled, halved lengthwise and sliced. Sprinkle in ⅓ cup (75 ml) sultanas or raisins, if desired.

8

FRIENDS FOR DINNER
Caribbean lamb stoba

Serves 4
Preparation time: 25 minutes
Cooking time: 1¾ hours

2 tablespoons (30 ml) sunflower oil
1½ pounds (750 g) boneless leg of lamb, cut into bite-sized cubes
2 onions, finely chopped
2 teaspoons (10 ml) finely grated gingerroot
1 Scotch bonnet chili, thinly sliced
1 red bell pepper, seeded and roughly chopped
2 teaspoons (10 ml) ground allspice
1 tablespoon (15 ml) ground cumin
1 cinnamon stick
1 pinch of grated nutmeg
1 can (14 ounces/398 ml) chopped tomatoes
10 ounces (300 g) cherry tomatoes
finely grated zest and juice of 2 limes
⅓ cup (75 ml) brown sugar
1½ cups (375 ml) fresh or frozen peas
salt and pepper

Heat half the oil in a large, heavy-bottomed saucepan. Brown the lamb in batches for 3–4 minutes. Remove with a slotted spoon and set aside.

Heat the remaining oil in the saucepan and add the onions, ginger, chili, red pepper and spices. Stir-fry for 3–4 minutes, then add the lamb with the canned and cherry tomatoes, lime zest and juice and sugar. Season and bring to a boil. Reduce the heat, cover tightly and simmer gently for 1½ hours or until the lamb is tender.

Stir in the peas 5 minutes before serving. Ladle onto warmed plates and serve with rice.

WATCHING MY WEIGHT
Lamb & flageolet bean stew

Serves 4
Preparation time: 5 minutes
Cooking time: 1 hour 20 minutes

- 1 teaspoon (5 ml) olive oil
- 11½ ounces (350 g) lean lamb, cubed
- 16 pickling onions, peeled
- 1 clove garlic, crushed
- 1 tablespoon (15 ml) all-purpose flour
- 2½ cups (600 ml) lamb stock (made with concentrated liquid stock)
- ½ can (7 ounces/200ml) chopped tomatoes
- 1 bouquet garni
- 2 cans (each 14 ounces/398 ml) flageolet beans, drained and rinsed
- 8 ounces (250 g) cherry tomatoes
- pepper

Heat the oil in an ovenproof casserole dish or saucepan, add the lamb and fry for 3–4 minutes, until browned all over. Remove the meat from the casserole dish and set aside.

Add the onions and garlic to the pan and fry for 4–5 minutes, until the onions are beginning to brown.

Return the lamb and any juices to the pan, then stir through the flour and add the stock, tomatoes, bouquet garni and beans. Bring to a boil, stirring, then cover and simmer for 1 hour, until the lamb is just tender.

Add the cherry tomatoes to the dish and season well with pepper. Continue to simmer for 10 minutes, then serve with steamed potatoes and green beans.

INSPIRE ME
Lamb & prune tagine with barley

Serves 4
Preparation time: 15 minutes
Cooking time: 1–1½ hours

- olive oil spray
- 1¼ pounds (625 g) lean lamb, diced
- 1 red onion, chopped
- 1 carrot, peeled and chopped
- 1 teaspoon (5 ml) paprika
- 1 teaspoon (5 ml) ground coriander
- 1 teaspoon (5 ml) fennel seeds
- 1¼-inch (3 cm) cinnamon stick
- 2 cloves garlic, crushed
- 2 bay leaves
- 2 tablespoons (30 ml) lime juice
- 3 cups (750 ml) chicken stock (see page 9)
- 3 ounces (75 g) dried prunes
- 1 can (14 ounces/398 ml) chopped tomatoes
- ⅓ cup (75 ml) pearl barley
- ⅓ cup (75 ml) chopped fresh coriander, plus extra sprigs to garnish
- 1 tablespoon (15 ml) lime juice
- 2¼ cups (550 ml) couscous
- salt and pepper

Heat a large saucepan or 8-cup (2 L) casserole dish, spray lightly with oil and cook the lamb briefly, in batches if necessary, until brown. Remove the lamb with a slotted spoon, add the onion and carrot to the pan and cook briefly to brown. Return the lamb, stir in all the remaining ingredients (except the couscous) and season to taste. Simmer, covered, for 1 hour or until the lamb is tender. At the end of cooking, stir in the coriander and lime juice.

Meanwhile, cook the couscous according to the instructions on the package and set aside for 5 minutes. Serve the hot tagine over the couscous and garnish with coriander sprigs.

FISH

A variety of simple and nutritious fish recipe suggestions for shrimp, salmon, cod, mackerel and tuna, many of which are fast and easy to prepare for an everyday meal.

FISH

 1 **BASIC**

 2 **GIVE IT A TWIST**

 3 **SAVE ME TIME**

 4 **SAVE ME MONEY**

 5 **KIDS WILL LOVE THESE**

SHRIMP PAGE 82

Lemongrass shrimp skewers

Noodles with shrimp & bok choy

Jumbo shrimp & zucchini linguine

Shrimp, zucchini & pea risotto

Shrimp & mango kebabs

SALMON PAGE 88

Seared salmon with avocado salad

Salmon with horseradish crust

Salmon fillets with sage & quinoa

Salmon & lentil salad

Sesame salmon burgers

COD PAGE 94

Cod with roasted tomatos

Chili & coriander fish parcels

Blackened cod with salsa

Baked cod with tomatoes & olives

Fish & chips

MACKEREL PAGE 100

Mackerel with baked beets

Bacon- & oat-topped mackerel

Spiced mackerel fillets

Mackerel with sweet potatoes

Mackerel with avocado salsa

TUNA PAGE 106

Tuna with green beans & broccoli

Spicy tuna fishcakes

Tuna, spinach & tomato penne

Tuna & corn pilaf

Tuna niçoise spaghetti

| 6 LEFTOVER TO LUNCH | 7 BUT I DON'T LIKE... | 8 FRIENDS FOR DINNER | 9 WATCHING MY WEIGHT | 10 INSPIRE ME |

Onion & bean soup with shrimp

Shrimp with green leaves

Shrimp & coconut rice

Jumbo shrimp with Japanese salad

Garlic chive flowers with shrimp

Salmon rösti cakes

Salmon & bulgur pilaf

Dill & mustard baked salmon

Asian salmon salad

Salmon with ginger & white fungus

Fish pie

Oven-steamed fish with greens

Seared cod with olive butter

Fried miso cod with bok choy

Cod rarebit

Mackerel with cider vichyssoise

Fish salad with lemongrass

Mackerel & asparagus pie

Mackerel with wild rice niçoise

Basque fish soup

Tuna pâté with toasted sourdough

Fusilli with tuna, capers & mint

Pot roasted tuna with lentils

Sesame tuna with spicy noodles

Tuna & pesto burgers

10 WAYS WITH SHRIMP

1

BASIC
Lemongrass shrimp skewers

Serves 4
Preparation time: 10 minutes, plus marinating
Cooking time: 8 minutes

> 5 stalks lemongrass
> 4 tablespoons (60 ml) sweet chili sauce, plus extra to serve
> 2 tablespoons (30 ml) chopped fresh coriander
> 2 tablespoons (30 ml) toasted sesame oil
> 20 raw tiger shrimp, peeled but tails left on

Take one of the lemongrass stalks and remove the outer leaves. Finely slice it and place it in a bowl along with the sweet chili sauce, coriander and oil. Place the shrimp in this marinade, cover and leave in the refrigerator to marinate for 1 hour or overnight.

Remove the shrimp from the marinade. Take the remaining 4 lemongrass stalks and remove a few of the outer layers to give you a thin lemongrass skewer. Make a hole through each shrimp at its thickest part using a metal skewer, then thread 5 of the shrimp onto a lemongrass stalk. Repeat with the remaining lemongrass and shrimp.

Place the shrimp skewers on a barbecue and cook for 4 minutes on each side or until the shrimp have turned pink and are firm to the touch.

Serve the shrimp straight from the barbecue with sweet chili sauce for dipping.

2

GIVE IT A TWIST
Noodles with shrimp & bok choy

Serves 4
Preparation time: 5 minutes
Cooking time: 12 minutes

> 8 ounces (250 g) dried medium egg noodles
> 3 tablespoons (45 ml) vegetable oil
> 2 tablespoons (30 ml) sesame seeds
> 1-inch (2.5 cm) piece of gingerroot, peeled and finely chopped
> 1 clove garlic, crushed
> 20 raw peeled jumbo shrimp
> 3 tablespoons (45 ml) light soy sauce
> 2 tablespoons (30 ml) sweet chili sauce
> 2 heads baby bok choy, leaves separated
> 4 green onions, finely sliced
> 1 handful of chopped fresh coriander
> 2 tablespoons (30 ml) toasted sesame oil

Cook the noodles according to the instructions on the package. Drain and set aside.

Heat a large frying pan and add 2 tablespoons (30 ml) of the vegetable oil. When really hot, add the noodles, flattening them down so that they cover the bottom of the pan. Cook over high heat for 3–4 minutes, until golden brown and crispy. Once they have colored on the first side, turn the noodles over and brown on the other side as well. Stir in the sesame seeds.

Meanwhile, heat the remaining oil in a wok, add the ginger and garlic and stir-fry for 1 minute, then add the shrimp and stir-fry for 2 minutes, until turning pink. Add the soy sauce and sweet chili sauce and bring to a boil, then reduce the heat and simmer for 1–2 minutes, until the shrimp are pink and firm. Finally, add the bok choy and stir until the leaves begin to wilt.

Place the noodles on a large plate and top with the shrimp and bok choy. Sprinkle with the green onions and coriander and drizzle with the sesame oil.

3

SAVE ME TIME

Jumbo shrimp & zucchini linguine

Serves 4
Preparation time: 10 minutes
Cooking time: 10–12 minutes

> 13 ounces (400 g) dried linguine
> 3 tablespoons (45 ml) olive oil
> 7 ounces (200 g) peeled raw jumbo shrimp
> 2 cloves garlic, crushed
> finely grated zest of 1 unwaxed lemon
> 1 fresh red chili, seeded and finely chopped
> 13 ounces (400 g) zucchini, coarsely grated
> ¼ cup (60 ml) unsalted butter, cut into cubes
> salt

Cook the pasta in a large saucepan of salted boiling water according to the package instructions, until al dente. Drain.

Meanwhile, heat the oil in a large frying pan over high heat until the surface of the oil seems to shimmer slightly. Add the shrimp, garlic, lemon zest and chili, season with salt and cook, stirring continuously for 2 minutes, until the shrimp turn pink. Add the zucchinis and butter, season with a little more salt and stir well. Cook, stirring continuously for 30 seconds.

Toss in the pasta and stir until the butter has melted and all the ingredients are well combined. Serve immediately.

4

SAVE ME MONEY

Shrimp, zucchini & pea risotto

Serves 4
Preparation time: 10 minutes
Cooking time: 25–30 minutes

> 2 tablespoons (30 ml) olive oil
> 1 small onion, finely chopped
> 1 clove garlic, crushed
> 1½ cups (375 ml) risotto rice
> 1 cup (250 ml) white wine
> about 6 cups (1.5 L) hot chicken stock (see page 9)
>   or fish stock (see page 8)
> 20 large raw peeled shrimp
> 1 large or 2 small zucchinis, cut into thin discs
> 1½ cups (375 ml) peas, thawed if frozen or blanched if fresh
> ½ cup (125 ml) butter
> 2 tablespoons (30 ml) chopped fresh mint
> grated zest of 1 lemon and juice of ½ lemon
> salt and pepper

Heat the oil in a frying pan, add the onion and fry until translucent. Add the garlic and risotto rice and fry for 2 minutes, stirring to coat the rice with the oil. Pour in the wine and leave to simmer until just 1 tablespoon (15 ml) of liquid is left.

Add the stock over medium heat, a ladleful at a time, stirring continuously. Allow each ladleful of stock to be absorbed by the rice before adding the next. Keep adding stock until the rice is cooked but still has a slight bite to it. This should take about 15–20 minutes.

Add the shrimp and zucchini just before the last couple of ladles of stock go in. Cook until the shrimp are pink and firm to the touch, about 3 minutes. Finally, stir in the peas, butter, mint and lemon zest. Season to taste with salt, pepper and lemon juice.

5

KIDS WILL LOVE THIS

Shrimp & mango kebabs

Serves 4
Preparation time: 10 minutes, plus marinating
Cooking time: 4–5 minutes

> 16 large raw tiger shrimp, peeled and deveined
> 1 tablespoon (15 ml) sunflower oil
> 4 tablespoons (60 ml) lemon juice
> 2 cloves garlic, crushed
> 1 teaspoon (5 ml) grated gingerroot
> 1 teaspoon (5 ml) chili powder
> 1 tablespoon (15 ml) liquid honey
> 1 teaspoon (5 ml) sea salt
> 1 large mango, peeled, pitted and cut into 16 bite-size pieces

Put the shrimp into a large bowl and add the oil, lemon juice, garlic, ginger, chili powder, honey and salt. Mix well and marinate for about 10 minutes.

Remove the shrimp from the marinade and thread 2 shrimp alternately between 2 pieces of mango on each of 8 presoaked wooden skewers.

Place the skewers under a preheated hot broiler, brush with the remaining marinade and grill for 2 minutes on each side or until the shrimp turn pink and are cooked through. Serve 2 skewers per person with some dressed mixed greens, if desired.

6

LEFTOVER TO LUNCH

Onion & bean soup with shrimp

Serves 4
Preparation time: 25 minutes
Cooking time: 20 minutes

> 2 tablespoons (30 ml) olive oil
> 10 green onions, roughly chopped, plus extra, finely chopped, to garnish
> 1 clove garlic, roughly chopped
> a few fresh thyme leaves
> 2 cans (each 14 ounces/398 ml) lima beans, drained and rinsed
> 3 cups (750 ml) chicken stock (see page 9) or fish stock (see page 8)
> ⅓ cup + 2 tablespoons (100 ml) whipping (35%) cream cream
> 20 raw peeled tiger shrimp, deveined
> salt and pepper
> 2 tablespoons (30 ml) finely chopped chives, to garnish

Heat 1 tablespoon (15 ml) of the oil in a saucepan. Add the roughly chopped green onions, garlic and thyme leaves and fry over gentle heat until soft. Add the beans, stock and cream. Bring the soup to the boil, then reduce the heat and simmer for 5 minutes.

Transfer the soup to a blender or food processor and blend until smooth. If it is a little thick, add a little more cream or stock. Season the soup with salt and pepper.

Place a frying pan over high heat and add the remaining oil. Season the shrimp with salt and pepper, then fry them in the pan for 4 minutes or until they turn pink.

Stack the shrimp in the center of 4 bowls and pour the soup around them. Garnish the dish with a few chopped green onions and the chives.

7

BUT I DON'T LIKE . . . SHRIMP

Shrimp with green leaves

Serves 4
Preparation time: 10 minutes
Cooking time: 5 minutes

olive oil spray
20 jumbo shrimp, with shells intact
1 clove garlic, chopped
4 ounces (125 g) plum tomatoes, chopped
2 ounces (50 g) arugula
2 ounces (50 g) spinach leaves, tough stalks removed
2 ounces (50 g) watercress, tough stalks removed
1 tablespoon (15 ml) lemon juice
salt and pepper

Heat a large saucepan, spray it with oil, add the shrimp and garlic and season to taste. Cover tightly and cook, shaking the pan from time to time, for about 3 minutes or until the shrimp turn pink and are cooked.

Add the tomatoes, arugula, spinach and watercress and stir until wilted. Squeeze in the lemon juice and check the seasoning before serving.

Serve immediately, with French bread if desired.

WHY NOT TRY... GARLIC MUSHROOMS WITH GREEN LEAVES

Replace the shrimp with 11½ ounces (350 g) whole button mushrooms and cook with the garlic as above. Remove the mushrooms from the pan while you wilt the leaves and tomatoes, then return them briefly to the pan. Serve topped with lemon zest and parsley.

SHRIMP ARE GRAY WHEN RAW, BUT THEY TURN AN ATTRACTIVE PINK WHEN COOKED. LANGOUSTINES ARE ACTUALLY MINI LOBSTERS BUT CAN BE COOKED IN THE SAME WAY AS SHRIMP.

8

FRIENDS FOR DINNER

Shrimp & coconut rice

Serves 4
Preparation time: 10 minutes, plus standing
Cooking time: 15 minutes

4 tablespoons (60 ml) peanut oil
1½ cups (375 ml) Thai fragrant (jasmine) rice
1 teaspoon (5 ml) cumin seeds
1 small cinnamon stick
4 kaffir lime leaves
1 can (14 ounces/400 ml) coconut milk
⅔ cup (150 ml) water
1 teaspoon (5 ml) salt
2 cloves garlic, crushed
1-inch (2.5 cm) piece gingerroot, peeled and grated
pinch of hot pepper flakes
1 pound (500 g) jumbo shrimp, peeled and deveined
2 tablespoons (30 ml) Thai fish sauce
1 tablespoon (15 ml) lime juice
2 tablespoons (30 ml) chopped fresh coriander leaves
¼ cup (60 ml) dry-roasted peanuts, chopped, to garnish

Heat half the oil in a saucepan and stir-fry the rice until all the grains are glossy. Add the cumin seeds, cinnamon stick, lime leaves, coconut milk, water and salt. Bring to a boil and simmer gently over a low heat for 10 minutes. Remove from the heat, cover and leave to rest for 10 minutes.

Meanwhile, heat the remaining oil in a wok and stir-fry the garlic, ginger and hot pepper flakes for 30 seconds. Add the shrimp and stir-fry for 3–4 minutes, until pink.

Stir in the coconut rice with the fish sauce, lime juice and coriander. Serve scattered with the peanuts.

9

WATCHING MY WEIGHT
Jumbo shrimp with Japanese salad

Serves 4
Preparation time: 10 minutes, plus cooling
Cooking time: 3 minutes

> 13 ounces (400 g) raw peeled jumbo shrimp
> 7 ounces (200 g) bean sprouts
> 4 ounces (125 g) snow peas, shredded
> 3½ ounces (100 g) water chestnuts, thinly sliced
> ½ iceberg lettuce, shredded
> 12 radishes, thinly sliced
> 1 tablespoon (15 ml) sesame seeds, lightly toasted
>
> **FOR THE DRESSING**
> 2 tablespoons (30 ml) rice vinegar
> ½ cup (125 ml) sunflower oil
> 1 teaspoon (5 ml) Chinese 5-spice powder (optional)
> 2 tablespoons (30 ml) mirin

Set a steamer over a pan of simmering water and steam the jumbo shrimp for 2–3 minutes, until cooked and pink. Set aside and leave to cool.

Make the dressing by mixing together all the ingredients in a small bowl.

Toss together the bean sprouts, snow peas, water chestnuts, lettuce and radishes and scatter with the shrimp and sesame seeds. Drizzle on the dressing and serve immediately.

10

INSPIRE ME
Garlic chive flowers with shrimp

Serves 4
Preparation time: 10 minutes
Cooking time: about 5 minutes

> 1–1½ tablespoons (15–22 ml) sunflower oil
> 2–3 cloves garlic, finely chopped
> 12 ounces (375 g) flowering garlic Chinese chives, cut into 3-inch (7 cm) long pieces (discard the hard ends of the stems)
> 1 tablespoon (15 ml) light soy sauce
> 2 tablespoons (30 ml) oyster sauce
> 8 ounces (250 g) small raw shrimp, peeled, roughly chopped
> a few slices of fresh red chili, to garnish

Heat the oil in a wok or large frying pan, add the garlic and stir-fry over a medium heat until lightly browned. Add the chives, light soy sauce and oyster sauce and stir-fry for 2–3 minutes.

Add the shrimp to the wok and stir-fry for 3 minutes or until cooked as you like. Spoon onto a serving plate and garnish with chili slices.

Serve immediately with boiled jasmine rice or cooked noodles.

10 WAYS WITH SALMON

1

BASIC
Seared salmon with avocado salad

Serves 4
Preparation time: 15 minutes
Cooking time: 10–12 minutes

  2 tablespoons (30 ml) olive oil
  4 salmon fillet, about 7 ounces (200 g) each, skin on
      and pin-boned
  1 large orange
  2 tablespoons (30 ml) extra virgin olive oil
  salt and pepper

  FOR THE AVOCADO SALAD
  2 ripe avocados, peeled and cut into ½-inch (1 cm) cubes
  1 red chili, seeded and finely chopped
  juice of 1 lime
  1 tablespoon (15 ml) roughly chopped fresh coriander
  1 tablespoon (15 ml) olive oil

Heat a small frying pan over high heat. When the pan is hot, add the olive oil. Season the salmon with salt and pepper and place it, skin side down, in the pan. Cook for 4 minutes, then turn the fish over and cook for a further 2 minutes.

   Heat another small frying pan. Cut the orange in half and place the orange halves, cut side down, in the pan. Sear the orange halves until they start to blacken. Remove the oranges from the pan and squeeze the juice into the frying pan. Bring the juice to a boil and reduce it until you have around 1 tablespoon (15 ml) left. Whisk in the extra virgin olive oil and season with salt and pepper.

   Place the avocados in a mixing bowl, add the remaining ingredients and season with salt and pepper. Spoon the avocado salad into the center of each plate. Place a piece of salmon on top and drizzle with the burnt orange vinaigrette.

2

GIVE IT A TWIST
Salmon with horseradish crust

Serves 4
Preparation time: 10 minutes
Cooking time: 12–15 minutes

  4 salmon fillets, about 7 ounces (200 g) each, skin on and pin-
      boned
  4 tablespoons (60 ml) mild horseradish sauce
  1¾ cups (375 ml) fresh breadcrumbs
  20 asparagus spears, trimmed
  1 tablespoon (15 ml) olive oil
  4–5 tablespoons (75 ml) (60–75 ml) crème fraîche or sour cream
  4 tablespoons (60 ml) lemon juice
  1 tablespoon (15 ml) chopped fresh parsley
  salt and pepper

Place the salmon fillets in a baking dish, skin side down. Spread the top of each fillet with 1 tablespoon (15 ml) of the horseradish sauce, then sprinkle with the breadcrumbs. Place in a preheated 350°F (180°C) oven for 12–15 minutes, until the fish is cooked and the breadcrumbs are golden brown.

   Meanwhile, blanch the asparagus in salted boiling water for 2 minutes. Drain and place in a very hot grill pan with the oil to char slightly. Season with salt and pepper.

   Mix together the crème fraîche, lemon juice and parsley and season with salt and pepper.

   Serve the salmon with the chargrilled asparagus and lemon crème fraîche.

3

Salmon fillets with sage & quinoa

Serves 4
Preparation time: 5 minutes
Cooking time: 15 minutes

1⅓ cups (325 ml) quinoa
7 tablespoons (100 ml) butter, at room temperature
8 fresh sage leaves, chopped
1 small bunch chives
grated zest and juice of 1 lemon
4 small salmon fillet steaks, about 4 ounces (125 g) each
1 tablespoon (15 ml) olive oil
salt and pepper

Cook the quinoa in unsalted boiling water for about 15 minutes or until cooked but firm.

Meanwhile, mix the butter with the sage, chives and lemon zest and add salt and pepper to taste.

Rub the salmon with the oil, season with pepper and cook in a preheated hot grill pan for about 6 minutes, turning carefully once. Remove and set aside to rest.

Drain the quinoa, stir in the lemon juice and season to taste. Spoon onto serving plates and top with the salmon, topping each piece with a knob of sage butter.

4

Salmon & lentil salad

Serves 4
Preparation time: 30 minutes, plus cooling and chilling
Cooking time: 35–45 minutes

1 pound (500 g) salmon fillet
2 tablespoons (30 ml) dry white wine
4 red bell peppers, halved and seeded
1 cup (250 ml) Puy lentils
1 large handful of fresh dill, chopped
1 bunch green onions, finely sliced
lemon juice, for squeezing
pepper

FOR THE DRESSING
2 green chilies, seeded and chopped
1 large handful of fresh flat-leaf parsley, chopped
1 large handful of fresh dill, chopped
2 cloves garlic
1 teaspoon (5 ml) Dijon mustard
½ cup (125 ml) lemon juice
1 tablespoon (15 ml) olive oil

Put the salmon on a sheet of foil and spoon the wine over. Gather up the foil and fold over at the top to seal. Place on a baking sheet and bake in a preheated 400°F (200°C) oven for 15–20 minutes, until cooked. Allow to cool, then flake, cover and chill.

Grill the peppers and peel away the skins, following the instructions on page 116. Reserve the pepper juices.

Make the dressing. Whiz the chilies, parsley, dill, garlic, mustard and lemon juice in a food processor until smooth. With the motor running, drizzle in the oil until the mixture is thick.

Put the lentils in a large saucepan with plenty of water, bring to a boil, then simmer gently for 15–20 minutes, until cooked but still firm to the bite. Drain them and place in a bowl with the red peppers and their juice. Add all the dill and most of the green onions. Season with pepper to taste.

Stir the dressing into the hot lentils and allow to infuse. To serve, top the lentils with the flaked salmon and gently mix through the lentils and dressing. Add a little lemon juice and the remaining green onions.

5

KIDS WILL LOVE THIS
Sesame salmon burgers

Serves 4
Preparation time: 10 minutes
Cooking time: 8 minutes

> 8 tablespoons (120 ml) sesame seeds
> 4 tablespoons (60 ml) black sesame seeds
> 4 salmon fillets, about 5 ounces (150 g) each, pin-boned and skinned
> 2 tablespoons (30 ml) olive oil
> 1 tablespoon (15 ml) toasted sesame oil
> 4 crusty sesame seed rolls
> ½ cucumber, cut into ribbons with a vegetable peeler
> 1 small red onion, finely sliced

Spread both types of sesame seeds on a large plate, then dip in the salmon fillets so that the top side of each is evenly coated. Heat the olive oil in a shallow frying pan and fry the salmon over medium heat for 4 minutes on each side or until golden and cooked through. Remove the pan from the heat and drizzle the toasted sesame oil over the top.

Halve the rolls and toast under a preheated broiler. Top each roll bottom with some cucumber and onion, then add a salmon fillet. Finish with the roll tops and serve immediately with extra cucumber and onion.

6

LEFTOVER TO LUNCH
Salmon rösti cakes

Serves 6
Preparation time: 30 minutes
Cooking time: 25–30 minutes

> 1 pound (500 g) white potatoes, peeled but left whole
> 2 tablespoons (30 ml) butter
> 8 ounces (250 g) salmon fillets
> 2 tablespoons (30 ml) sunflower oil
> ¾ cup (175 ml) crème fraîche or sour cream
> 3 green onions, finely sliced
> 2 tablespoons (30 ml) chopped chives
> lemon wedges, to serve

Bring a large pan of lightly salted water to a boil. Cook the potatoes for 10 minutes, until beginning to soften. Drain and set aside to cool.

Heat the butter in a small frying pan and add the salmon. Cover with a tight-fitting lid and reduce the heat to very low. Cook for 8–10 minutes, until the salmon is just cooked. Remove from the heat and set aside until the salmon is cool enough to handle. Flake the salmon and place in a bowl with the pan juices.

Grate the cooled potatoes, add to the bowl with the salmon and toss together to mix. Divide the mixture into 6 parts and form into flattened patties. Heat the oil in a large nonstick frying pan and cook the rösti over medium heat for 2–3 minutes on each side, until golden and cooked through, turning with a spatula.

Meanwhile, place the crème fraîche in a bowl with the green onions and chives and mix well. Drain the rösti on paper towels, then spoon on the crème fraîche and serve with lemon wedges.

7

BUT I DON'T LIKE ...
SALMON

Salmon & bulgur pilaf

Serves 4
Preparation time: 10 minutes
Cooking time: 10–15 minutes

15 ounces (475 g) boneless skinless salmon
1¾ cups (425 ml) bulgur
½ cup (125 ml) frozen peas
2 cups (500 ml) broad green beans, chopped
2 tablespoons (30 ml) chopped chives
2 tablespoons (30 ml) chopped fresh flat-leaf parsley
salt and pepper

TO SERVE
2 lemons, halved
low-fat yogurt

Cook the salmon in a steamer or microwave for about 10 minutes. Alternatively, wrap it in foil and cook in a preheated 350°F (180°C) oven for 15 minutes.

Meanwhile, cook the bulgur according to the instructions on the package and boil the peas and beans. Alternatively, cook the bulgur, peas and beans in the steamer with the salmon.

Flake the salmon and mix it into the bulgur with the peas and beans. Fold in the chives and parsley and season to taste. Serve immediately with the lemon halves and yogurt.

WHY NOT TRY...
HAM & BULGUR PILAF

Pan-fry 10 ounces (300 g) diced lean ham instead of the salmon. Replace the runner beans with the same quantity of ordinary green beans and fold in 2 tablespoons (30 ml) chopped mint along with the chives and parsley.

> # SALMON IS A GREAT SUPPER SOLUTION — WHY NOT MAKE FRIDAY SALMON NIGHT?

8

FRIENDS FOR DINNER

Dill & mustard baked salmon

Serves 4
Preparation time: 20 minutes
Cooking time: 45–50 minutes

3 tablespoons (45 ml) chopped fresh dill
2 tablespoons (30 ml) grainy mustard
2 tablespoons (30 ml) lime juice
1 tablespoon (15 ml) granulated sugar
⅔ cup (150 ml) whipping (35%) cream
2 small fennel bulbs, thinly sliced
2 tablespoons (30 ml) olive oil
1½ pounds (750 g) salmon fillet, skinned
4 hard-boiled eggs, quartered
8 ounces (250 g) puff pastry
beaten egg yolk, to glaze
salt and pepper

Mix together the dill, mustard, lime juice and sugar in a bowl. Stir in the cream and a little seasoning.

Put the fennel in an 8-cup (2 L) shallow, baking dish or pie plate. Drizzle with the oil and bake in a preheated 400°F (200°C) oven for 20 minutes, turning once or twice during cooking, until softened.

Cut the salmon into 8 chunky pieces and add to the dish with the egg quarters, tucking them between the fennel slices so that all the ingredients are evenly mixed. Spoon the cream mixture over and return to the oven for 15 minutes.

Roll out the pastry on a lightly floured surface and cut out eight 2½-inch (6 cm) squares. Brush the tops with egg yolk to glaze and make diagonal markings over the surface of the pastry with the tip of a sharp knife. Sprinkle with pepper.

Place a double thickness of waxed or parchment paper over the dish of salmon and put the pastry squares on the paper. Bake for 10–15 minutes until the pastry is risen and golden. Slide the pastry squares onto the salmon and serve with a herb salad.

9

WATCHING MY WEIGHT
Asian salmon salad

Serves 4
Preparation time: 20 minutes
Cooking time: 8–10 minutes

- 1 cup (250 ml) long-grain rice
- 4 salmon fillets, each about 4 ounces (125 g)
- 3 tablespoons (45 ml) tamari sauce
- 3½ ounces (100 g) sugar snap peas, halved lengthwise
- 1 large carrot, cut into matchsticks
- 4 green onions, thinly sliced
- 3½ ounces (100 g) bean sprouts
- 2 tablespoons (30 ml) sunflower oil
- 3 tablespoons (45 ml) sesame seeds
- 2 teaspoons (10 ml) Thai fish sauce (nam pla) (optional)
- 2 teaspoons (10 ml) rice vinegar or white wine vinegar
- 1 small bunch fresh coriander or basil, leaves roughly torn

Half-fill a saucepan with water and bring to a boil. Add the rice and simmer for 8 minutes.

Meanwhile, put the salmon on a foil-lined broiler pan and drizzle with 1 tablespoon (15 ml) of the tamari sauce. Cook under a preheated broiler for 8–10 minutes, turning once, until the fish is browned and flakes easily.

Add the sugar snap peas to the rice and cook for 1 minute. Drain, rinse with cold water and drain again. Tip into a salad bowl. Add the carrot, green onions and bean sprouts to the salad bowl.

Heat 1 teaspoon (5 ml) of the oil in a nonstick frying pan, add the sesame seeds and fry until just beginning to brown. Add 1 tablespoon (15 ml) tamari sauce and quickly cover the pan so the seeds do not ping out. Remove the pan from the heat and leave to stand for 1–2 minutes, then mix in the remaining tamari sauce, oil, fish sauce (if using) and vinegar.

Add the sesame mixture to the salad and toss together. Take the skin off the salmon and flake into pieces, discarding any bones. Add to the salad with the torn herb leaves and serve.

10

INSPIRE ME
Salmon with ginger & white fungus

Serves 4
Preparation time: 10 minutes
Cooking time: 15–17 minutes

- 1 handful of dried white fungus
- 4 salmon fillets, about 8 ounces (250 g) each
- 2 carrots, cut into matchsticks
- 2-inch (5 cm) piece of gingerroot, peeled, finely shredded
- 20 sun-dried goji berries (optional)
- ¼ teaspoon (1 ml) ground black pepper
- 3 tablespoons (45 ml) light soy sauce
- 4 whole coriander plants
- 4 handfuls of watercress, cleaned, shaken dry, to serve

Soak the dried fungus in boiling-hot water for 3–4 minutes or until soft, then drain. Remove and discard the hard stalks and roughly chop.

Place the salmon fillets on a baking dish and sprinkle with the carrots, ginger, goji berries (if using), pepper, 1 tablespoon (15 ml) of the soy sauce and the fungus. Snap each coriander plant in half and place one on top of each fillet. Cover with foil and bake in a preheated 350°F (180°C) oven for 15–17 minutes, or until a skewer will slide easily into the flesh and come out clean.

Remove the coriander plants. Place a fish fillet with some of the sauce on a warm serving plate. Pile a handful of watercress next to it. Serve the remaining light soy sauce separately in a small bowl. Alternatively, place each fish over boiled rice or cooked noodles, or serve with a vegetable dish such as stir-fried vegetables.

10 WAYS WITH COD

BASIC
Cod with roasted tomatos

Serves 4
Preparation time: 15 minutes
Cooking time: 1¼ hours

> 4 ripe tomatoes, halved
> a few sprigs fresh thyme
> 2 tablespoons (30 ml) olive oil
> 4 cod fillets, about 7 ounces (200 g) each, skin on and pin-boned
> 4 slices ciabatta bread
> 1 clove garlic
> salt and pepper

> **FOR THE DRESSING**
> 1 large handful of fresh basil
> 4 tablespoons (60 ml) olive oil
> 2 tablespoons (30 ml) freshly grated Parmesan cheese, plus some shavings to garnish (optional)

Place the tomatoes on a baking sheet, season with salt and pepper, sprinkle with the thyme sprigs and drizzle with 1 tablespoon (15 ml) of the oil. Roast in a preheated 325°F (160°C) oven for 1 hour until soft, then turn the oven up to 350°F (180°C). Season the cod and roast along with the tomatoes in the oven for 10–12 minutes or until the fish is cooked and the tomatoes have softened.

Brush both sides of the bread with the remaining oil. Preheat a grill pan and grill the bread until golden brown on both sides. Then rub both sides with the clove garlic.

Place the ingredients for the dressing in a small food processor and blend until smooth. You can also do this using a handheld blender.

Top the toasted ciabatta bread with the tomatoes and serve with the cod. Drizzle a little of the dressing over the top and garnish with some Parmesan shavings, if desired.

GIVE IT A TWIST
Chili & coriander fish parcels

Serves 1
Preparation time: 15 minutes, plus marinating and chilling
Cooking time: 15 minutes

> 4 ounces (125 g) cod, coley or haddock fillet
> 2 teaspoons (10 ml) lemon juice
> 1 tablespoon (15 ml) fresh coriander leaves
> 1 clove garlic
> 1 green chili, seeded and chopped
> ¼ teaspoon (1 ml) granulated sugar
> 2 teaspoons (10 ml) natural yogurt

Place the fish in a non-metallic dish and sprinkle with the lemon juice. Cover and leave in the refrigerator to marinate for 15–20 minutes.

Put the coriander, garlic and chili in a food processor or blender and process until the mixture forms a paste. Add the sugar and yogurt and briefly process to blend.

Lay the fish on a sheet of foil. Coat the fish on both sides with the paste. Gather up the foil loosely and turn over at the top to seal. Return to the refrigerator for at least 1 hour.

Place the parcel on a baking tray and bake in a preheated 400°F (200°C) oven for about 15 minutes, until the fish is just cooked.

SAVE ME TIME
Blackened cod with salsa

Serves 4
Preparation time: 15 minutes, plus resting
Cooking time: 8 minutes

   1 large orange
   1 clove garlic, crushed
   2 large tomatoes, skinned, seeded and diced
   2 tablespoons (30 ml) chopped fresh basil
   2 ounces (50 g) pitted black olives, chopped
   5 tablespoons (75 ml) extra virgin olive oil
   4 thick cod fillets, about 6 ounces (175 g) each
   1 tablespoon (15 ml) jerk seasoning
   salt and pepper
   arugula leaves, to serve

Peel and segment the orange, holding it over a bowl to catch the juices. Halve the segments. Mix them with the garlic, tomatoes, basil, olives and 4 tablespoons (60 ml) of the oil, season to taste with salt and pepper and set the salsa aside to infuse.

   Wash and pat dry the fish and pull out any small bones with a pair of tweezers. Brush with the remaining oil and coat well with the jerk seasoning.

   Heat a large heavy-bottomed frying pan and fry the cod fillets, skin side down, for 5 minutes. Turn them over and cook for a further 3 minutes. Transfer to a low 300°F (150°C) oven to rest for about 5 minutes.

   Serve the fish with the salsa and some arugula leaves.

SAVE ME MONEY
Baked cod with tomatoes & olives

Serves 4
Preparation time: 5 minutes
Cooking time: 15 minutes

   8 ounces (250 g) cherry tomatoes, halved
   3½ ounces (100 g) pitted black olives
   2 tablespoons (30 ml) capers in brine, drained
   4 sprigs fresh thyme, plus extra to garnish
   4 cod fillets, about 6 ounces (175 g) each
   2 tablespoons (30 ml) extra virgin olive oil
   2 tablespoons (30 ml) balsamic vinegar
   salt and black pepper

Combine the tomatoes, olives, capers and thyme sprigs in a roasting pan. Nestle the cod fillets in the pan, drizzle over the oil and balsamic vinegar and season to taste with salt and pepper.

   Bake in a preheated 400°F (200°C) oven for 15 minutes.

   Transfer the fish, tomatoes and olives to warmed plates. Spoon the pan juices over the fish. Serve immediately with a mixed greens salad.

TO EAT SUSTAINABLY AND PROTECT FISH STOCKS, ALWAYS TRY TO BUY LINE-CAUGHT COD.

5

KIDS WILL LOVE THIS
Fish & chips

Serves 4
Preparation time: 25 minutes
Cooking time: 30 minutes

> 1 cup (250 ml) self-rising flour, plus extra for dusting
> ½ teaspoon (2 ml) baking powder
> ¼ teaspoon (1 ml) ground turmeric
> ¾ cup + 2 tablespoons (200 ml) cold water
> 3 pounds (1.5 kg) large potatoes
> 1½ pounds (750 g) piece cod or haddock fillet, pin-boned and skinned
> sunflower oil, for deep-frying
> salt and pepper

Mix together the flour, baking powder, turmeric and a pinch of salt in a bowl and make a well in the center. Add half the water to the well. Gradually whisk the flour into the water to make a smooth batter, then whisk in the remaining water.

Cut the potatoes into ¾-inch (1.5 cm) slices, then cut across to make chunky chips. Put them in a bowl of cold water. Pat the fish dry on paper towels and cut into 4 portions. Season lightly and dust with extra flour. Thoroughly drain the chips and pat them dry on paper towels.

Pour the oil into a deep-fat fryer or large saucepan to a depth of at least 3 inches (7 cm) and heat to 350–375°F (180–190°C), or until a spoonful of batter turns golden in 30 seconds. Fry half the chips for 10 minutes, or until golden. Drain and keep warm while you cook the remainder. Keep all the chips warm while you fry the fish.

Dip 2 pieces of fish in the batter and lower them into the hot oil. Fry gently for 4–5 minutes or until crisp and golden. Drain and keep warm while you fry the other pieces. Serve with the chips and some peas.

6

LEFTOVER TO LUNCH
Fish pie

Serves 6–8
Preparation time: 30 minutes
Cooking time: 55–60 minutes

> 12 ounces (375 g) salmon fillet
> 12 ounces (375 g) cod loin
> 2⅓ cups (575 ml) 1% or 2% milk
> 1 bay leaf
> 1 leek, thinly sliced
> 1¼ pounds (625 g) potatoes, thinly sliced
> 3 tablespoons (45 ml) chopped fresh dill
> ¼ cup (60 ml) butter
> ⅓ cup + 1 tablespoon (90 ml) all-purpose flour
> 3½ ounces (100 g) aged Cheddar cheese, grated
> salt and pepper

Put the salmon and cod into a frying pan, pour in enough of the milk to just cover it, then add the bay leaf and a little seasoning. Bring to a boil then cover and simmer for 8 minutes until the fish flakes when pressed with a knife, adding the leeks for the last 2 minutes. Meanwhile, cook the potatoes in a saucepan of boiling water for 3–4 minutes until just tender. Drain, rinse in cold water and drain again.

Lift the fish out of the milk and flake the flesh into large pieces, discarding the skin and any bones. Transfer to a 5-cup (1.2 L), 2-inch (5 cm) deep baking dish. Strain the milk into a container with the remaining milk and discard the bay leaf. Arrange the leeks on top of the fish and sprinkle with the dill.

Heat the butter in a clean pan, stir in the flour, then gradually whisk in the milk. Bring to a boil, whisking, until thickened and smooth. Season and stir in three-quarters of the cheese. Pour half the sauce over the fish. Arrange the potato slices overlapping on top, pour the remaining sauce over, then sprinkle with the remaining cheese. Allow to cool, then chill until required.

When ready to serve, remove the cover and cook the fish pie in a preheated 350°F (180°C) oven for 40–45 minutes, until the top is golden brown and the pie is piping hot. Serve with green beans, if desired.

BUT I DON'T LIKE ...
COD
Oven-steamed fish with greens

Serves 2
Preparation time: 15 minutes
Cooking time: 25 minutes

- ½ ounce (15 g) gingerroot
- ¼ teaspoon (1 ml) hot pepper flakes
- 1 clove garlic, thinly sliced
- 2 tablespoons (30 ml) rice wine vinegar
- 2 chunky cod fillets, each 150–200 g (5–7 oz), skinned
- ⅔ cup (150 ml) hot fish stock (see page 8)
- ½ cucumber
- 2 tablespoons (30 ml) light soy sauce
- 2 tablespoons (30 ml) oyster sauce
- 1 tablespoon (15 ml) granulated sugar
- ½ bunch green onions, cut into 1-inch (2.5 cm) long pieces
- ½ cup (125 ml) fresh coriander, roughly chopped
- 1½ cups (375 ml) cooked rice

Peel and slice the ginger as finely as possible. Cut across into thin shreds and mix with the hot pepper flakes, garlic and 1 teaspoon (5 ml) of the vinegar. Spoon over the pieces of cod, rubbing it in gently.

Lightly oil a wire rack and position over a small roasting pan. Pour the stock into the pan and place the cod fillets on the rack. Cover with foil and carefully transfer to a preheated 350°F (180°C) oven for 20 minutes or until cooked through.

Meanwhile, peel the cucumber, cut in half and scoop out the seeds. Cut the flesh into small, chip-sized pieces. Mix together the soy sauce, oyster sauce, sugar and remaining vinegar in a small bowl.

Remove the fish from the pan and keep warm. Drain the juices from the pan and reserve. Add the cucumber, green onions, coriander and rice to the pan and heat through, stirring continuously, for about 5 minutes until hot. Stir in enough of the reserved juices to make the rice slightly moist.

Pile onto serving plates, top with the fish and serve with the sauce spooned over.

WHY NOT TRY...
OVEN-STEAMED CHICKEN WITH GREENS

Replace the fish with 4 skinless chicken breast fillets. Use chicken stock (see page 9) instead of the fish stock. Make several deep scores in the chicken, then cook as per the second step but for 30–40 minutes. Replace the oyster sauce with the same quantity of hoisin sauce.

FRIENDS FOR DINNER
Seared cod with olive butter

Serves 4
Preparation time: 20 minutes
Cooking time: 10–12 minutes

- 5 ounces (150 g) sugar snap peas
- 1 pound (500 g) zucchini, sliced diagonally
- 1 tablespoon (15 ml) olive oil
- finely grated zest and juice of 1 lemon
- 4 cod fillets, about 4 ounces (125 g) each
- 2 ounces (50 g) pitted mixed olives, roughly chopped
- ¼ cup (60 ml) butter
- 1 small bunch fresh basil, roughly torn
- salt and pepper

Put the sugar snap peas and zucchini on a large piece of oiled foil, sprinkle with the lemon zest and plenty of seasoning, then top with the fish. Drizzle with lemon juice and sprinkle with a little extra seasoning. Seal the edges of the foil to make an airtight parcel. Chill until required.

Beat the olives with the butter and half the basil. Season with pepper, then spoon onto a piece of waxed paper. Wrap tightly and roll into a small log shape. Chill until required.

When ready to serve, put the fish parcel in a broiler pan, open the foil and top the fish with 4 slices of olive butter. Cook under a preheated hot broiler for 8–10 minutes, until the fish is browned and flakes when pressed with a knife. Lift out the fish and cook the vegetables for a few minutes more, until they are just tender and lightly browned.

Spoon the vegetables onto serving plates and top with the fish fillets and any pan juices. Top with the remaining butter, cut into thin slices, and garnish with the remaining basil.

9

WATCHING MY WEIGHT
Fried miso cod with bok choy

Serves 4
Preparation time: 10 minutes, plus cooling and marinating
Cooking time: 13–15 minutes

    4 cod fillets, about 6 ounces (175 g) each
    olive oil, for brushing
    4 heads baby bok choy, halved lengthwise and blanched in boiling
        water for 1–2 minutes

    FOR THE MISO SAUCE
    6 tablespoons (90 ml) miso paste
    ¼ cup (60 ml) soy sauce
    ¼ cup (60 ml) sake
    ¼ cup (60 ml) mirin
    ¼ cup (60 ml) granulated or superfine sugar

Make the miso sauce. Put all the ingredients into a small saucepan and heat gently until the sugar has dissolved. Simmer gently for about 5 minutes, stirring frequently. Remove from the heat and set aside to cool.

Arrange the cod fillets in a dish into which they fit snugly and cover with the cold miso sauce. Rub the sauce over the fillets so that they are completely covered and leave to marinate for at least 6 hours, preferably overnight.

Heat a frying pan or grill over medium heat, remove the cod fillets from the miso sauce and cook the fish for about 2–3 minutes. Carefully turn them over and cook for a further 2–3 minutes. Remove and keep warm.

Heat a clean pan. Brush a little oil over the cut side of the bok choy and arrange them, cut side down, in the pan. Cook for about 2 minutes, until hot and lightly charred. Transfer to a serving plate with the cod and serve immediately.

10

INSPIRE ME
Cod rarebit

Serves 4
Preparation time: 5 minutes, plus cooling
Cooking time: 15 minutes

    2 tablespoons (30 ml) whole-grain mustard
    3 tablespoons (45 ml) beer or milk
    8 ounces (250 g) Cheddar cheese, grated
    2 tablespoons (30 ml) olive oil
    4 cod fillets, about 7 ounces (200 g) each, pin-boned
    salt and pepper

Mix together the mustard, beer or milk and cheese in a small saucepan. Over low heat, allow the cheese to melt. Stir occasionally and don't let it boil, as the cheese will curdle. Remove the pan from the heat and leave to cool and thicken.

Heat a frying pan over high heat with the oil. Season the fish and place it into the pan, skin side down. Cook for 4–5 minutes, until the skin is crispy, then turn the fish over and cook for a further minute on the other side.

Spread the cheese mixture over the 4 pieces of cod and place under a preheated broiler. Grill until golden brown.

10 WAYS WITH MACKEREL

1

BASIC

Mackerel with baked beets

Serves 4
Preparation time: 15 minutes
Cooking time: 1 hour 5 minutes

> 4 small mackerel, filleted
> 1 tablespoon (15 ml) olive oil
> salt and pepper
>
> **FOR THE BEETS**
> 2 large raw beets
> 2 cloves garlic, sliced
> 4 sprigs fresh thyme
> 2 tablespoons (30 ml) olive oil, plus extra for drizzling
>
> **FOR THE HORSERADISH CREAM (OPTIONAL)**
> ⅔ cup (150 ml) crème fraîche or sour cream
> 2 tablespoons (30 ml) mayonnaise
> 2 tablespoons (30 ml) finely chopped chives
> 1–2 tablespoons (15–30 ml) creamed horseradish

Wash the beets well. Wrap the beets in a foil parcel with the garlic, thyme, salt and pepper to taste and oil. Place in a preheated 350°F (180°C) oven for around 1 hour, until the beets are cooked and a knife can easily be inserted into the center. Once cool enough to handle, peel the beets. Cut into bite-size pieces, drizzle with a little oil and season with salt and pepper. Set aside. Mix together all the horseradish cream ingredients, if using, and season with salt and pepper.

Place the fish on a nonstick baking sheet, skin side up. Brush the skin with the oil and season with salt and pepper. Cook under a preheated broiler on this side until the skin is crispy, about 3 minutes, then carefully turn over and cook for a further 2 minutes on the other side.

Serve the mackerel with the baked beets and horseradish cream, if using.

2 ◎

GIVE IT A TWIST

Bacon- & oat-topped mackerel

Serves 4
Preparation time: 15 minutes
Cooking time: 10 minutes

> 4 mackerel, heads removed, boned
> 4 teaspoons (20 ml) finely chopped fresh rosemary leaves
> 2 slices smoked back bacon, finely diced
> 6 tablespoons (90 ml) old-fashioned (large-flake) rolled oats
> ¼ cup (60 ml) walnuts, roughly chopped
> finely grated zest and juice of 1 lemon
> 2 tablespoons (30 ml) olive oil
> 2 teaspoons (10 ml) hot horseradish
> 6 tablespoons (90 ml) Greek yogurt
> salt and pepper

Arrange the mackerel fillets skin side down on a baking sheet lined with oiled parchment paper or foil. Mix the rosemary, bacon, oats, walnuts and lemon zest together, season with salt and pepper, then spoon on top of the fish. Drizzle with the lemon juice and oil. Cover and chill until required.

Mix the horseradish and yogurt in a small bowl with a little salt and pepper, cover and chill until required.

When ready to serve, remove the cover and bake the mackerel in a preheated 425°F (220°C) oven for 10 minutes, until the topping is crisp and golden and the fish flakes easily when pressed with a knife. Serve with salad and the horseradish sauce.

3 🕐

SAVE ME TIME
Spiced mackerel fillets

Serves 4
Preparation time: 4 minutes
Cooking time: 5–6 minutes

- 2 tablespoons (30 ml) olive oil
- 1 tablespoon (15 ml) smoked paprika
- 1 teaspoon (5 ml) cayenne pepper
- 4 mackerels, scaled, filleted and pin-boned
- 2 limes, quartered
- salt and pepper

Mix together the oil, paprika and cayenne with a little salt and pepper. Make 3 shallow cuts in the skin of the mackerel and brush on the spiced oil.

Place the lime quarters and mackerel on a hot barbecue, skin side down first, and cook for 4–5 minutes, until the skin is crispy and the limes are charred. Turn the fish over and cook for a further minute on the other side. Serve with with arugula salad.

4

SAVE ME MONEY
Mackerel with sweet potatoes

Serves 2
Preparation time: 15 minutes
Cooking time: 1 hour

- 12 ounces (375 g) sweet potatoes, scrubbed and cut into ¾-inch (1.5 cm) chunks
- 1 red onion, thinly sliced
- 4 tablespoons (60 ml) chili oil
- sprigs fresh thyme
- 1½ ounces (40 g) sun-dried tomatoes in oil, drained and thinly sliced
- 4 large mackerel fillets, pin-boned
- ⅓ cup + 2 tablespoons (100ml) natural yogurt
- 1 tablespoon (15 ml) each chopped fresh coriander and mint
- salt and pepper
- lemon wedges, to serve

Scatter the chunks of sweet potato in a shallow, baking dish with the onion. Add the oil, thyme and a little salt and mix together. Bake in a preheated 400°F (200°C) oven for 40–45 minutes, turning once or twice, until the potatoes are just tender and beginning to brown.

Stir in the tomatoes. Fold each mackerel fillet in half, skin side out, and place on top of the potatoes. Return to the oven for a further 12–15 minutes or until the fish is cooked through.

Meanwhile, mix together the yogurt, herbs and a little salt and pepper to make a raita. Transfer the fish and potatoes to warm plates, spoon over the raita and serve with lemon wedges.

OILY FISH, SUCH AS MACKEREL, ARE A SOURCE OF OMEGA-3 FATTY ACIDS.

5

KIDS WILL LOVE THIS
Mackerel with avocado salsa

Serves 4
Preparation time: 10 minutes
Cooking time: 6–8 minutes

8 mackerel fillets
2 lemons, plus extra wedges to serve
salt and pepper

FOR THE AVOCADO SALSA
2 avocados, peeled, pitted and finely diced
juice and zest of 1 lime
1 red onion, finely chopped
½ cucumber, finely diced
1 handful of fresh coriander leaves, finely chopped

Make 3 diagonal slashes across each mackerel fillet on the skin side and season well with salt and pepper. Cut the lemons in half, then squeeze the juice over the fish.

Lay on a broiler pan, skin side up, and cook under a preheated broiler for 6–8 minutes or until the skin is lightly charred and the flesh is just cooked through.

Meanwhile, to make the salsa, mix together the avocados and lime juice and zest, then add the onion, cucumber and coriander. Toss well to mix and season to taste with salt and pepper.

Serve the mackerel hot with the avocado salsa and lemon wedges for squeezing over.

6

LEFTOVER TO LUNCH
Mackerel with cider vichyssoise

Serves 3–4 as a main course, 8 as a starter
Preparation time: 15 minutes
Cooking time: 35 minutes

1¼ pounds (625 g) leeks
¼ cup (60 ml) butter
1¼ pounds (625 g) new potatoes, diced
2⅓ cups (575 ml) strong cider
2½ cups (600 ml) fish stock (see page 8)
2 teaspoons (10 ml) Dijon mustard
10 ounces (300 g) smoked mackerel fillets
5 tablespoons (75 ml) chopped chives
plenty of freshly ground nutmeg
¾–1 cup (175–250 ml) crème fraîche or sour cream
salt and pepper
chive sprigs, to garnish

Trim the leeks and chop, keeping the white and green parts separate. Melt the butter in a large saucepan and gently fry the white parts and half the green parts for 5 minutes. Add the potatoes, then stir in the cider, stock and mustard and bring almost to a boil. Reduce the heat and simmer gently for 20 minutes, until the potatoes are soft but still holding their shape.

Flake the smoked mackerel into small pieces, discarding any skin and stray bones. Add to the pan with the chopped chives, nutmeg and remaining green leeks. Simmer gently for 5 minutes.

Stir in half the crème fraîche and season to taste with salt and pepper. Spoon into bowls, top with the remaining crème fraîche and garnish with chive sprigs.

BUT I DON'T LIKE ...
MACKEREL
Fish salad with lemongrass

Serves 4
Preparation time: 20 minutes
Cooking time: 15–20 minutes

> 1 tablespoon (15 ml) sunflower oil
> 1¼ pounds (625 g) mackerel or whiting, gutted, scored with a
>   sharp knife 3–4 times
> ¼ teaspoon (1 ml) sea salt
> ¼ teaspoon (1 ml) ground black pepper
> 3 stalks lemongrass, about 6 inches (15 cm) each, finely sliced
> 4–5 shallots, finely sliced
> 3 green onions, finely sliced
> 1-inch (2.5 cm) piece gingerroot, peeled, finely shredded
> 3–4 kaffir lime leaves, finely shredded
> ½ handful of fresh mint leaves
> 2½ tablespoons (37 ml) light soy sauce
> 4 tablespoons (60 ml) lime juice
> 1–1½ long red chilies, stemmed, seeded, finely chopped
> mixed salad leaves, to serve

Line a baking sheet with foil, then drizzle and rub the surface with a little oil. Rub the fish with oil, salt and pepper and place on the baking sheet.

Bake in a preheated 350°F (180°C) oven uncovered, for 15–20 minutes or until the fish is cooked. Remove the heads (if left on) and all the bones. Break the fish, including the skin, into bite-size chunks and put these in a mixing bowl.

Mix with the lemongrass, shallots, green onions, ginger, kaffir lime leaves, mint leaves, soy sauce, lime juice and chilies. Taste and adjust the seasoning. Divide among 4 serving plates next to a pile of mixed salad leaves.

WHY NOT TRY...
TUNA SALAD WITH LEMONGRASS

Replace the makerel with 1 pound (500 g) of very fresh tuna steak (sashimi grade) and omit the sunflower oil, salt, kaffir lime leaves and mint leaves. Chill the tuna in the refrigerator for 2–3 hours, then finely dice it. Mix with the pepper, lemongrass, shallots, green onions, ginger, soy sauce and 2 tablespoons (30 ml) lime juice. No cooking is required.

FRIENDS FOR DINNER
Mackerel & asparagus pie

Serves 4
Preparation time: 20 minutes, plus chilling
Cooking time: 30–40 minutes

> 8 asparagus spears, trimmed and blanched
> 8 ounces (250 g) smoked mackerel, skinned
> 2 eggs
> ⅓ cup + 2 tablespoons (100 ml) 1% or 2% milk
> ⅓ cup + 2 tablespoons (100 ml) whipping (35%) cream
> salt and pepper
>
> **FOR THE PASTRY**
> 1⅔ cups (400 ml) all-purpose flour, plus extra for dusting
> ⅓ cup (75 ml) lightly salted butter, chilled and diced
> 1 egg, plus 1 egg yolk

Put the flour, butter, egg and egg yolk in a food processor and blend until a soft dough is formed. If the pastry won't come together, add a drop of cold water. Take the dough out of the processor and knead lightly for 1 minute, until it is smooth. Place it in a freezer bag or wrap in plastic wrap and chill in the refrigerator for at least 30 minutes. Alternatively, make the pastry by hand by rubbing the butter into the flour until it resembles breadcrumbs, then work in the eggs.

Roll the pastry out on a well-floured work surface until it is about ⅛ inch (3 mm) thick and line a 10-inch (25 cm) round, fluted tart pan. Trim off the excess pastry. Chill the lined tart pan for 1 hour.

Line the tart with a piece of parchment paper, cover with beans, then place in a preheated 350°F (180°C) oven for 10–12 minutes, until lightly golden. Remove from the oven and take away the paper and beans. Place back in the oven for a further 2 minutes to dry out the base of the pastry case. Remove from the oven.

Slice each asparagus spear into 3 diagonal pieces. Flake the fish into the pastry case and add the asparagus. Mix together the eggs, milk and cream. Season with salt and pepper. Pour the mixture into the pastry case for 20–25 minutes, bake until the mixture has set.

9

WATCHING MY WEIGHT
Mackerel with wild rice niçoise

Serves 3–4
Preparation time: 20 minutes, plus cooling
Cooking time: 25 minutes

½ cup (125 ml) wild rice
2 cups (500 ml) green beans, halved
10 ounces (300 g) large mackerel fillets, pin-boned
6 tablespoons (90 ml) olive oil
12 black olives
8 canned anchovy fillets, drained and halved
8 ounces (250 g) cherry tomatoes, halved
3 hard-boiled eggs, cut into quarters
1 tablespoon (15 ml) lemon juice
1 tablespoon (15 ml) Dijon mustard
2 tablespoons (30 ml) chopped chives
salt and pepper

Cook the rice in plenty of boiling water for 20–25 minutes or until it is tender. (The grains will start to split open when they're just cooked.) Add the green beans and cook for 2 minutes.

Meanwhile, lay the mackerel on a foil-lined broiler pan and brush with 1 tablespoon (15 ml) of the oil. Cook under a preheated broiler for 8–10 minutes or until cooked through. Leave to cool.

Drain the rice and beans and mix together in a salad bowl with the olives, anchovies, tomatoes and eggs. Flake the mackerel, discarding any stray bones, and add to the bowl.

Mix the remaining oil with the lemon juice, mustard, chives and a little salt and pepper, and add to the bowl. Toss the ingredients lightly together, cover and chill until ready to serve.

10

INSPIRE ME
Basque fish soup

Serves 6
Preparation time: 20 minutes
Cooking time: 45 minutes

2 tablespoons (30 ml) olive oil
1 onion, finely chopped
½ green pepper, cored, seeded and diced
½ red bell pepper, cored, seeded and diced
1 zucchini, diced
2 cloves garlic, finely chopped
8 ounces (250 g) potatoes, cut into chunks
½ teaspoon (2 ml) smoked paprika
⅔ cup (150 ml) red wine
4 cups (1 L) fish stock (see page 8)
1 can (14 ounces/400 g) chopped tomatoes
1 tablespoon (15 ml) tomato paste
2 whole mackerel, gutted, rinsed with cold water inside and out
salt and cayenne pepper

Heat the oil in a large saucepan, add the onion and fry gently for 5 minutes, until softened. Add the peppers, zucchini, garlic and potato and fry for 5 minutes, stirring continuously. Mix in the paprika and cook for 1 minute.

Pour in the wine, stock, tomatoes, tomato paste, salt and cayenne. Bring to a boil, stirring continuously, then add the whole mackerel. Cover and simmer gently for 20 minutes, until the fish flakes easily when pressed with a knife.

Lift the fish out with a slotted spoon and put on a plate. Simmer the soup, uncovered, for a further 15 minutes. Peel the skin off the fish, then lift the flesh away from the backbone. Flake into pieces, checking carefully for any bones.

Return the mackerel flakes to the pan. Reheat and ladle into shallow bowls. Serve with lemon wedges and crusty bread.

10 WAYS WITH TUNA

1

BASIC
Tuna with green beans & broccoli

Serves 4
Preparation time: 8 minutes
Cooking time: 15 minutes

1 pound (500 g) new potatoes
8 ounces (250 g) slender green beans, topped and tailed
7 ounces (200 g) young broccoli, stems peeled off if necessary
4 fresh tuna steaks, about 6 ounces (175 g) each
1 tablespoon (15 ml) olive oil
½ cup (125 ml) toasted hazelnuts, roughly chopped
salt and pepper

FOR THE DRESSING
4 tablespoons (60 ml) hazelnut oil
1 tablespoon (15 ml) lemon juice
1 teaspoon (5 ml) Dijon mustard

Cook the potatoes, beans and broccoli in lightly salted water until tender but still with a slight bite to them. Then plunge into ice-cold water to stop the cooking process. Drain and cut the potatoes into quarters lengthwise.

Mix all the dressing ingredients together and season with salt and pepper. Heat a grill pan over very high heat. Season the steaks and rub with oil. Place in the pan and sear on 1 side for about 1 minute, then turn over and sear again for a further minute (or longer if you want your tuna cooked through rather than pink).

Toss the potatoes, beans and broccoli in the dressing. Sprinkle with the hazelnuts and serve with the tuna.

2

GIVE IT A TWIST
Spicy tuna fishcakes

Serves 4
Preparation time: 10 minutes
Cooking time: 20 minutes

8 ounces (250 g) russet or baking potatoes, peeled and cut into cubes
2 cans (each 6 ounces/170 g) tuna, drained and flaked
2 ounces (50 g) Cheddar cheese, grated
4 green onions, finely chopped
1 small clove garlic, crushed
2 teaspoons (10 ml) dried thyme
1 small egg, beaten
½ teaspoon (2 ml) cayenne pepper
4 teaspoons (20 ml) seasoned flour
vegetable oil, for frying
salt and pepper

TO SERVE
lemon wedges
watercress

Cook the potatoes in lightly salted boiling water for 10 minutes, until tender. Drain, mash and set aside to cool down.

Beat the tuna, Cheddar, green onions, garlic, thyme and egg into the mashed potato, add the cayenne pepper and season with salt and pepper.

Divide the mixture into 8 portions and make into thick patties. Sprinkle the flour over them and fry in a shallow layer of hot oil for 5 minutes on each side, until they are crisp and golden. Serve with lemon wedges and watercress.

3 🕐

Tuna, spinach & tomato penne

Serves 4
Preparation time: 4 minutes
Cooking time: 10 minutes

- 11½ ounces (350 g) dried penne pasta
- 2 tablespoons (30 ml) olive oil, plus extra for drizzling
- 1 onion, finely sliced
- 1 clove garlic, crushed
- 1 pound (500 g) cherry tomatoes, halved
- 1 pinch of sugar (optional)
- 8 ounces (250 g) baby spinach, washed
- 2 cans (each 6½ ounces/185 g) solid tuna in olive oil, drained
- salt and pepper

Cook the pasta according to the instructions on the package.

Meanwhile, heat the oil in a saucepan, add the onion and fry gently until soft. Add the garlic and tomatoes and fry for a further 3–4 minutes, until the tomatoes just start to break up. Season the sauce with salt and pepper and a little sugar if it is needed.

Stir the spinach into the sauce. Gently stir in the tuna, trying not to break it up too much, then drain and stir in the pasta. Drizzle a little more olive oil over the dish before serving.

4

Tuna & corn pilaf

Serves 4
Preparation time: 10 minutes
Cooking time: 15–20 minutes

- 2 tablespoons (30 ml) olive oil
- 1 onion, chopped
- 1 red pepper, cored, seeded and diced
- 1 clove garlic, crushed
- 1¾ cups (425 ml) converted rice
- 3 cups (750 ml) chicken stock (see page 9)
- 1 can (11 ounces/325 ml) corn, drained
- 1 can (6 ounces/ 170 g) tuna in spring water, drained
- salt and pepper
- 6 chopped green onions, to garnish

Heat the oil in a saucepan, add the onion, red pepper and garlic and cook until soft. Stir in the rice, then add the stock and season to taste with salt and pepper.

Bring to a boil, then reduce the heat and simmer, stirring occasionally, for 10–15 minutes, until all the stock has been absorbed and the rice is tender.

Stir in the corn and tuna and cook briefly over low heat to heat through. Serve immediately, garnished with the green onions.

WATER-PACKED CANNED TUNA CONTAINS THE MOST OMEGA-3 OILS. SOME OF THE OMEGA-3 IN FISH CANNED IN OIL IS DRAINED AWAY AS YOU PREPARE IT.

5

KIDS WILL LOVE THIS
Tuna niçoise spaghetti

Serves 4
Preparation time: 10 minutes
Cooking time: 10 minutes

> 4 eggs
> 11½ ounces (350 g) dried spaghetti
> 3 can (each 6 ounces/170 g) tuna in brine, drained
> 3½ ounces (100 g) green beans, trimmed and blanched
> 2 ounces (50 g) kalamata olives, pitted
> 3½ ounces (100 g) semi-dried tomatoes
> 1 teaspoon (5 ml) grated lemon zest
> 2 tablespoons (30 ml) lemon juice
> 3 tablespoons (45 ml) capers
> salt and pepper

Put the eggs in a saucepan of cold water and bring to a boil. Cook for 10 minutes, then plunge into cold water to cool. Shell the eggs, then roughly chop and set aside.

Meanwhile, cook the pasta in a large saucepan of salted boiling water according to the package instructions, until al dente.

Mix together the tuna, beans, olives, semi-dried tomatoes, lemon zest and juice and capers in a bowl. Season with pepper.

Drain the pasta and return to the pan. Add the tuna mixture and gently toss to combine. Serve immediately, garnished with the eggs.

6

LEFTOVER TO LUNCH
Tuna pâté with toasted sourdough

Serves 4
Preparation time: 10 minutes
Cooking time: 5 minutes

> 2 cans (each 6 ounces/170 g) tuna in brine
> 3 tablespoons (45 ml) mayonnaise
> 1 tablespoon (15 ml) ketchup
> 2 tablespoons (30 ml) lemon juice
> 1 tablespoon (15 ml) chopped fresh parsley
> 1 sourdough loaf, thinly sliced
> ¼ cup (60 ml) butter
> 1 tablespoon (15 ml) olive oil
> 1 tablespoon (15 ml) balsamic vinegar
> 3 ounces (75 g) arugula leaves, washed and drained
> 2 tablespoons (30 ml) roughly chopped capers
> 10 semi-sun-dried tomatoes, halved
> 10 pitted black olives, halved
> salt and pepper

Drain the tuna and place it in a small food processor along with the mayonnaise, ketchup and lemon juice. Blend until smooth, then stir in the parsley and season with salt and pepper. Alternatively, you can make this by hand just by mixing the ingredients together. Spoon the pâté into individual pots.

Place the sourdough slices in a preheated grill pan to toast or under a preheated broiler. Spread with butter.

Mix together the oil and vinegar and lightly dress the arugula leaves. Toss in the capers, semi-sun-dried tomatoes and olives.

Serve a pot of the tuna pâté along with the warm buttered toast and arugula salad.

7

BUT I DON'T LIKE . . .
TUNA

Fusilli with tuna, capers & mint

Serves 4
Preparation time: 10 minutes
Cooking time: 10–12 minutes

> 1 can (10 ounces/300 g) tuna in olive oil
> 4 tablespoons (60 ml) extra virgin olive oil, plus extra for drizzling
> finely grated zest of 1 lemon
> 2 cloves garlic, crushed
> 2 tablespoons (30 ml) capers in brine, drained and rinsed
> ½ red chili, seeded and finely chopped
> 2 tablespoons (30 ml) roughly chopped fresh mint
> 13 ounces (400 g) dried fusilli
> salt

Put the tuna with its oil in a large serving bowl. Break it up with a fork, then stir in the remaining ingredients, except for the pasta. Season with salt. Cover and leave to infuse while you cook the pasta.

Cook the pasta in a large saucepan of salted boiling water for about 10–12 minutes, or according to the package instructions, until al dente.

Drain the pasta and toss into the sauce. Serve immediately with a bottle of extra virgin olive oil for anyone to drizzle a little extra over their serving.

WHY NOT TRY... PENNE WITH GRILLED VEGETABLES, CAPERS & MINT

Replace the tuna with 10 ounces (300 g) mixed bottled grilled vegetables in olive oil, such as peppers, zucchini and eggplant. Drain the vegetables, reserving the oil from the jars. Roughly chop and put in a bowl with 4 tablespoons (60 ml) of the reserved oil and the remaining ingredients as above. Season with salt. Cover and leave to infuse while you cook 13 ounces (400 g) dried penne, instead of the fusilli, as above. Drain and toss with the sauce.

8

FRIENDS FOR DINNER

Pot roasted tuna with lentils

Serves 4
Preparation time: 15 minutes
Cooking time: 50 minutes–1 hour 10 minutes

> ½ teaspoon (2 ml) celery salt
> 1½ pounds (750 g) tuna, in 1 slender piece
> 1 fennel bulb
> 3 tablespoons (45 ml) olive oil
> 1 cup (250 ml) black lentils, rinsed
> ⅔ cup (150 ml) white wine
> 1 cup (250 ml) fish or vegetable stock (see page 8)
> 4 tablespoons (60 ml) chopped fresh fennel or dill
> 2 tablespoons (30 ml) capers, rinsed and drained
> 1 can (14 ounces/398 ml) chopped tomatoes
> salt and pepper

Mix the celery salt with a little pepper and rub all over the tuna. Cut the fennel bulb in half, then into thin slices.

Heat the oil in an ovenproof casserole dish and fry the tuna on all sides until browned. Drain. Add the sliced fennel to the pan and fry gently until softened.

Add the lentils and wine and bring to a boil. Boil until the wine has reduced by about half. Stir in the stock, fennel or dill, capers and tomatoes and return to a boil. Cover with a lid and transfer to a preheated 350°F (180°C) oven for 15 minutes.

Return the tuna to the casserole dish and cook gently for a further 20 minutes, until the lentils are completely tender. The tuna should still be slightly pink in the center. If you prefer your tuna to be well done, return it to the oven for a further 15–20 minutes. Check the seasoning and serve.

9

WATCHING MY WEIGHT
Sesame tuna with spicy noodles

Serves 4
Preparation time: 10 minutes
Cooking time: 10 minutes

10 ounces (300 g) rice vermicelli noodles
⅓ cup (75 ml) sesame seeds
4 tuna steaks, about 5 ounces (150 g) each

FOR THE CHILI DRESSING
2 cloves garlic, chopped
2-inch (5 cm) piece gingerroot, peeled and grated
4 tablespoons (60 ml) sweet chili sauce
½ cup (125 ml) fresh coriander leaves, plus extra to garnish
2 tablespoons (30 ml) oil
1 chili, chopped
2 tablespoons (30 ml) sesame oil
2 tablespoons (30 ml) rice vinegar

Make the dressing by mixing together all the ingredients. Meanwhile, cook the noodles according to the instructions on the package and set aside.

Press the sesame seeds into both sides of the tuna. Heat a large, heavy frying pan and dry-fry the tuna for 1-2 minutes on each side, depending on the thickness, until it is just pink in the middle.

Slice the tuna. Spoon the dressing over the hot noodles and put the sliced tuna on top. Garnish with coriander leaves and serve immediately.

10

INSPIRE ME
Tuna & pesto burgers

Serves 4
Preparation time: 5 minutes
Cooking time: 4–6 minutes

4 ciabatta rolls
4 tuna steaks, about 6 ounces (175 g) each
1 tablespoon (15 ml) extra virgin olive oil, plus extra to drizzle
1 lemon, halved
2 tomatoes, sliced
4 tablespoons (60 ml) basil pesto
2 ounces (50 g) mixed salad leaves
salt and pepper

Heat a ridged grill pan until hot. Split the rolls in half, add to the pan and cook for 1–2 minutes on each side, until lightly charred. Transfer to serving plates.

Brush the tuna steaks lightly with the oil and season with salt and pepper. Add to the pan and cook for 1 minute on each side.

Transfer each tuna steak to the base of a roll and squeeze over a little lemon juice from the lemon halves. Divide the tomato slices, pesto and salad leaves between the roll bases and drizzle over a little extra oil. Replace the roll tops and serve immediately.

VEGETABLES

A variety of meat-free recipe ideas using red peppers, spinach, mushrooms, butternut squash and eggplant, all bursting with flavor, that both vegetarians and meat-eaters alike will enjoy.

VEGETABLES

 1 BASIC

 2 GIVE IT A TWIST

 3 SAVE ME TIME

 4 SAVE ME MONEY

 5 KIDS WILL LOVE THESE

RED PEPPERS PAGE 116

 Roasted stuffed peppers

 Red pepper & pecorino pesto

 Red pepper & feta rolls with olives

 Corn & pepper frittata

 Red pepper & cheese tortellini

SPINACH PAGE 122

 Spinach & Gorgonzola salad

 Spinach & pea frittata

 Gnocchi with spinach & Gorgonzola

 Spinach & ricotta cannelloni

 Spinach & potato gratin

MUSHROOMS PAGE 128

 Mixed mushrooms on toast

 Mushrooms à la grecque

 Mushroom stroganoff

 Golden mushroom & leek pies

 Mushroom toad in the hole

BUTTERNUT SQUASH PAGE 134

 Cheesy butternut squash soup

 Butternut squash, tofu & pea curry

 Beet & squash spaghetti

 Squash, kale & mixed bean stew

 Butternut squash risotto

EGGPLANT PAGE 140

 Eggplant pesto toasties

 Baby eggplant with chili

 Pasta with eggplant & pine nuts

 Eggplant with goat cheese gratin

 Rigatoni with eggplant & ricotta

|
6 |
7 |
8 |
9 |
10 |

6 LEFTOVER TO LUNCH

7 BUT I DON'T LIKE...

8 FRIENDS FOR DINNER

9 WATCHING MY WEIGHT

10 INSPIRE ME

Red pepper soup

Pasta baked red peppers

Red pepper & Munster tarts

Yellow split pea & pepper patties

Panzanella

Spinach & haddock soup

Cheese & spinach pie

Spinach lasagna

Spicy fried rice with spinach salad

Spinach & feta phyllo pie

Mushroom truffle soup

Onion & mushroom quesadillas

Mixed mushroom tart

Mushroom ramen

Mushroom & ginger wontons

Butternut squash & rosemary soup

Swordfish with squash couscous

Roasted squash & sage pizza

Squash with red bean sauce

Thai squash & coriander soup

Eggplant dip with flatbreads

Caponata ratatouille

Baked eggplant & mozzarella

Spicy eggplant Goan curry

Eggplant pâté

10 WAYS WITH RED PEPPERS

1

BASIC

Roasted stuffed peppers

Serves 4
Preparation time: 10 minutes
Cooking time: 55 minutes–1 hour

- 4 large bell red peppers
- 2 cloves garlic, crushed
- 1 tablespoon (15 ml) chopped fresh thyme, plus extra to garnish
- 4 plum tomatoes, halved
- 4 tablespoons (60 ml) extra virgin olive oil
- 2 tablespoons (30 ml) balsamic vinegar
- salt and pepper

Cut the red peppers in half lengthwise, then scoop out and discard the cores and seeds. Put the pepper halves, cut sides up, in a roasting pan lined with foil or a ceramic baking dish. Divide the garlic and thyme between them and season with salt and pepper.

Put a tomato half in each pepper and drizzle with the oil and vinegar. Roast in a preheated 425°F (220°C) oven for 55 minutes–1 hour, until the peppers are soft and charred.

Serve with some crusty bread to mop up the juices and a baby greens salad, if desired.

2

GIVE IT A TWIST

Red pepper & pecorino pesto

Serves 4
Preparation time: 10 minutes
Cooking time: 25 minutes

- 5 red bell peppers
- 1 tablespoon (15 ml) extra virgin olive oil, plus extra to serve
- ¼–⅓ cup (60–75 ml) blanched almonds
- 1 clove garlic, peeled
- 1¼ ounces (30 g) pecorino cheese, freshly grated
- 13 ounces (400 g) dried penne
- 2½ ounces (65 g) wild arugula
- salt and pepper

Rub the peppers with the oil and cook under a preheated very hot broiler, turning occasionally, until black and blistered all over. Transfer the peppers to a bowl, cover with plastic wrap and leave to steam for 5 minutes. This will make it easier to peel off the skins.

When the peppers are cool enough to handle, peel off the skins. Cut one of the peppers into strips, trimming off the white core and seeds as you go, and reserve. Trim the remaining peppers.

Put the trimmed peppers in a food processor with the almonds, garlic and pecorino and process until smooth. Season with salt and pepper. Transfer to a serving bowl.

Cook the pasta in a large saucepan of salted boiling water according to the package instructions, until it is al dente. Drain the pasta and add it to the sauce with the reserved pepper strips and arugula. Toss through the pasta. Serve immediately with a generous drizzle of extra virgin olive oil.

3

SAVE ME TIME
Red pepper & feta rolls with olives

Serves 4
Preparation time: 10 minutes, plus cooling
Cooking time: 7–8 minutes

- **2 red bell peppers, cored, seeded and quartered lengthwise**
- **3½ ounces (100 g) feta cheese, thinly sliced or crumbled**
- **16 fresh basil leaves**
- **16 black olives, pitted and halved**
- **2 tablespoons (30 ml) pine nuts, toasted**
- **1 tablespoon (15 ml) pesto**
- **1 tablespoon (15 ml) fat-free French dressing**

Place the peppers skin side up on a baking sheet under a hot broiler and cook for 7–8 minutes, until the skins are blackened. Remove the peppers and place them in a plastic bag. Fold over the top to seal and leave to cool for 20 minutes, then remove the skins.

Lay the skinned pepper quarters on a board and layer the feta, basil leaves, olives and pine nuts on each one.

Carefully roll up the peppers and secure with a cocktail stick. Place 2 pepper rolls on each serving plate.

Whisk together the pesto and French dressing in a small bowl and drizzle over the pepper rolls. Serve with arugula and some crusty bread to mop up the juices.

4

SAVE ME MONEY
Corn & pepper frittata

Serves 4
Preparation time: 10 minutes
Cooking time: about 10 minutes

- **2 tablespoons (30 ml) olive oil**
- **4 green onions, thinly sliced**
- **1 can (7 ounces/200ml) corn, drained**
- **5 ounces (150 g) bottled roasted red peppers in oil, drained and cut into strips**
- **4 eggs, lightly beaten**
- **4 ounces (125 g) aged Cheddar cheese, grated**
- **1 small handful of chives, finely chopped**
- **salt and pepper**

Heat the oil in a frying pan, add the green onions, corn and red peppers and cook for 30 seconds.

Add the eggs, Cheddar, chives, and salt and pepper to taste and cook over medium heat for 4–5 minutes, until the base is set. Remove from the hob, place under a preheated broiler and cook for 3–4 minutes or until golden and set. Cut into wedges and serve immediately with a green salad and crusty bread.

5

KIDS WILL LOVE THIS
Red pepper & cheese tortellini

Serves 4
Preparation time: 10 minutes, plus cooling
Cooking time: 15 minutes

- 2 red bell peppers
- 2 cloves garlic, chopped
- 8 green onions, finely sliced
- 1 pound (500 g) fresh cheese-stuffed tortellini or any other fresh stuffed tortellini of your choice
- ¾ cup (175 ml) olive oil
- 1 ounce (25 g) Parmesan cheese, finely grated
- salt and pepper

Cut the peppers into large pieces, removing the cores and seeds. Lay skin side up under a preheated broiler and cook until the skin blackens and blisters. Transfer to a plastic bag, tie the top to enclose and leave to cool, then peel away the skin.

Place the peppers and garlic in a food processor and blend until fairly smooth. Stir in the green onions and set aside.

Cook the tortellini in a large saucepan of boiling water according to the package instructions, until al dente. Drain and return to the pan.

Toss the pepper mixture into the pasta and add the oil and grated Parmesan. Season to taste with salt and pepper and serve immediately.

6

LEFTOVER TO LUNCH
Red pepper soup

Serves 4
Preparation time: 15 minutes
Cooking time: 35 minutes

- 2 onions, finely chopped
- 2 tablespoons (30 ml) olive oil
- 1 clove garlic, crushed
- 3 red bell peppers, seeded and roughly chopped
- 2 zucchini, finely chopped
- 3¾ cups (925 ml) vegetable stock (see page 8) or water
- salt and pepper

TO GARNISH
- natural yogurt or whipping (35%) cream
- chopped chives

Put the onions in a large saucepan with the oil and gently fry for 5 minutes or until softened and golden brown. Add the garlic and cook gently for 1 minute.

Add the red peppers and half the zucchini and fry them for 5–8 minutes or until softened and brown.

Add the stock or water to the pan with salt and pepper and bring to a boil. Reduce the heat, cover the pan and simmer gently for 20 minutes.

When the vegetables are tender, blend the mixture, in batches, to a smooth soup and return to the pan. Season to taste, reheat and serve topped with the remaining chopped zucchini and garnished with yogurt or a swirl of cream and chopped chives. This vibrant and warming soup is ideal for any meal and tastes just as good cold.

BUT I DON'T LIKE ...
RED PEPPERS
Pasta baked red peppers

Serves 4
Preparation time: 20 minutes
Cooking time: 35–45 minutes

> 4 red bell peppers, halved, cored and seeded
> 4 ounces (125 g) mini macaroni, cooked
> 2 plum tomatoes, chopped
> 4 ounces (125 g) Cheddar cheese, grated
> 2 green onions, sliced
> 2 tablespoons (30 ml) chopped fresh parsley
> 3 tablespoons (45 ml) olive oil
> salt and pepper

Place the halved peppers in an ovenproof dish, with the hollowed-out side facing up. Mix the macaroni, tomatoes, cheese, green onions and parsley in a bowl. Spoon into the peppers, drizzle with the olive oil and season to taste.

Bake in a preheated 350°F (180°C) oven for 35–45 minutes or until the macaroni filling is golden and bubbling.

WHY NOT TRY...
BAKED STUFFED MUSHROOMS

Remove and finely chop the stalks from 4 large mushrooms. Grill the mushrooms for 5 minutes, until just softened. Finely chop 1 small onion and mix with the chopped mushroom stalks, 2 ounces (50 g) cooked macaroni, 3 tablespoons (45 ml) chopped walnuts, 1 tablespoon (15 ml) chopped parsley, 3 tablespoons (45 ml) cubed Cheddar cheese and 1 tablespoon (15 ml) tomato paste. Season, then bind with a little beaten egg. Pile on top of the mushrooms, drizzle with a little olive oil, then cook under a preheated medium broiler for 15–20 minutes, until the top of the stuffing is crisp and has started to char at the edges.

CAPSICUM IS THE GENERIC NAME FOR THE PEPPER FAMILY. CAPSICUMS VARY FROM MILD RED BELL PEPPERS, TO GREEN, YELLOW AND HOT CHILI PEPPERS.

FRIENDS FOR DINNER
Red pepper & Munster tarts

Serves 4
Preparation time: 15 minutes, plus chilling
Cooking time: 35–40 minutes

> 13 ounces (400 g) ready-made shortcrust pastry
> 1 tablespoon (15 ml) vegetable oil
> 1 tablespoon (15 ml) butter
> 1 red onion, finely chopped
> ⅔ cup (150 ml) half-and-half (10%) cream
> 2 eggs
> 2 cloves garlic, crushed
> ⅓ cup (75 ml) chives, snipped, plus extra to garnish
> 1 small red bell pepper, roasted, peeled and thinly sliced
> 3 ounces (75 g) Munster cheese, roughly chopped
> salt and pepper
> fresh basil leaves, to garnish

Roll out the pastry on a lightly floured surface and use to line four 4-inch (10 cm) tart tins. Prick the bases, line with circles of parchment paper and fill with baking beans, then chill for 30 minutes.

Place the tarts on a baking sheet and bake blind in a preheated 375°F (190°C) oven for 8 minutes. Remove the paper and beans and bake for a further 2–3 minutes or until the shells are crisp and beginning to brown. Remove from the oven and set aside until required.

Heat the oil and butter in a pan and fry the red onion until caramelized. Set aside until required. Beat the cream, eggs, salt and pepper together. Add the crushed garlic and chives, and chill the mixture until required.

When ready to serve, divide the onion and the roasted red pepper strips between the pastry shells. Pour in the cream and egg mixture and sprinkle the Munster on top. Cook the tarts on the middle shelf of a preheated 375°F (190°C) oven for 20–25 minutes or until just cooked. Garnish with basil leaves and snipped chives, if desired.

9

WATCHING MY WEIGHT
Yellow split pea & pepper patties

Serves 4
Preparation time: 10–15 minutes, plus chilling
Cooking time: 40–50 minutes

- 3 cloves garlic
- 1⅓ cups (325 ml) yellow split peas
- 3 cups (750 ml) vegetable stock (see page 8)
- olive oil spray
- 2 red bell peppers, halved and seeded
- 1 yellow bell pepper, halved and seeded
- 1 red onion, quartered
- 1 tablespoon (15 ml) chopped fresh mint, plus extra leaves to garnish
- 2 tablespoons (30 ml) capers, rinsed and chopped
- flour, for dusting
- salt and pepper
- ready-made tzatziki or raita, to serve

Peel and halve a garlic clove and cook it with the split peas in the stock for 40 minutes. Check the seasoning and leave to cool slightly.

Meanwhile, lightly spray a roasting pan with oil. Put the remaining garlic cloves in the pan with the peppers and onion and cook in a preheated 400°F (200°C) oven for 20 minutes. Squeeze the roasted garlic cloves from their skins and chop with the roasted vegetables.

Mix the split peas with the roasted vegetables, mint and capers. Flour your hands and shape the mixture into patties. Refrigerate until ready to cook.

Heat a frying pan and spray with oil. Cook the patties, in batches if necessary, leaving them to cook undisturbed for 2 minutes on each side. Serve either hot or cold, garnished with mint leaves, with tzatziki or raita on the side.

10

INSPIRE ME
Panzanella

Serves 4
Preparation time: 15 minutes
Cooking time: 10–15 minutes

- 3 red bell peppers, cored, seeded and quartered
- 12 ounces (375 g) ripe plum tomatoes, skinned
- 6 tablespoons (90 ml) extra virgin olive oil
- 3 tablespoons (45 ml) white wine vinegar
- 2 cloves garlic, crushed
- 4 ounces (125 g) stale ciabatta bread, broken into small chunks
- 2 ounces (50 g) pitted black olives
- 1 small handful of fresh basil leaves, shredded
- salt and pepper

Place the peppers, skin side up, on a foil-lined broiler pan and grill under a preheated broiler for 10–15 minutes or until the skins are blackened.

Meanwhile, quarter the tomatoes and scoop out the pulp, placing it in a sieve over a bowl to catch the juices. Set the tomato quarters aside. Press the pulp with the back of a spoon to extract as much juice as possible. Beat the oil, vinegar, garlic and salt and pepper into the tomato juice.

When cool enough to handle, peel the skins from the peppers and discard. Roughly slice the peppers and place in a bowl with the tomato quarters, bread, olives and basil. Add the dressing and toss the ingredients together. Chill until required.

10 WAYS WITH SPINACH

1

BASIC
Spinach & Gorgonzola salad

Serves 4
Preparation time: 5 minutes, plus cooling
Cooking time: 3 minutes

- 1 tablespoon (15 ml) liquid honey
- 4 ounces (125 g) walnut halves
- 8 ounces (250 g) young green beans, trimmed
- 7 ounces (200 g) baby spinach leaves
- 5 ounces (150 g) Gorgonzola cheese, crumbled

FOR THE DRESSING
- 4 tablespoons (60 ml) walnut oil
- 2 tablespoons (30 ml) extra virgin olive oil
- 1–2 tablespoons (15–30 ml) sherry vinegar
- salt and pepper

Heat the honey in a small frying pan, add the walnuts and stir-fry over medium heat for 2–3 minutes, until the nuts are glazed. Tip on to a plate and leave to cool.

Meanwhile, cook the beans in a saucepan of lightly salted boiling water for 3 minutes. Drain, refresh under cold water and shake dry. Put in a large bowl with the spinach leaves.

Whisk all the dressing ingredients together in a small bowl and season with salt and pepper. Pour over the salad and toss well. Arrange the salad in serving bowls, scatter over the Gorgonzola and glazed walnuts and serve immediately.

2

GIVE IT A TWIST
Spinach & pea frittata

Serves 4
Preparation time: 10 minutes
Cooking time: 25 minutes

- 1 tablespoon (15 ml) olive oil
- 1 onion, thinly sliced
- 5 ounces (150 g) baby spinach leaves
- 4 ounces (125 g) shelled fresh or frozen peas
- 6 eggs
- salt and pepper

Heat the oil in a heavy-bottomed, ovenproof, nonstick 9-inch (23 cm) frying pan over low heat. Add the onion and cook for 6–8 minutes, until softened, then stir in the spinach and peas and cook for a further 2 minutes or until any moisture released by the spinach has evaporated.

Beat the eggs in a bowl and season lightly with salt and pepper. Stir in the cooked vegetables, then pour the mixture into the pan and quickly arrange the vegetables so that they are evenly dispersed. Cook over low heat for 8–10 minutes or until all but the top of the frittata is set.

Transfer the pan to a preheated very hot broiler and cook about 4 inches (10 cm) from the heat source until the top is set but not colored. Give the pan a shake to loosen the frittata, then transfer to a plate to cool. Serve slightly warm or at room temperature, accompanied by a green salad.

3

SAVE ME TIME
Gnocchi with spinach & Gorgonzola

Serves 3–4
Preparation time: 5 minutes
Cooking time: 10 minutes

8 ounces (250 g) baby spinach leaves
1¼ cups (300 ml) vegetable stock (see page 8)
1 pound (500 g) potato gnocchi
5 ounces (150 g) Gorgonzola cheese, cut into small pieces
3 tablespoons (45 ml) whipping (35%) cream
plenty of freshly grated nutmeg
pepper

Wash the spinach leaves thoroughly, if necessary. Pat them dry on paper towels.

Bring the stock to a boil in a large saucepan. Tip in the gnocchi and return to a boil. Cook for 2–3 minutes or until plumped up and tender.

Stir in the cheese, cream and nutmeg and heat until the cheese melts to make a creamy sauce. Add the spinach to the pan and cook gently for 1–2 minutes, turning the spinach with the gnocchi and sauce until wilted. Pile onto serving plates and season with plenty of black pepper.

4 🐷

SAVE ME MONEY
Spinach & ricotta cannelloni

Serves 4
Preparation time: 25 minutes
Cooking time: 35 minutes

1 pound (500 g) frozen spinach, defrosted
10 ounces (300 g) ricotta cheese
1 clove garlic, crushed
2 tablespoons (30 ml) half-and-half (10%) cream
1 pinch of freshly grated nutmeg
16 dried cannelloni tubes
cooking spray, for oiling
1 ounce (25 g) Parmesan cheese, freshly grated
salt and pepper

FOR THE TOMATO SALSA
1 pound (500 g) ripe tomatoes, diced
1 clove garlic, crushed
3 ounces (75 g) pitted black olives, chopped
2 tablespoons (30 ml) capers in brine, drained
1 tablespoon (15 ml) chopped fresh parsley
2 tablespoons (30 ml) extra virgin olive oil

Squeeze the excess water from the spinach and put in a bowl. Add the ricotta, garlic, cream, nutmeg and salt and pepper, and stir together until evenly combined.

Cook the cannelloni tubes in a large saucepan of boiling water for 5 minutes or until just al dente. Drain well and immediately refresh under cold water. Pat dry with paper towels.

Lightly oil 4 individual gratin dishes with cooking spray. Cut down one side of each cannelloni tube and open out flat. Spoon 2 tablespoons (30 ml) of the spinach and ricotta mixture down one side and roll the pasta up to form tubes once more. Divide between the prepared dishes.

Combine all the salsa ingredients in a bowl, then spoon over the cannelloni. Scatter with the Parmesan. Cover the dishes with foil and bake in a preheated 400°F (200°C) oven for 20 minutes. Remove the foil and bake for a further 10 minutes until bubbling and golden. Serve immediately.

5

KIDS WILL LOVE THIS
Spinach & potato gratin

Serves 4
Preparation time: 10 minutes
Cooking time: 35 minutes

- 1¼ pounds (625 g) potatoes, thinly sliced
- 1 pound (500 g) spinach leaves
- 7 ounces (200 g) mozzarella cheese, grated
- 4 tomatoes, sliced
- 3 eggs, beaten
- 1¼ cups (300 ml) whipping (30 %) cream
- salt and pepper

Cook the potato slices in a large saucepan of salted boiling water for 5 minutes, then drain well.

Meanwhile, cook the spinach in a separate saucepan of boiling water for 1–2 minutes. Drain and squeeze out all the excess water.

Grease a large baking dish and line the bottom with half the potato slices. Cover with the spinach and half the mozzarella, seasoning each layer well with salt and pepper. Cover with the remaining potato slices and arrange the tomato slices on top. Sprinkle with the remaining mozzarella.

Whisk the eggs and cream together in a bowl and season well with salt and pepper. Pour over the ingredients in the dish.

Bake in a preheated 350°F (180°C) oven for about 30 minutes. Serve immediately with a salad and bread.

6

LEFTOVER TO LUNCH
Spinach & haddock soup

Serves 6
Preparation time: 30 minutes
Cooking time: about 1 hour

- 2 tablespoons (30 ml) butter
- 1 onion, roughly chopped
- 1 baking potato, about 8 ounces (250 g), diced
- 4 cups (1 L) vegetable or chicken stock (see pages 8–9)
- ¼ teaspoon (1 ml) grated nutmeg
- 7½ ounces (225 g) young spinach leaves, rinsed and drained
- 1¼ cups (300 ml) 1% or 2% milk
- 13 ounces (400 g) smoked haddock
- 9 quail eggs
- 2 hen egg yolks
- ⅔ cup (150 ml) whipping (35%) cream
- salt and pepper

Heat the butter in a saucepan, add the onion and fry gently for 5 minutes, until softened. Add the potato, cover and cook for 10 minutes, stirring occasionally.

Pour in the stock, add the nutmeg and salt and pepper, then bring to a boil. Cover and simmer for 20 minutes, until the potato is soft. Reserve a few tiny spinach leaves and add the rest to the pan. Re-cover the pan and cook for 5 minutes, until just wilted.

Purée the soup in batches in a blender or food processor until smooth, then pour back into the saucepan, mix in the milk and set aside.

Cut the haddock into 2 pieces, then cook in a steamer for 8–10 minutes until the fish flakes when pressed with a knife. Put the quail eggs into a small saucepan of cold water, bring to a boil and simmer for 2–3 minutes, drain, rinse with cold water and peel off the shells. Cut each in half.

Mix the 2 hen egg yolks with the cream. Stir into the soup and bring just to a boil, still stirring. Taste and adjust the seasoning if needed. Flake the fish, discarding the skin and bones, make small mounds in the base of 6 shallow serving bowls and top with the quail egg halves. Ladle the soup around the fish and eggs and garnish with tiny spinach leaves and pepper.

7

BUT I DON'T LIKE ...
SPINACH
Cheese & spinach pie

Serves 4
Preparation time: 10 minutes
Cooking time: 25 minutes

> ¼ cups (60 ml) butter
> 1 small onion, finely chopped
> 1 clove garlic, crushed
> 2 teaspoons (10 ml) chopped fresh thyme
> 8 ounces (250 g) frozen spinach, defrosted
> ¾ cup (175 ml) half-and-half (10%) cream
> 2 eggs, beaten
> 1 ounce (25 g) Parmesan cheese, freshly grated
> 8 inch (20 cm) frozen pie crust (cook from frozen)
> salt and pepper

Melt the butter in a large frying pan, add the onion, garlic, thyme and salt and pepper to taste and cook for 5 minutes. Squeeze out all the excess water from the spinach, add to the pan and cook, stirring, for 2–3 minutes, until heated through.

Beat together the cream, eggs, cheese and a pinch of salt and pepper in a bowl. Spoon the spinach mixture into the pie shell, carefully pour in the cream mixture and bake on a preheated baking sheet in a preheated 400°F (200°C) oven for 20 minutes, until set. Serve with a green salad.

WHY NOT TRY...
MUSHROOM & SOUR CREAM TART

Cook the onion, garlic and thyme in the butter as above, then add 12 ounces (375 g) halved button mushrooms to the pan and cook until browned. Omit the spinach and continue as above, but replace the half-and-half cream with sour cream.

SPINACH CAN BE EATEN RAW IN SALADS WHEN YOUNG AND TENDER. BUT REMEMBER THAT A MOUND OF LEAVES WILL BECOME ONLY A TABLESPOON OF COOKED SPINACH.

8

FRIENDS FOR DINNER
Spinach lasagna

Serves 6–8
Preparation time: 35 minutes, plus infusing
Cooking time: 45–50 minutes

> 4 tablespoons (60 ml) olive oil
> 2 cloves garlic, crushed
> 2 teaspoons (10 ml) chopped fresh thyme
> 1 pound (500 g) button mushrooms, trimmed and sliced
> 1 pound (500 g) frozen spinach, defrosted
> cooking spray, for oiling
> 7 ounces (200 g) fresh lasagna sheets
> salt and pepper
>
> **FOR THE CHEESE SAUCE**
> 5 cups (1.25 L) 1% or 2% milk
> 2 fresh bay leaves
> ¼ cup (60 ml) unsalted butter, plus extra for greasing
> ⅓ cup + 1 tablespoon (90 ml) all-purpose flour
> 8 ounces (250 g) Cheddar cheese, grated

First make the sauce. Put the milk and bay leaves in a saucepan and heat to boiling point. Remove from the heat and leave to infuse for 20 minutes. Discard the bay leaves.

Melt the butter in a separate saucepan, add the flour and cook over medium heat, stirring constantly, for 1 minute. Gradually stir in the milk and continue to cook, stirring continuously, until the mixture boils. Reduce the heat and simmer for 2 minutes. Remove from the heat, add most of the Cheddar and stir until melted.

Meanwhile, heat the oil in a frying pan, add the garlic, thyme, mushrooms and salt and pepper and cook over medium heat, stirring frequently, for 5 minutes, until tender. Squeeze out the excess water from the spinach and roughly chop. Stir into the mushroom mixture. Remove from the heat.

Lightly oil a 10-cup (2.5 L) lasagna dish with cooking spray. Spread a quarter of the cheese sauce over the base and add one-third of the mushroom and spinach mixture and a lasagna sheet. Repeat these layers twice more. Add a final layer of sauce to cover the lasagna and scatter over the remaining cheese. Bake in a preheated 375°F (190°C) oven for 35–40 minutes until browned.

9

WATCHING MY WEIGHT
Spicy fried rice with spinach salad

Serves 3–4
Preparation time: 10 minutes
Cooking time: 10 minutes

> 4 eggs
> 2 tablespoons (30 ml) sherry
> 2 tablespoons (30 ml) light soy sauce
> 1 bunch green onions
> 4 tablespoons (60 ml) peanut oil
> ⅔ cup (150 ml) unsalted cashews
> 1 green bell pepper, seeded and finely chopped
> ½ teaspoon (2 ml) Chinese 5-spice powder
> 2 cups (500 ml) cooked long-grain rice
> 5 ounces (150 g) baby spinach leaves
> 3½ ounces (100 g) mung beans or 2 ounces (50 g) pea shoots
> salt and pepper
> sweet chili sauce, to serve

Beat the eggs with the sherry and 1 tablespoon (15 ml) of the soy sauce in a small bowl. Cut 2 of the green onions into 3-inch (7 cm) long pieces, then cut lengthwise into fine shreds. Leave in a bowl of very cold water to curl up slightly. Finely chop the remaining green onions, keeping the white and green parts separate.

Heat half the oil in a large frying pan or wok and fry the cashews and green parts of the green onions, turning in the oil, until the cashews are lightly browned. Drain with a slotted spoon.

Add the white parts of the green onions to the pan and stir-fry for 1 minute. Add the beaten eggs and cook, stirring constantly, until the egg starts to scramble into small pieces, rather than one omelet.

Stir in the green pepper and 5-spice powder with the remaining oil and cook for 1 minute, then tip in the cooked rice and spinach with the remaining soy sauce, mixing the ingredients together well until thoroughly combined and the spinach has wilted.

Return the cashews and green onions to the pan with the bean sprouts or pea shoots and season to taste. Pile onto serving plates, scatter with the drained green onion curls and serve with sweet chili sauce.

10

INSPIRE ME
Spinach & feta phyllo pie

Serves 6
Preparation time: 20 minutes
Cooking time: about 1 hour

> 1½ pounds (750 g) fresh spinach leaves, rinsed
> 8 ounces (250 g) feta cheese, roughly crumbled
> ½ teaspoon (2 ml) hot pepper flakes
> 3 ounces (75 g) Parmesan cheese, finely grated
> 2 ounces (50 g) pine nuts, toasted
> ½ ounce (15 g) dill, chopped
> ½ ounce (15 g) tarragon, chopped
> 3 eggs, beaten
> 1 pinch of grated nutmeg
> 8 ounces (250 g) phyllo pastry
> 5–8 tablespoons (75–120 ml) olive oil
> 1 tablespoon (15 ml) sesame seeds
> salt and pepper

Cook the spinach in a large saucepan, with just the water left on the leaves after rinsing, over low heat until wilted and soft. Drain well, pressing out the juices.

Mix the feta into the spinach with the hot pepper flakes, Parmesan, pine nuts and herbs. Mix in the beaten eggs with plenty of salt, pepper and grated nutmeg.

Unwrap the phyllo pastry and, working quickly, brush the top sheet of pastry with a little olive oil. Lay in the bottom of a lightly greased 8-inch (20 cm) cake pan with the edges overlapping the rim of the pan. Brush the next sheet of pastry and lay it in the opposite direction to cover the base of the pan. Repeat with 4–6 sheets of pastry, saving 3 sheets to make a top crust.

Spoon the spinach mixture into the phyllo pastry shell, pushing it in with the back of the spoon and to level.

Cut the remaining pastry into 2-inch (5 cm) wide strips. One by one, brush them with oil and place them on top of the spinach in a casual folded arrangement. Fold the overhanging phyllo toward the middle of the pie, sprinkle with sesame seeds and bake in a preheated 375°F (190°C) oven for 50–60 minutes. Leave to cool. When ready to serve, remove from the pan and serve with salad.

10 WAYS WITH MUSHROOMS

1

BASIC
Mixed mushrooms on toast

Serves 4
Preparation time: 10 minutes
Cooking time: 5 minutes

- 2 tablespoons (30 ml) butter
- 3 tablespoons (45 ml) extra virgin olive oil, plus extra to serve
- 1½ pounds (750 g) mixed mushrooms, such as oyster, shiitake, portabello and button, trimmed and sliced
- 2 cloves garlic, crushed
- 1 tablespoon (15 ml) chopped fresh thyme
- grated zest and juice of 1 lemon
- 2 tablespoons (30 ml) chopped fresh parsley
- 4 slices of sourdough bread
- 3½ ounces (100 g) mixed salad leaves
- salt and pepper
- **fresh Parmesan cheese shavings, to serve**

Melt the butter with the oil in a large frying pan. As soon as the butter stops foaming, add the mushrooms, garlic, thyme, lemon zest and salt and pepper and cook over medium heat, stirring continuously, for 4–5 minutes, until tender. Scatter the parsley over and squeeze on a little lemon juice.

Meanwhile, toast the bread, then arrange it on serving plates. Top the sourdough toast with an equal quantity of the salad leaves and mushrooms, and drizzle on a little more oil and lemon juice. Scatter with Parmesan shavings and serve immediately.

2

GIVE IT A TWIST
Mushrooms à la grecque

Serves 1
Preparation time: 10 minutes, plus standing
Cooking time: 10 minutes

- ½ cup (125 ml) olive oil
- 2 large onions, sliced
- 3 cloves garlic, finely chopped
- 1 pound 3 ounces (575 g) button mushrooms, halved
- 8 plum tomatoes, roughly chopped, or 1 can (14 ounces/398 ml) chopped tomatoes
- 3½ ounces (100 g) pitted black olives
- 2 tablespoons (30 ml) white wine vinegar
- salt and pepper
- chopped parsley, to garnish

Heat 2 tablespoons (30 ml) of the oil in a large frying pan, add the onions and garlic and cook until soft and starting to brown. Add the mushrooms and tomatoes and cook, stirring gently, for about 4–5 minutes. Remove from the heat.

Transfer the mushroom mixture to a serving dish and garnish with the olives.

Whisk the remaining oil with the vinegar in a small bowl, season to taste with salt and pepper and drizzle over the salad. Garnish with the chopped parsley, cover and leave to stand at room temperature for 30 minutes to allow the flavors to mingle before serving.

3 🕐

SAVE ME TIME
Mushroom stroganoff

Serves 4
Preparation time: 10 minutes
Cooking time: 10 minutes

- 1 tablespoon (15 ml) butter
- 2 tablespoons (30 ml) olive oil
- 1 onion, thinly sliced
- 4 cloves garlic, finely chopped
- 1 pound (500 g) chestnut or cremini mushrooms, sliced
- 2 tablespoons (30 ml) whole-grain mustard
- 1 cup (250 ml) crème fraîche or sour cream
- salt and pepper
- 3 tablespoons (45 ml) chopped fresh parsley, to garnish

Melt the butter with the oil in a large frying pan, add the onion and garlic and cook until soft and starting to brown.

Add the mushrooms to the pan and cook until soft and starting to brown. Stir in the mustard and crème fraîche and just heat through. Season to taste with salt and pepper, then serve immediately, garnished with the chopped parsley.

4

SAVE ME MONEY
Golden mushroom & leek pies

Serves 4
Preparation time: 15 minutes
Cooking time: 25–30 minutes

- 2 tablespoons (30 ml) butter
- 2 leeks, thinly sliced
- 10 ounces (300 g) chestnut or cremini mushrooms, quartered
- 10 ounces (300 g) button mushrooms, quartered
- 1 tablespoon (15 ml) all-purpose flour
- 1 cup (250 ml) 1% or 2% milk
- ⅔ cup (150 ml) whipping (35%) cream
- 3½ ounces (100 g) aged Cheddar cheese, grated
- 4 tablespoons (60 ml) finely chopped fresh parsley
- 2 sheets, rolled out puff pastry, defrosted if frozen
- 1 egg, beaten

Melt the butter in a large saucepan, add the leeks and cook for 1–2 minutes. Add the mushrooms and cook for 2 minutes. Stir in the flour and cook, stirring, for 1 minute, then gradually add the milk and cream and cook, stirring continuously, until the mixture thickens.

Add the Cheddar and the parsley and cook, stirring, for 1–2 minutes. Remove from the heat.

Cut 4 rounds from the pastry sheets to cover 4 individual pie plates. Divide the mushroom mixture between the dishes. Brush the rims with the beaten egg, then place the pastry rounds on top. Press down around the rims and crimp the edges with a fork. Cut a couple of slits in the top of each pie to let the steam out. Brush the pastry with the remaining egg.

Bake in a preheated 425°F (220°C) oven for 15–20 minutes, until the pastry is golden brown. Serve the pies immediately.

5

KIDS WILL LOVE THIS
Mushroom toad in the hole

Serves 4
Preparation time: 5 minutes
Cooking time: 25–30 minutes

4 large or 13 ounces (400 g) smaller portobello or shütake mushrooms
2 tablespoons (30 ml) butter
5 tablespoons (75 ml) olive oil
3 cloves garlic, sliced
2 tablespoons (30 ml) chopped fresh rosemary or thyme
1 cup (250 ml) all-purpose flour
2 eggs
2 tablespoons (30 ml) horseradish sauce
1⅔ cups (400 ml) 1% or 2% milk
salt and pepper

FOR THE BEER GRAVY
2 onions, sliced
2 teaspoons (10 ml) sugar
1 tablespoon (15 ml) all-purpose flour
1 cup + 2 tablespoons (275 ml) beer
⅔ cup (150 ml) vegetable stock (see page 8)

Heat the oven to 450°F (230°C). Put the mushrooms, stalk side up, in a large, shallow baking dish.

Melt the butter with 4 tablespoons (60 ml) of the oil in a frying pan. Add the garlic and herbs and a little salt and pepper and stir for about 30 seconds. Pour the sauce over the mushrooms and bake in the oven for 2 minutes.

Meanwhile, put the flour in a bowl and slowly whisk in the eggs, horseradish, milk and a little salt and pepper until really smooth.

Pour the batter over the mushrooms and return to the oven for 20–25 minutes, until the batter has risen and is golden.

Meanwhile, make the gravy. Heat the rest of the oil in a frying pan. Add the onions and sugar and fry for 10 minutes, until deep golden, stir in the flour, then pour in the beer and stock and add a sprinkling of salt and pepper. Stir for 5 minutes.

Cut up the toad and pour the beer gravy generously over the top of each serving.

THERE ARE SO MANY TYPES OF MUSHROOM AVAILABLE, FROM THE DELICATE JAPANESE ENOKI TO THE MEATY PORTOBELLO.

6

LEFTOVER TO LUNCH
Mushroom truffle soup

Serves 6
Preparation time: 15 minutes, plus chilling and soaking
Cooking time: 40 minutes

1 tablespoon (15 ml) dried porcini mushrooms
4 tablespoons (60 ml) boiling water
⅓ cups (75 ml) butter
2 onions, chopped
2 cloves garlic, crushed
2 tablespoons (30 ml) chopped fresh thyme
2 pounds (1 kg) portobello mushrooms, trimmed and chopped
4 cups (1 L) vegetable stock (see page 8)
1 cup (250 ml) half-and-half (10%) cream, plus extra to serve
salt and pepper
chopped chives, to garnish

FOR THE TRUFFLE BUTTER
⅔ cup (150 ml) butter, softened
2 teaspoons (10 ml) truffle paste

First make the truffle butter. Beat the butter and truffle paste together in a bowl until smooth. Form into a log, wrap in plastic wrap and chill in the freezer for 30 minutes. Cut into slices.

Meanwhile, soak the porcini mushrooms in the water for 15 minutes. Drain well, reserving the soaking liquid, then chop the porcini.

Melt half the butter in a saucepan, add the onions, garlic and thyme and cook over low heat, stirring occasionally, for 10 minutes. Add the remaining butter and the fresh mushrooms and porcini and cook over medium heat, stirring frequently, for 5 minutes, until the mushrooms are softened. Stir in the stock and the reserved soaking liquid and bring to a boil, then reduce the heat, cover and simmer gently for 20 minutes.

Transfer to a food processor or blender and process until really smooth. Return to the pan, stir in the cream, season and heat through without boiling. Spoon the soup into bowls and serve each portion topped with slices of the truffle butter and chopped chives.

7

BUT I DON'T LIKE ...
MUSHROOMS

Onion & mushroom quesadillas

Serves 4
Preparation time: 10 minutes
Cooking time: about 30 minutes

3 tablespoons (45 ml) olive oil
2 red onions, thinly sliced
1 teaspoon (5 ml) granulated sugar
7 ounces (200 g) button mushrooms, sliced
8 flour tortillas
5 ounces (150 g) Cheddar cheese, grated
1 small handful of fresh parsley, chopped
salt and pepper

Heat 2 tablespoons (30 ml) of the oil in a large frying pan, add the onions and cook until soft. Add the sugar and cook for 3 minutes or until caramelized. Remove the onions with a slotted spoon and set aside. Heat the remaining oil in the pan, add the mushrooms and cook for 3 minutes or until golden brown. Set aside.

Heat a nonstick frying pan and add 1 tortilla. Scatter over a quarter of the red onions, mushrooms, Cheddar and parsley. Season to taste with salt and pepper. Cover with another tortilla and cook until browned on the underside. Turn over and cook until browned on the other side. Remove from the pan and keep warm.

Repeat with the remaining tortillas and ingredients. Cut into wedges and serve with a salad.

WHY NOT TRY...
SPINACH & BRIE QUESADILLAS

Replace the mushrooms with 7 ounces (200 g) cooked, chopped spinach leaves and use 5 ounces (150 g) Brie, cut into slices, instead of the Cheddar. Cook and serve as above.

8

FRIENDS FOR DINNER
Mixed mushroom tart

Serves 6
Preparation time: 45 minutes, plus chilling and cooling
Cooking time: 50–55 minutes

¼ cup (60 ml) butter
6 shallots, finely chopped
2 cloves garlic, crushed
2 teaspoons (10 ml) chopped fresh thyme
11½ ounces (350 g) mixed mushrooms, such as shiitake, oyster, brown and field, trimmed and sliced
1¼ cups (300 ml) sour cream
3 eggs, lightly beaten
1 ounce (25 g) Parmesan cheese, freshly grated
salt and pepper
arugula leaves, to serve

FOR THE PASTRY
1⅔ cups (400 ml) all-purpose flour, plus extra for dusting
½ teaspoon (2 ml) salt
4 ounces (125 ml) chilled unsalted butter, diced
1 egg yolk
2 tablespoons (30 ml) cold water

First make the pastry. Sift the flour and salt into a bowl. Add the butter and rub in with your fingertips until the mixture resembles fine breadcrumbs. Add the egg yolk and water and bring the mixture together. Wrap in plastic wrap and chill for 30 minutes.

Roll the pastry out on a lightly floured work surface. Use to line a 10-inch (25 cm) fluted tart pan. Prick the base with a fork and chill for 30 minutes. Line the pastry with parchment paper and beans and bake in a preheated 400°F (200°C) oven for 15 minutes. Remove the paper and beans and bake for a further 15 minutes. Leave to cool.

Meanwhile, melt the butter in a frying pan, add the shallots, garlic and thyme and cook over low heat, stirring frequently, for 5 minutes. Increase the heat, add the mushrooms and salt and pepper and cook, stirring continuously, for 4–5 minutes, until browned. Leave to cool. Scatter over the tart shell. Beat the sour cream, eggs, Parmesan and salt and pepper together and pour over the top. Bake for 20–25 minutes, until golden and just set.

Serve warm with some arugula leaves.

9

WATCHING MY WEIGHT
Mushroom ramen

Serves 4
Preparation time: 10 minutes
Cooking time: 15 minutes

> 10 ounces (300 g) dried ramen noodles
> 6 cups (1.5 L) vegetable stock (see page 8)
> ⅓ cup (75 ml) dark soy sauce
> 3 tablespoons (45 ml) mirin
> 11½ ounces (350 g) mixed mushrooms, trimmed
> 4 green onions, trimmed and thinly sliced
> 10 ounces (300 g) silken tofu, drained and diced

Cook the noodles according to the package instructions. Drain well in a colander, refresh under cold water and set aside.

Combine the stock, soy sauce and mirin in a saucepan and bring to a boil, then reduce the heat and simmer gently for 5 minutes. Add the mushrooms and simmer gently for a further 5 minutes. Add the green onions and tofu.

Meanwhile, boil a full kettle of water. Set the noodles, still in the colander, over a sink and pour the boiling water over. Divide the noodles between serving bowls and add the soup. Serve immediately.

10

INSPIRE ME
Mushroom & ginger wontons

Serves 4
Preparation time: 30 minutes, plus cooling
Cooking time: 10–12 minutes

> 2 tablespoons (30 ml) vegetable oil
> 1 clove garlic, crushed
> 1 teaspoon (5 ml) grated gingerroot
> 8 ounces (250 g) mixed mushrooms, trimmed and finely chopped
> 1 tablespoon (15 ml) dark soy sauce
> 1 tablespoon (15 ml) chopped fresh coriander
> 16 wonton wrappers
> salt and pepper

> **FOR THE SZECHUAN CHILI DRESSING**
> 1 teaspoon (5 ml) hot pepper flakes
> ⅔ cup (150 ml) vegetable stock (see page 8)
> 1 tablespoon (15 ml) rice wine vinegar
> 1 tablespoon (15 ml) light soy sauce
> 2 teaspoons (10 ml) granulated or superfine sugar
> ¼ teaspoon (1 ml) freshly ground Szechuan pepper

Heat the oil in a frying pan, add the garlic and ginger and cook over medium heat, stirring continuously, for 2–3 minutes. Add the mushrooms and soy sauce and cook, stirring, for 3–4 minutes, until golden. Remove from the heat, season and stir in the coriander. Leave to cool.

Meanwhile, make the dressing. Put all the ingredients in a saucepan and heat over low heat, stirring, until hot but not boiling. Keep warm.

Put a teaspoon (5 ml) of the mushroom mixture in the center of each wonton wrapper. Brush a little water around the filling and fold the wontons in half diagonally, pressing the edges together to seal.

Bring a large saucepan of lightly salted water to a rolling boil, add the wontons and cook for 2–3 minutes, until they rise to the surface. Gently drain and transfer to warmed serving bowls. Drizzle on the dressing and serve immediately.

10 WAYS WITH BUTTERNUT SQUASH

1

BASIC

Cheesy butternut squash soup

Serves 6
Preparation time: 25 minutes
Cooking time: about 1 hour

    2 tablespoons (30 ml) olive oil
    1 onion, roughly chopped
    1 butternut squash, about 1½ pounds (750 g), halved, seeded,
        peeled and cut into chunks
    1–2 cloves garlic, finely chopped
    2 large sprigs fresh sage
    4 cups (1 L) vegetable or chicken stock (see pages 8–9)
    2½ ounces (65 g) Parmesan rinds
    salt and pepper

    TO SERVE
    oil for deep frying
    1 small bunch fresh sage
    grated Parmesan cheese

Heat the oil in a saucepan, add the onion and fry for 5 minutes, until softened and just beginning to turn golden. Add the squash, garlic and sage and fry for 5 minutes, stirring.

Pour in the stock and add the Parmesan rinds and salt and pepper. Bring to a boil, then cover and simmer for 45 minutes, until the squash is tender.

Scoop out and discard the sage and Parmesan rinds. Allow the soup to cool slightly, then purée in batches in a blender or food processor until smooth. Return to the saucepan and reheat. Add a little extra stock if needed, then taste and adjust the seasoning.

Fill a small saucepan halfway with oil and heat until a cube of day-old bread sizzles the minute it is added. Then tear the sage leaves from the stems and add to the oil, frying for 1–2 minutes, until crisp. Lift out with a slotted spoon and put on paper towels.

Ladle the soup into bowls, top with some of the crispy sage and a sprinkling of grated Parmesan, serving the remaining leaves and extra Parmesan in small bowls for diners to add their own as desired.

2

GIVE IT A TWIST

Butternut squash, tofu & pea curry

Serves 4
Preparation time: 15 minutes
Cooking time: 25 minutes

    1 tablespoon (15 ml) sunflower oil
    1 tablespoon (15 ml) Thai red curry paste
    1 pound (500 g) peeled, seeded butternut squash, cubed
    1¾ cups (425 ml) vegetable stock (see page 8)
    1 can (14 ounces/400 ml) coconut milk
    6 kaffir lime leaves, bruised, plus extra shredded leaves to garnish
    1½ cups (375 ml) frozen peas
    10 ounces (300 g) firm tofu, diced
    2 tablespoons (30 ml) light soy sauce
    juice of 1 lime
    chopped fresh coriander, to garnish
    finely chopped red chili, to garnish

Heat the oil in a wok or deep frying pan, add the curry paste and stir-fry over low heat for 1 minute. Add the squash, stir-fry briefly, then add the stock, coconut milk and bruised lime leaves. Bring to a boil, then cover, reduce the heat and simmer gently for 15 minutes, until the squash is cooked.

Stir in the peas, tofu, soy sauce and lime juice and simmer for a further 5 minutes, until the peas are cooked. Spoon into serving bowls; garnish with shredded lime leaves and chopped coriander.

3

SAVE ME TIME
Beets & squash spaghetti

Serves 4
Preparation time: 8 minutes
Cooking time: 10 minutes

   10 ounces (300 g) dried spaghetti or fusilli
   5 ounces (150 g) fine green beans
   1 pound (500 g) butternut squash, peeled, seeded and cut into
      ½-inch (1 cm) cubes
   4 tablespoons (60 ml) olive oil
   1 pound (500 g) raw beets, cut into ½-inch (1 cm) cubes
   2 ounces (50 g) walnuts, crushed
   5 ounces (150 g) goat cheese, diced
   2 tablespoons (30 ml) lemon juice
   freshly grated Parmesan cheese, to serve (optional)

Cook the pasta in lightly salted boiling water for 10 minutes or until just cooked. Add the beans and squash for the final 2 minutes of cooking time.

Meanwhile, heat the oil in a large frying pan, add the beets and cook, stirring occasionally, for 10 minutes until cooked but still firm.

Toss the drained pasta mixture with the beets, walnuts and goat cheese. Squeeze the lemon juice over and serve immediately with a bowl of Parmesan, if desired.

4

SAVE ME MONEY
Squash, kale & mixed bean stew

Serves 6
Preparation time: 15 minutes
Cooking time: 45 minutes

   1 tablespoon (15 ml) olive oil
   1 onion, finely chopped
   2 cloves garlic, finely chopped
   1 teaspoon (5 ml) smoked paprika
   1 pound (500 g) butternut squash, sliced, seeded, peeled and
      diced
   2 small carrots, diced
   1 pound (500 g) tomatoes, skinned (optional), roughly chopped
   1 can (14 ounces/398 ml) mixed beans, drained
   3½ cups (875 ml) vegetable or chicken stock (see pages 8–9)
   ⅔ cup (150 ml) crème fraîche or sour cream
   3½ ounces (100 g) kale, torn into bite-size pieces
   salt and pepper

Heat the oil in a saucepan, add the onion and fry gently for 5 minutes. Stir in the garlic and smoked paprika and cook briefly, then add the squash, carrots, tomatoes and drained beans.

Pour in the stock, season with salt and pepper and bring to a boil, stirring. Cover and simmer for 25 minutes, until the vegetables are tender.

Stir the crème fraîche into the soup, then add the kale, pressing it just beneath the surface of the stock. Cover and cook for 5 minutes, until the kale has just wilted. Ladle into bowls and serve with warm garlic bread.

5

KIDS WILL LOVE THIS
Butternut squash risotto

Serves 4
Preparation time: 15 minutes
Cooking time: about 25 minutes

- 2 tablespoons (30 ml) olive oil
- 1 onion, finely chopped
- 1 pound (500 g) butternut squash, peeled, seeded and roughly chopped
- 1 cup (250 ml) Arborio rice
- 3½ cups (875 ml) rich chicken stock (see page 9)
- ½ cup (125 ml) freshly grated Parmesan cheese, plus extra to serve
- 4 tablespoons (60 ml) pine nuts, toasted
- 8 ounces (250 g) fresh spinach leaves

Heat the oil in a large heavy frying pan and cook the onion and squash over low to medium heat for 10 minutes, until softened. Add the rice and cook for 1 minute, then add half the stock. Bring to a boil, then reduce the heat and simmer gently for 5 minutes, until almost all the stock has been absorbed, stirring occasionally.

Continue to add the stock ⅔ cup (150 ml) at a time and cook over gentle heat until almost all the stock has been absorbed before adding more. Once the rice is tender, remove the pan from the heat, add the Parmesan, pine nuts and spinach and stir well to combine and wilt the spinach, returning to the heat for 1 minute if necessary.

Serve in warmed serving bowls with extra freshly grated Parmesan on top.

BUTTERNUT SQUASH IS GOLDEN-FLESHED AND IS CLASSIFIED AS A FRUIT RATHER THAN A VEGETABLE. IT HAS A SWEET AND NUTTY TASTE AND IS HIGHLY VERSATILE.

6

LEFTOVER TO LUNCH
Butternut squash & rosemary soup

Serves 4
Preparation time: 15 minutes
Cooking time: 1¼ hours

- 1 butternut squash
- 2 tablespoons (30 ml) olive oil
- a few fresh sprigs rosemary, plus extra to garnish
- 5 ounces (150 g) red lentils, washed
- 1 onion, finely chopped
- 3½ cups (875 ml) vegetable stock (see page 8)
- salt and pepper

Cut the squash in half and use a spoon to scoop out the seeds and fibrous flesh. Peel and cut the squash into small chunks and place in a roasting pan. Sprinkle on the oil and rosemary, and season well with salt and pepper. Roast in a preheated 400°F (200°C) oven for 45 minutes.

Meanwhile, place the lentils in a saucepan, cover with water, bring to a boil and boil rapidly for 10 minutes. Strain, then return the lentils to a clean saucepan with the onion and stock and simmer for 5 minutes. Season to taste.

Remove the squash from the oven, mash the flesh with a fork and add to the soup. Simmer for 25 minutes and then ladle into bowls. Garnish with more rosemary before serving.

7

BUT I DON'T LIKE ...
BUTTERNUT SQUASH
Swordfish with squash couscous

Serves 4
Preparation time: 15 minutes, plus marinating
Cooking time: 40 minutes

> 1 butternut squash, peeled, seeded and cut into ¾-inch
>   (1.5 cm) cubes
> 4 tablespoons (60 ml) olive oil
> 1 tablespoon (15 ml) cumin seeds
> 1 teaspoon (5 ml) ground coriander
> 1 teaspoon (5 ml) ground cumin
> 1 teaspoon (5 ml) paprika
> 4 swordfish steaks, about 7 ounces (200 g) each and ¾ inch
>   (1.5 cm) thick
> 1½ cups (375 ml) couscous
> 1 tablespoon (15 ml) harissa paste
> 1⅔ cups (400 ml) boiling chicken or vegetable stock
>   (see pages 8–9)
> 4 tablespoons (60 ml) lemon juice
> salt and pepper

Place the squash on a rimmed baking sheet and drizzle with
1 tablespoon (15 ml) of the oil. Season with salt and pepper and
sprinkle with the cumin seeds. Roast in a preheated 350°F
(180°C) oven for 30 minutes, until the squash is tender.

Meanwhile, mix together the coriander, ground cumin,
paprika and 2 tablespoons (30 ml) of the oil. Rub the mixture over
the swordfish steaks and leave in the refrigerator to marinate for
30 minutes.

Place the couscous in a heatproof bowl. Mix the harissa paste
with the boiling stock and pour it over the couscous. Cover the
bowl with plastic wrap and leave for 5–8 minutes, then fluff the
couscous up with a fork to separate the grains. Mix in the lemon
juice and remaining oil and season with salt and pepper. Finally,
stir in the roasted butternut squash.

Place the marinated swordfish in a very hot grill pan and cook
for 3–4 minutes on each side. Serve immediately with the warm
couscous.

WHY NOT TRY...
TUNA WITH HERB SALSA

Marinate 4 fresh tuna steaks, about 7 ounces (200 g) each, in a
mixture of 1 teaspoon (5 ml) ground coriander, 1 teaspoon
(5 ml) ground cumin, a few hot pepper flakes, 1 crushed clove
garlic and 2 tablespoons (30 ml) olive oil. Leave in the refrigerator
to marinate for 40 minutes, then cook as the swordfish for
2–3 minutes on each side. Meanwhile, mix together 1 tablespoon
(15 ml) each lemon juice, chopped oregano, chopped parsley and
roughly chopped capers, 1 crushed clove garlic and 2 tablespoons
(30 ml) olive oil. Season and serve with the tuna.

8

FRIENDS FOR DINNER
Roasted squash & sage pizza

Serves 2
Preparation time: 20 minutes, plus rising
Cooking time: 45–55 minutes

> cooking spray, for oiling
> 1 recipe Basic Pizza Dough (see page 7)
> white bread flour, for dusting
> 1 pound (500 g) butternut squash, peeled
> 1 onion, sliced
> 1 tablespoon (15 ml) extra virgin olive oil
> 2 cloves garlic, finely chopped
> 1 pinch of hot pepper flakes
> 1 tablespoon (15 ml) chopped fresh sage
> 8 ounces (250 g) mozzarella cheese, sliced
> 4 tablespoons (60 ml) freshly grated Parmesan cheese
> salt and pepper

Lightly oil a bowl with cooking spray. Turn the dough out on a
lightly floured work surface. Knead for 10 minutes, until smooth
and elastic. Put in the prepared bowl, cover and leave to rise in a
warm place for 1 hour, until doubled in size.

Meanwhile, cut the squash in half and scoop out and discard
the seeds and fibres. Cut into 1-inch (2.5 cm) cubes. Put in a
roasting pan, add the onion, half the oil, the garlic, hot pepper
flakes, sage and salt and pepper and toss well. Roast in a
preheated 450°F (230°C) oven for 25 minutes, until tender,
stirring halfway through.

Put 2 heavy pizza pans in the oven and heat for 5 minutes.
Knock the air out of the dough. Divide in half. Roll the halves out
to 10-inch (25 cm) rounds. Transfer to the heated pizza pans.
Divide the squash mixture and cheeses between the dough. Bake
for 10–15 minutes, until the bases are crisp and golden. Serve
immediately.

9

WATCHING MY WEIGHT
Squash with red bean sauce

Serves 4
Preparation time: 10 minutes
Cooking time: 15 minutes

2⅓ cups (575 ml) vegetable stock (see page 8)
2 pounds (1 kg) mixed squash, such as butternut and acorn,
    quartered and seeded
4 ounces (125 g) baby spinach leaves
rice, to serve

FOR THE SAUCE
4 tablespoons (60 ml) olive oil
4 cloves garlic, thinly sliced
1 red bell pepper, cored, seeded and finely chopped
2 tomatoes, chopped
1 can (14 ounces/398 ml) red kidney beans, drained and rinsed
1–2 tablespoons (15–30 ml) hot pepper sauce
1 small handful of fresh coriander leaves, chopped
salt

Bring the stock to a boil in a large saucepan. Add the squash, reduce the heat and cover. Simmer gently for about 15 minutes or until the squash is just tender.

Meanwhile, to make the sauce, heat the oil in a frying pan, add the garlic and red pepper and fry for 5 minutes, stirring frequently, until very soft. Add the tomatoes, red kidney beans, hot pepper sauce and a little salt and simmer for 5 minutes, until pulpy. Set aside.

Drain the squash from the stock, reserving the stock, and return to the pan. Scatter on the spinach leaves, then cover and cook for about 1 minute, until the spinach has wilted in the steam.

Pile the vegetables onto servings of boiled rice. Stir ½ cup (125 ml) of the reserved stock into the sauce with the coriander. Spoon over the vegetables.

10

INSPIRE ME
Thai squash & coriander soup

Serves 6
Preparation time: 25 minutes
Cooking time: 55 minutes

1 tablespoon (15 ml) sunflower oil
1 onion, roughly chopped
1 tablespoon (15 ml) Thai red curry paste
1–2 cloves garlic, finely chopped
1-inch (2.5 cm) piece gingerroot, peeled and finely chopped
1 butternut squash, about 1½ pounds (750 g), halved, seeded,
    peeled and diced
1 can (14 ounces/400 ml) full-fat coconut milk
3 cups (750 ml) vegetable or chicken stock (see pages 8–9)
2 teaspoons (10 ml) Thai fish sauce
pepper
1 small bunch fresh coriander

Heat the oil in a saucepan, add the onion and fry gently for 5 minutes, until softened. Stir in the curry paste, garlic and ginger and cook for 1 minute. Then mix in the squash, coconut milk, stock and fish sauce. Add a little pepper (don't add salt as the fish sauce is so salty), then bring to a boil.

Cover the pan and simmer for 45 minutes, stirring occasionally, until the squash is soft. Leave to cool slightly. Reserve a few sprigs of coriander for garnish, then tear the remainder into pieces and add to the soup. Purée the soup in batches in a blender or food processor until smooth. Pour back into the saucepan and reheat, tearing in the reserved coriander sprigs. Ladle into bowls and serve.

10 WAYS WITH EGGPLANT

1

BASIC
Eggplant pesto toasties

Serves 4
Preparation time: 15 minutes
Cooking time: 8–20 minutes

1 large eggplant
4 tablespoons (60 ml) extra virgin olive oil
4 slices sourdough bread
2 beefsteak tomatoes, thickly sliced
7 ounces (200 g) mozzarella cheese, sliced
salt and pepper

FOR THE PESTO
1⅓–1½ cups (325–375 ml) basil leaves
1 clove garlic, crushed
4 tablespoons (60 ml) pine nuts
¾ cup + 2 tablespoons (100 ml) extra virgin olive oil
2 tablespoons (30 ml) freshly grated Parmesan cheese

First make the pesto. Put the basil, garlic, pine nuts, oil and salt and pepper in a food processor and process until fairly smooth. Transfer to a bowl, stir in the Parmesan and adjust the seasoning. Set aside until required.

Cut the eggplant into ½-inch (1 cm) thick slices. Season the oil with salt and pepper and brush over the eggplant slices. Heat a ridged grill pan until hot. Add the eggplant slices, in batches if necessary, and cook for 4–5 minutes on each side, until charred and tender.

Meanwhile, grill the sourdough bread. Top the grilled bread with an eggplant slice. Spread with the pesto. Top with tomato and mozzarella slices and more pesto. Cook under a preheated hot broiler for 1–2 minutes, until bubbling and golden.

2

GIVE IT A TWIST
Baby eggplant with chili

Serves 4
Preparation time: 20 minutes
Cooking time: 25–30 minutes

1 pound (500 g) baby eggplant
5 tablespoons (75 ml) sunflower oil
6 cloves garlic, finely chopped
1 tablespoon (15 ml) finely chopped gingerroot
8 green onions, cut diagonally into 1-inch (2.5 cm) long pieces
2 red chilies, seeded and finely sliced
3 tablespoons (45 ml) light soy sauce
1 tablespoon (15 ml) Chinese rice wine
1 tablespoon (15 ml) palm sugar
1 small handful of fresh mint leaves
1 small handful of roughly chopped fresh coriander
3½ ounces (100 g) canned water chestnuts, roughly chopped
2 ounces (50 g) roasted peanuts, roughly chopped

Cut the eggplant in half lengthwise and place on an ovenproof plate. Place a trivet or steamer rack in a wok and pour in about 2 inches (5 cm) of water. Bring the water to a boil and lower the eggplant plate onto the trivet or rack.

Reduce the heat, cover and steam for 25–30 minutes (replenishing the water in the wok if needed), until the eggplant are cooked through and soft to the touch. Remove the eggplant from the wok, transfer to a serving platter and allow to cool.

Meanwhile, heat the oil in a nonstick frying pan. Add the garlic, ginger, green onions and chilies and stir-fry for 2–3 minutes. Remove from the heat and stir in the soy sauce, rice wine and sugar.

Toss the mint leaves, coriander and water chestnuts with the eggplant and pour the garlic and ginger mixture evenly over the top. Sprinkle on the peanuts, toss gently and serve immediately with lime wedges and steamed egg noodles or rice, if desired.

SAVE ME TIME
Pasta with eggplant & pine nuts

Serves 4
Preparation time: 10 minutes
Cooking time: 15 minutes

- ½ cup (125 ml) olive oil
- 2 eggplants, diced
- 2 red onions, sliced
- ½ cup (125 ml) pine nuts
- 3 cloves garlic, crushed
- 5 tablespoons (75 ml) sun-dried tomato paste
- ⅔ cup (150 ml) vegetable stock (see page 8)
- 10 ounces (300 g) cracked pepper-, tomato- or mushroom-flavored fresh ribbon pasta
- 3½ ounces (100 g) pitted black olives
- salt and pepper
- 3 tablespoons (45 ml) roughly chopped fresh flat-leaf parsley, to garnish

Heat the oil in a large frying pan, add the eggplants and onions and cook for 8–10 minutes, until tender and golden. Add the pine nuts and garlic and cook, stirring, for 2 minutes. Stir in the sun-dried tomato paste and stock and simmer for 2 minutes.

Meanwhile, cook the pasta in a large saucepan of salted boiling water for 2 minutes or until al dente.

Drain the pasta and return to the pan. Add the vegetable mixture and olives, season to taste with salt and pepper and toss together over medium heat for 1 minute, until combined. Serve scattered with the chopped parsley.

SAVE ME MONEY
Eggplant with goat cheese gratin

Serves 6
Preparation time: 10 minutes
Cooking time: 1 hour 10 minutes

- cooking spray, for oiling
- 2 cans (14 ounces/398 ml each) chopped tomatoes
- 2 large cloves garlic, crushed
- 4 tablespoons (60 ml) extra virgin olive oil
- 1 teaspoon (5 ml) granulated sugar
- 2 tablespoons (30 ml) chopped fresh basil
- 2 eggplants
- 8 ounces (250 g) soft goat cheese, sliced or crumbled
- 2 ounces (50 g) Parmesan cheese, freshly grated
- salt and pepper

Lightly oil a 6-cup (1.5 L) baking dish with cooking spray. Put the tomatoes, garlic, half the oil, sugar, basil and salt and pepper in a saucepan and bring to a boil. Reduce the heat and simmer for 30 minutes, until reduced and thickened.

Cut each eggplant lengthwise into 6 thin slices. Season the remaining oil with salt and pepper, then brush the eggplant slices with the seasoned oil.

Cook under a preheated hot broiler for 3–4 minutes on each side, until charred and tender.

Arrange one-third of the eggplant slices, overlapping them slightly, in the base of the prepared dish. Add one-third of the tomato sauce and one-third of the goat cheese and Parmesan. Repeat these layers, finishing with the two cheeses. Bake in a preheated 400°F (200°C) oven for 30 minutes, until bubbling and golden.

5

KIDS WILL LOVE THIS
Rigatoni with eggplant & ricotta

Serves 4
Preparation time: 5 minutes
Cooking time: 35 minutes

> **2 large eggplants**
> **olive oil, for frying**
> **2 cloves garlic, finely chopped**
> **2 cans (14 ounces/398 ml each) chopped tomatoes**
> **20 fresh basil leaves, torn**
> **13 ounces (400 g) dried rigatoni**
> **7 ounces (200 g) ricotta cheese**
> **3 tablespoons (45 ml) freshly grated pecorino cheese**
> **salt and pepper**

Cut the eggplant into quarters lengthwise, then each quarter in half lengthwise. Cut the pieces into finger-sized lengths.

Heat ½ inch (1 cm) of oil in a large frying pan over high heat until the surface of the oil seems to shimmer. Add the eggplant, in batches, and fry until golden. With a slotted spoon, remove and drain on paper towels.

Heat 1 tablespoon (15 ml) of oil in a large, heavy frying pan over medium heat, add the garlic and cook, stirring, for 30 seconds. Stir in the eggplants and season, then stir in the tomatoes. Bring to a boil, then reduce the heat and simmer, uncovered, for 20 minutes, until the sauce has thickened. Remove from the heat, stir in half the basil and adjust the seasoning.

When the sauce is almost ready, cook the pasta in a large saucepan of salted boiling water according to the package instructions, until al dente. Drain, reserving a ladleful of the cooking water. Add the pasta to the sauce and stir over low heat. Pour in the reserved pasta cooking water and continue stirring until the pasta is well coated and looks silky. Serve immediately with a scattering of ricotta, pecorino and the remaining basil.

6

LEFTOVER TO LUNCH
Eggplant dip with flatbreads

Serves 6
Preparation time: 15 minutes, plus cooling
Cooking time: 15 minutes

> **1 large eggplant**
> **4 tablespoons (60 ml) extra virgin olive oil**
> **1 teaspoon (5 ml) ground cumin**
> **⅔ cup (150 ml) Greek yogurt**
> **1 small clove garlic, crushed**
> **2 tablespoons (30 ml) chopped fresh coriander**
> **1 tablespoon (15 ml) lemon juice**
> **4 flour tortillas**
> **salt and pepper**

Cut the eggplant lengthwise into ¼-inch (5 mm) thick slices. Mix 3 tablespoons (45 ml) of the oil with the cumin and salt and pepper and brush all over the eggplant slices. Cook in a preheated ridged grill pan or under a preheated hot broiler for 3–4 minutes on each side, until charred and tender. Leave to cool, then finely chop.

Mix the eggplant into the yogurt in a bowl, then stir in the garlic, coriander, lemon juice, the remaining oil and salt and pepper to taste. Transfer to a serving bowl.

Cook the tortillas in the preheated grill pan or under the preheated hot broiler for 3 minutes on each side, until toasted. Cut into triangles and serve immediately with the eggplant dip.

7

BUT I DON'T LIKE ...
EGGPLANT
Caponata ratatouille

Serves 6
Preparation time: 20 minutes
Cooking time: 35–40 minutes

- 1½ pounds (750 g) eggplant
- 1 large onion
- 1 tablespoon (15 ml) olive oil
- 3 stalks celery, coarsely chopped
- a little wine (optional)
- 2 large beef tomatoes, skinned and seeded
- 1 teaspoon (5 ml) chopped fresh thyme
- ¼–½ teaspoon (1–2 ml) cayenne pepper
- 2 tablespoons (30 ml) capers
- 1 handful of pitted green olives
- 4 tablespoons (60 ml) white wine vinegar
- 1 tablespoon (15 ml) sugar
- 1–2 tablespoons (15–30 ml) cocoa powder (optional)
- pepper

TO GARNISH
toasted chopped almonds
chopped fresh parsley

Cut the eggplant and onion into ½-inch (1 cm) chunks. Heat the oil in a nonstick frying pan until very hot, add the eggplant and fry for about 15 minutes, until very soft. Add a little boiling water to prevent sticking if necessary.

Meanwhile, place the onion and celery in a saucepan with a little water or wine. Cook for 5 minutes, until tender but still firm.

Add the tomatoes, thyme, cayenne pepper and eggplant. Cook for 15 minutes, stirring occasionally. Add the capers, olives, wine vinegar, sugar and cocoa powder (if using) and cook for 2–3 minutes.

Season with pepper and serve garnished with almonds and parsley. Serve hot or cold as a side dish, starter or a main dish, with polenta and hot crusty bread, if desired.

WHY NOT TRY...
RED PEPPER & POTATO CAPONATA

Omit the eggplant, thyme and cocoa powder from the recipe above. Grill 2 red and 2 yellow bell peppers until the skins have blackened, then discard the skin and roughly chop the flesh. Cook the onions and celery as above, then follow the remainder of the recipe, adding the skinned peppers and 1 pound (500 g) cooked and halved new potatoes instead of the eggplant.

8

FRIENDS FOR DINNER
Baked eggplant & mozzarella

Serves 4
Preparation time: 10 minutes
Cooking time: about 25 minutes

- 2 eggplant, sliced in half lengthwise
- 3 tablespoons (45 ml) olive oil
- 1 onion, chopped
- 1 clove garlic, crushed
- 1 can (8 ounces/225 ml) chopped tomatoes
- 1 tablespoon (15 ml) tomato paste
- 10 ounces (300 g) mozzarella cheese, cut into thin slices
- salt and pepper
- fresh basil, to garnish

Brush the eggplants with 2 tablespoons (30 ml) of the oil and arrange, cut side up, on a baking sheet. Roast in a preheated 400°F (200°C) oven for 20 minutes.

Meanwhile, heat the remaining oil in a frying pan, add the onion and garlic and cook until the onion is soft and starting to brown. Add the tomatoes and tomato paste and simmer for 5 minutes or until the sauce has thickened.

Remove the eggplants from the oven and cover each half with some sauce and 2 of the mozzarella slices. Season to taste with salt and pepper and return to the oven for 4–5 minutes to melt the cheese. Serve immediately, scattered with basil leaves.

EGGPLANT ARE ALSO DELICIOUS WHEN GRILLED ON THE BARBECUE.

9

WATCHING MY WEIGHT

Spicy eggplant Goan curry

Serves 4
Preparation time: 15 minutes
Cooking time: 20 minutes

- 1 teaspoon (5 ml) cayenne pepper
- 2 fresh green chilies, seeded and sliced
- ½ teaspoon (2 ml) ground turmeric
- 4 cloves garlic, crushed
- 1-inch (2½ cm) piece gingerroot, peeled and grated
- 1¼ cups (300 ml) warm water
- 1 teaspoon (5 ml) cumin seeds, toasted
- 4 teaspoons (20 ml) coriander seeds, toasted
- 1 can (14 ounces/400 g) coconut milk
- 1 tablespoon (15 ml) tamarind paste
- 1 large eggplant, thinly sliced lengthwise
- salt and pepper

Mix the cayenne, chilies, turmeric, garlic and ginger with the warm water.

Crush the cumin and coriander seeds together, add them to the sauce and simmer for 10 minutes, until thickened. Season to taste. Stir in the coconut milk and tamarind paste.

Arrange the eggplant slices in a foil-lined broiler pan and brush the tops with some of the curry sauce. Cook under a preheated hot broiler until golden. Serve the eggplant slices in the curry sauce and, if desired, with naan bread or chapattis.

10

INSPIRE ME

Eggplant pâté

Serves 6
Preparation time: 10 minutes, plus soaking
Cooking time: 15 minutes

- 1 ounce (25 g) dried porcini mushrooms
- 6 tablespoons (90 ml) olive oil
- 1 pound (500 g) eggplant, cut into 1-cm (½ inch) cubes
- 1 small red onion, chopped
- 2 teaspoons (10 ml) cumin seeds
- 6 ounces (175 g) chestnut mushrooms
- 2 cloves garlic, crushed
- 3 pickled walnuts, halved
- 1 small handful of fresh coriander
- salt and pepper

Place the dried mushrooms in a bowl and cover with boiling water. Leave to soak for 10 minutes.

Meanwhile, heat the oil in a large frying pan. Add the eggplant and onion and fry gently for 8 minutes, until the vegetables are softened and browned.

Drain the dried mushrooms and add to the pan with the cumin seeds, fresh mushrooms and garlic. Fry for a further 5–7 minutes until the eggplant is very soft.

Transfer the mixture to a food processor or blender with the pickled walnuts and coriander, season to taste with salt and pepper and process until broken up but not completely smooth. Transfer to a serving dish and chill until required. Serve the pâté on thick slices of bread or hot toast.

PIZZA, PASTA & NOODLES

Experiment with flavors using these quick and easy recipes for homemade pizza, lasagna, ravioli, spaghetti and rice noodles. (See page 7 for basic pizza dough and homemade pasta dough recipes.)

PIZZA, PASTA & NOODLES

1 BASIC

2 GIVE IT A TWIST

3 SAVE ME TIME

4 SAVE ME MONEY

5 KIDS WILL LOVE THESE

HOMEMADE PIZZA PAGE 150

Cherry tomato pizza

Pizza Fiorentina

Quick prosciutto & arugula pizza

Tortilla pizza with salami

Pizza with speck & dolcelatte

LASAGNA PAGE 156

Classic meat lasagna

Chicken & mushroom lasagna

Tuna layered lasagna with arugula

Goat cheese & pepper lasagna

Mushroom & spinach lasagna

RAVIOLI PAGE 162

Tomato & cream ravioli

Arugula, potato & lemon ravioli

Spinach & ricotta ravioli

Tortellini with creamy ham & peas

Duck tortellini

SPAGHETTI PAGE 168

Spaghetti with easy tomato sauce

Pesto Trapenese

No-cook tomato spaghetti

Spaghetti puttanesca

Spaghetti with meatballs

RICE NOODLES PAGE 174

Vietnamese rolls

Spicy mixed noodles

Ginger rice noodles

Crispy rice noodles

Crab & noodle Asian wraps

6 	7	8	9 	10
LEFTOVER TO LUNCH	**BUT I DON'T LIKE...**	**FRIENDS FOR DINNER**	**WATCHING MY WEIGHT**	**INSPIRE ME**

Mini scone pizzas

Halloumi & fig pastry pizza

Eggplant, basil & ricotta pizza

Pizza scrolls

Asparagus & Taleggio pizza

Open seafood lasagna

Vegetable lasagna

Wild mushroom lasagna

Lean lasagna

Parma ham lasagna

Feel-good broth

Warm ravioli salad with beets

Wild mushroom ravioli

Italian tortellini in brodo

Homemade pasta with squash & sage

Spaghetti & zucchini frittata

Chili & lemon shrimp with pasta

Spaghetti with lobster sauce

Broad bean & lemon spaghetti

Squid, tomato & chili spaghetti

Glass noodle soup

Indonesian shrimp salad

Beef & flat noodle soup

Lime- & chili-marinated chicken

Northern Thai salad

10 WAYS WITH HOMEMADE PIZZA

BASIC
Cherry tomato pizza

Serves 4
Preparation time: 15 minutes, plus making the pizza dough
Cooking time: 7–8 minutes per pizza

- 7 ounces (200 g) cherry tomatoes
- 2 cloves garlic, crushed
- 1 large pinch of hot pepper flakes
- 2 tablespoons (30 ml) olive oil, plus extra for glazing
- 1 recipe Basic Pizza Dough (see page 7)
- all-purpose flour, for dusting
- 5 ounces (150 g) buffalo mozzarella cheese, drained and torn into large pieces
- 2 ounces (50 g) wild arugula leaves
- salt

Put the tomatoes in a large bowl and crush them between your fingers. Add the garlic and hot pepper flakes, then stir in half the oil. Season with salt, cover and leave to infuse.

Heat a baking sheet in a preheated 475°F (240°C) oven. Place 1 pizza dough ball on a well-floured, 9-inch (23 cm) pizza pan. Push down on the dough with your fingertips, pressing it out to fill the pan, leaving the border slightly thicker. If you get any tears, forcefully pinch the dough around the hole back together.

Spoon a quarter of the tomato mixture over the base, then brush the border with oil to glaze. Remove the heated baking sheet from the oven, slide the tin onto it, then quickly return to the oven. Bake for 7–8 minutes, until crisp and risen. Scatter with a quarter each of the mozzarella and arugula and serve immediately. As the first pizza cooks, prepare the next for the oven.

GIVE IT A TWIST
Pizza Fiorentina

Serves 4
Preparation time: 10 minutes, plus making the pizza dough
Cooking time: 7–8 minutes per pizza

- 1 tablespoon (15 ml) olive oil, plus extra for drizzling and glazing
- 2 cloves garlic, crushed
- 1 pound (500 g) baby spinach leaves
- 1 recipe Basic Pizza Dough (see page 7)
- all-purpose flour, for dusting
- ¾ cup (175 ml) tomato sauce
- 7 ounces (200 g) mozzarella cheese (drained weight), chopped
- 20 black olives
- 4 eggs
- salt and pepper

Heat the oil in a large frying pan with the garlic for 15 seconds, then add the spinach and cook over high heat for 1–2 minutes, until just wilted. Season lightly with salt and pepper.

Heat a baking sheet in a preheated 475°F (240°C) oven. Place 1 pizza dough ball on a 9-inch (23 cm) pizza pan. Push down on the dough with your fingertips, pressing it out to fill the pan, leaving the border slightly thicker. If you get any tears, forcefully pinch the dough around the hole back together.

Spoon 3 tablespoons (45 ml) of sauce over the base and scatter with a quarter of the mozzarella, spinach and olives. Crack 1 egg onto the pizza, drizzle with oil and season lightly with salt and pepper. Brush the border with oil to glaze. Remove the baking sheet from the oven, slide the pan onto it, then quickly return to the oven. Bake for 7–8 minutes, until crisp and risen. Serve immediately. As the first pizza cooks, prepare the next for the oven.

3

Quick prosciutto & arugula pizza

Serves 4
Preparation time: 10 minutes
Cooking time: 10 minutes

- 4 ready-made mini pizza bases
- 2 cloves garlic, halved
- 8 ounces (250 g) reduced-fat mozzarella cheese, shredded
- 8 cherry tomatoes, quartered
- 5 ounces (150 g) prosciutto, sliced
- 2 ounces (50 g) arugula leaves, washed
- balsamic vinegar, to taste
- salt and pepper

Rub the top surfaces of the pizza bases with the cut faces of the garlic cloves.

Put the pizza bases on a baking sheet, top with mozzarella and tomatoes and bake in a preheated 400°F (200°C) oven for 10 minutes until the bread is golden.

Top the pizzas with slices of prosciutto and arugula leaves, season to taste with salt, pepper and balsamic vinegar and serve.

4

Tortilla pizza with salami

Makes 2
Preparation time: 5 minutes
Cooking time: 8–10 minutes per pizza

- 2 large flour tortillas or flatbreads
- 4 tablespoons (60 ml) tomato pasta sauce
- 3½ ounces (100 g) spicy salami slices
- 5 ounces (150 g) mozzarella cheese, thinly sliced
- 1 tablespoon (15 ml) fresh oregano leaves, plus extra to garnish
- salt and pepper

Lay the tortillas or flatbreads on 2 large baking sheets. Top each with half the pasta sauce, spreading it up to the edge. Arrange half the salami, mozzarella slices and oregano leaves over the top.

Bake in a preheated 400°F (200°C) oven for 8–10 minutes, until the cheese is melted and golden. Serve garnished with extra oregano leaves.

CREATING YOUR OWN PIZZA FROM SCRATCH WILL MAKE SURE THAT WHAT YOU EAT IS FAR MORE HEALTHY AND TASTY THAN ANYTHING YOU ARE ABLE TO BUY FROM A TAKEOUT OR SUPERMARKET.

5

KIDS WILL LOVE THIS

Pizza with speck & dolcelatte

Serves 4
Preparation time: 15 minutes, plus infusing and making the pizza dough
Cooking time: 7–8 minutes per pizza

> ¾ cup (175 ml) tomato sauce
> 5 large fresh basil leaves, torn, plus extra to garnish
> 1 clove garlic, crushed
> 1 tablespoon (15 ml) extra virgin olive oil, plus extra for glazing
> 1 recipe Basic Pizza Dough (see page 7)
> all-purpose flour, for dusting
> 4 ounces (125 g) mozzarella cheese (drained weight), torn into chunks
> 12 slices speck or proscuitto
> 3 ounces (75 g) dolcelatte or other mild creamy blue cheese, broken into pieces
> salt

Combine the sauce, basil, garlic and oil in a bowl. Season with salt, cover and leave to infuse for 15 minutes.

Heat a baking sheet in a preheated 475°F (240°C) oven. Place 1 pizza dough ball on a well-floured, 9-inch (23 cm) pizza pan. Push down on the dough with your fingertips, pressing it out to fill the pan, leaving the border slightly thicker. If you get any tears, forcefully pinch the dough around the hole back together.

Spoon 3 tablespoons (45 ml) of the tomato sauce mix over the base and scatter with a quarter of the mozzarella. Brush the border with oil to glaze. Remove the heated baking sheet from the oven, slide the pan onto it, then quickly return to the oven. Bake for 7–8 minutes, until crisp and risen. Top with 3 slices of speck, then half the dolcelatte. Serve immediately, garnished with a little torn basil. As the first pizza cooks, prepare the next for the oven.

6

LEFTOVER TO LUNCH

Mini scone pizzas

Serves 4
Preparation time: 25 minutes
Cooking time: 15–20 minutes

> 2 cups (500 ml) self-raising whole-wheat flour
> ¼ cup (60 ml) butter, cubed
> ⅔ cup (150 ml) milk
> ⅔ cup (150 ml) tomato sauce
> 3 tablespoons (45 ml) tomato purée
> 2 tablespoons (30 ml) chopped fresh basil
> 4 thick slices good-quality ham, shredded
> 4 ounces (125 g) pitted black olives, halved
> 5 ounces (150 g) mozzarella cheese, grated

Sift the flour into a bowl and rub in the butter until the mixture resembles fine breadcrumbs. Make a well in the center and stir in enough of the milk to give a fairly soft dough. Turn it out on to a lightly floured surface and knead gently. Cut into 4 pieces, then knead again to shape each into a rough round. Roll out 4 rough circles, each about 15 cm (6 inches) wide, and place on a baking sheet.

Mix the tomato sauce and paste with the basil. Divide between the scone bases and spread to within 1 cm (½ inch) of the edges. Pile each with the ham and olives, then sprinkle with the mozzarella.

Drizzle with a little oil and bake in a preheated 400°F (200°C) oven for 15–20 minutes, until the bases are risen and the cheese is golden. Wrap in foil and serve warm or cold.

BUT I DON'T LIKE ...
HOMEMADE PIZZA

Halloumi & fig
pastry pizza

Serves 2
Preparation time: 10 minutes
Cooking time: 25 minutes

> 1 sheet frozen puff pastry, 10 inches (25 cm) square, defrosted
> 3 tablespoons (45 ml) ready-made pesto
> 4 fresh figs, quartered
> 7 ounces (200 g) halloumi cheese, thinly sliced
> 2 ounces (50 g) pitted black olives, halved
> 2 tablespoons (30 ml) freshly grated Parmesan cheese
> a few fresh mint leaves, to garnish
> salt and pepper

Lay the pastry on a baking sheet and score a ½-inch (1 cm) border around the edge. Prick the base with a fork and spread the pesto in the center.

Arrange the figs, halloumi and olives over the pesto, season with salt and pepper, and scatter over the Parmesan.

Place the baking sheet on another preheated baking sheet (this will ensure the pastry is crispy) and bake in a preheated 400°F (200°C) oven for 10 minutes. Reduce the temperature to 325°F (160°C) and bake for a further 15 minutes, until the base is crispy. Scatter the mint leaves over to garnish and serve with an arugula salad.

WHY NOT TRY... MINI PUFF PASTRIES

Use a 2-inch (5 cm) pastry cutter to cut out rounds from the pastry sheet. Top each with a spoonful of olive tapenade and a slice of fresh fig, then divide 5 ounces (150 g) crumbled goat cheese between the rounds. Scatter over the Parmesan and bake as above for 8–10 minutes. Serve warm.

FRIENDS FOR DINNER

Eggplant, basil
& ricotta pizza

Serves 4
Preparation time: 10 minutes, plus making the pizza dough
Cooking time: 50 minutes

> ⅔ cup (150 ml) tomato sauce
> 5 large basil leaves, torn
> 1 clove garlic, crushed
> 2–3 small–medium eggplants, sliced lengthwise into ¼-inch (5 mm) thick slices
> 1 recipe Basic Pizza Dough (see page 7)
> all-purpose flour, for dusting
> 4 ounces (125 g) ricotta cheese, broken into small chunks
> 3 ounces (75 g) mozzarella cheese (drained weight), roughly chopped
> olive oil, for glazing
> salt
> fresh basil leaves, to garnish

Combine the tomato sauce, basil and garlic in a bowl. Season lightly with salt, cover and leave to infuse while you cook the eggplants.

Heat a ridged grill pan over high heat until smoking hot. Add the eggplant, in batches, and cook for 2 minutes on each side, until charred on the outside and soft all the way through.

Heat a baking sheet in a preheated 475°F (240°C) oven. Place 1 pizza dough ball on a well-floured, 9-inch (23 cm) pizza pan. Push down on the dough with your fingertips, pressing it out to fill the pan, leaving the border slightly thicker. If you get any tears, forcefully pinch the dough around the hole back together.

Spoon 2 tablespoons (30 ml) of the tomato sauce mixture over the base, top with a quarter of the eggplant, then scatter with a quarter each of the cheeses. Brush the border with oil to glaze. Remove the heated baking sheet from the oven, slide the pan onto it, then quickly return to the oven. Bake for 7–8 minutes, until it is crisp and has risen. Serve immediately, garnished with basil leaves. As the first pizza cooks, prepare the next for the oven.

WATCHING MY WEIGHT
Pizza scrolls

Makes 8
Preparation time: 25 minutes, plus proving
Cooking time: 12–15 minutes

   2 packages (about ¼ ounce /7 g each) fast-acting dried yeast
   1 teaspoon (5 ml) granulated sugar
   1 cup (250 ml) milk, warmed
   1¼ cups (300 ml) rice flour, plus extra for dusting
   ¾ cup (175 ml) potato flour
   1 teaspoon (5 ml) baking powder
   1 teaspoon (5 ml) xanthan gum
   1 pinch of salt
   1 tablespoon (15 ml) sunflower oil
   1 egg, beaten

   FOR THE FILLING
   4 tablespoons (60 ml) tomato sauce
   7 ounces (200 g) grated mixed cheese, such as mozzarella
      and Cheddar
   3 ounces (75 g) wafer-thin ham, shredded
   1 handful of fresh basil, chopped

Place the yeast, sugar and milk in a bowl and set aside for about
10 minutes, until frothy. In a large bowl, stir together the flours,
baking powder, xanthan gum and salt.

Mix the oil and egg into the yeast mixture and pour this into
the flour mixture, using a fork to bring the mixture together. Tip
it out onto a surface dusted lightly with rice flour and knead for
5 minutes, adding a little flour if the mixture becomes sticky.
Place in a lightly oiled bowl, cover with a damp cloth and leave
to rise in a warm place for about 40 minutes or until well risen.

Roll the dough out on the floured surface into a rectangle
approximately 12 x 10 inches (30 x 25 cm). Spread with the
tomato sauce, then sprinkle over the other fillings. Roll the pizza
up from one long edge, then slice into 8 pieces.

Arrange the rolled-up pizza scrolls side by side on a lightly
oiled heavy rimmed baking sheet or pan. They should be pushed
up against each other so the sides are touching. Place in a
preheated 425°F (220°C) oven for 12–15 minutes, until golden.
Eat warm from the oven.

INSPIRE ME
Asparagus & Taleggio pizza

Makes 2
Preparation time: 15 minutes, plus rising
Cooking time: 10–15 minutes per pizza

   cooking spray, for oiling
   1 recipe Basic Pizza Dough (see page 7)
   white bread flour, for dusting
   5 tablespoons (75 ml) tomato sauce
   1 tablespoon (15 ml) ready-made red pesto
   1 pinch of salt
   8 ounces (250 g) Taleggio cheese, sliced
   6 ounces (175 g) slim asparagus, trimmed
   2 tablespoons (30 ml) olive oil
   black pepper

Lightly oil a bowl with cooking spray. Turn the dough out on a
lightly floured work surface. Knead for 10 minutes until smooth
and elastic. Put in the prepared bowl, cover and leave to rise in a
warm place for 1 hour until doubled in size.

Put a heavy-based baking sheet on the middle shelf of
a preheated 450°F (230°C) oven and heat for 5 minutes.
Meanwhile, mix the tomato sauce, pesto and salt together in a
bowl.

Knock the air out of the dough. Divide in half. Roll one half
out to a 25-cm (10 inch) round. Transfer to the heated baking
sheet. Spread half the tomato sauce mixture over the pizza base.
Top with half the Taleggio slices and asparagus and drizzle with
half the oil. Bake for 10–15 minutes until the base is crisp and
golden. Season with pepper and serve immediately. Repeat to
make the second pizza.

10 WAYS WITH LASAGNA

1

BASIC
Classic meat lasagna

Serves 6–8
Preparation time: 20 minutes, plus infusing
Cooking time: 27–35 minutes

> 3 cups (750 ml) milk
> 1 bay leaf
> ¼ cup (60 ml) unsalted butter
> ⅓ cup + 1 tablespoon (90 ml) all-purpose flour
> large pinch of freshly grated nutmeg
> 1 pound (500 g) Bolognese sauce
> 8 ounces (250 g) dried lasagna sheets or 1 recipe 2-Egg Pasta
>   Dough (see page 7), rolled out to lasagna sheets
> 5 tablespoons (75 ml) freshly grated Parmesan cheese
> salt and pepper

Make the béchamel sauce. Bring the milk and bay leaf to a simmer. Take off the heat and infuse for 20 minutes. Strain. Melt the butter over very low heat. Add the flour and cook, stirring continuously, for 2 minutes until a light biscuity color. Remove from the heat and slowly add the infused milk, stirring away lumps as you go. Return to the heat and simmer, stirring continuously, for 2–3 minutes. Add the nutmeg and season.

If your bolognese was made earlier, reheat. Meanwhile, cook the pasta, in batches, in salted boiling water until al dente (according to package instructions for dried pasta or for 2 minutes if using fresh). Drain, refresh in cold water and lay on a tea towel.

Cover the base of an ovenproof dish with one-third of the bolognese, top with a layer of pasta and cover with half the remaining bolognese, then one-third of the béchamel. Repeat with a layer of pasta, the remaining Bolognese and half the remaining béchamel. Finish with the remaining pasta, then the remaining béchamel and scatter with Parmesan. Bake in a preheated 425°F (220°C) oven for 20 minutes, until golden brown.

2

GIVE IT A TWIST
Chicken & mushroom lasagna

Serves 4–6
Preparation time: 45 minutes
Cooking time: 1 hour 25 minutes

> 8 chicken thighs
> ⅔ cup (150 ml) dry white wine
> 1¼ cups (300 ml) chicken stock (see page 9)
> few stems fresh thyme
> 2 tablespoons (30 ml) olive oil
> 2 onions, thinly sliced
> 2 cloves garlic, finely chopped
> 3½ ounces (100 g) exotic mushrooms
> 4 ounces (125 g) shiitake mushrooms, sliced
> ¼ cup (60 ml) butter
> ⅓ cup + 1 tablespoon (90 ml) all-purpose flour
> ¾ cup + 2 tablespoons (200 ml) whipping (35%) cream
> 8 ounces (250 g) package of 6 fresh lasagna sheets
> 1½ ounces (40 g) Parmesan cheese, freshly grated
> salt and pepper

Pack the chicken into the base of a saucepan, add the wine, stock and thyme and season. Bring to a boil, cover and simmer for 45 minutes until tender.

Meanwhile, heat the oil in a frying pan, add the onions and fry for 5 minutes, until golden. Mix in the garlic and cook for 2–3 minutes, then add the mushrooms and fry for another 2–3 minutes.

Lift the chicken out of the pan, drain and set aside. Pour the stock into a measuring cup. Make up to 2⅓ cups (575 ml) with water if needed. Wash and dry the pan, then melt the butter in it. Stir in the flour, then whisk in the stock and bring to a boil, stirring continuously, until thickened. Stir in the cream and adjust the seasoning, if needed.

Soak the lasagna sheets in boiling water for 5 minutes. Skin and bone the chicken and dice the meat. Drain the lasagna sheets.

Pour a thin layer of sauce into the base of a 8 x 11 x 2-inch (20 x 28 x 5 cm) ovenproof dish, then cover with 2 sheets of the lasagna. Spoon over half the mushroom mixture and half the chicken, then cover with a thin layer of sauce. Repeat the layers, then cover with the remaining lasagna and sauce. Sprinkle with the Parmesan and set aside until required.

Cook in a preheated 375°F (190°C) oven for 40 minutes, until the top is golden. Serve with salad and garlic bread.

3 🕐

SAVE ME TIME
Tuna layered lasagna with arugula

Serves 4
Preparation time: 10 minutes
Cooking time: 10 minutes

> 8 dried lasagna sheets
> 1 tablespoon (15 ml) olive oil
> 1 bunch green onions, sliced
> 2 zucchinis, diced
> 1 pound (500 g) cherry tomatoes, quartered
> 2 cans (each 6 ounces/170 g) tuna in water, drained
> 2½ ounces 65 g) wild arugula
> 4 teaspoons (20 ml) ready-made green pesto
> pepper
> fresh basil leaves, to garnish

Cook the pasta sheets, in batches, in a large saucepan of salted boiling water according to the package instructions, until al dente. Drain and return to the pan to keep warm.

Meanwhile, heat the oil in a frying pan over medium heat, add the green onions and zucchini and cook, stirring continuously, for 3 minutes. Remove from the heat, add the tomatoes, tuna and arugula and gently toss together.

Place a little of the tuna mixture on 4 serving plates and top with a pasta sheet. Spoon over the remaining tuna mixture, then top with the remaining pasta sheets. Season with plenty of pepper and top with a spoonful of pesto and some basil leaves.

4

SAVE ME MONEY
Goat cheese & pepper lasagna

Serves 4
Preparation time: 20 minutes, plus standing
Cooking time: 50 minutes–1 hour

> 1 can or jar (11 ounces/325 ml) of pimientos
> 6 tomatoes, skinned and roughly chopped
> 1 yellow bell pepper, seeded and finely chopped
> 2 zucchini, thinly sliced
> 3 ounces (75 g) sun-dried tomatoes, thinly sliced
> 3½ ounces (100 g) sun-dried tomato pesto
> ⅔ cup (150 ml)) basil
> 4 tablespoons (60 ml) olive oil
> 5 ounces (150 g) soft fresh goat cheese
> 2⅓ cups (575 ml) store-bought or homemade cheese sauce
> 5 ounces (150 g) dried egg lasagna
> 6 tablespoons (90 ml) grated Parmesan cheese
> salt and pepper

Drain the pimientos and roughly chop. Mix in a bowl with the tomatoes, yellow pepper, zucchini, sun-dried tomatoes and pesto. Tear the basil leaves and add to the bowl with the oil and a little salt and pepper. Mix the ingredients together thoroughly.

Spoon a quarter of the ingredients into a 7-cup (1.75 L) shallow, ovenproof dish and dot with a quarter of the goat cheese and 4 tablespoons (60 ml) of the cheese sauce. Cover with one-third of the lasagna sheets in a layer, breaking them to fit where necessary. Repeat the layering, finishing with a layer of the tomato mixture and goat cheese.

Spoon the remaining cheese sauce on top and sprinkle with the Parmesan. Bake in a preheated 375°F (190°C) oven for 50–60 minutes, until deep golden. Leave to stand for 10 minutes before serving with a leafy salad.

KIDS WILL LOVE THIS
Mushroom & spinach lasagna

Serves 4
Preparation time: 20 minutes, plus standing
Cooking time: 25–30 minutes

- 8 ounces (250 g) package of 6 fresh lasagna sheets
- 3 tablespoons (45 ml) olive oil
- 1 pound (500 g) mixed mushrooms such as shiitake, oyster and chestnut, sliced
- 2 cloves garlic, finely chopped
- 7 ounces (200 g) mascarpone cheese
- 4 ounces (125 g) baby spinach leaves
- 5 ounces (150 g) Taleggio cheese, rinf removed, cut into cubes
- salt and pepper

Place the lasagna a sheets in a large roasting pan and cover with boiling water. Leave to stand for 5 minutes or until tender, then drain off the water.

Heat the oil in a large frying pan and fry the mushrooms for 5 minutes. Add the garlic and mascarpone and turn up the heat. Cook for another minute, until the sauce is thick. Season with salt and pepper. Steam the spinach for 2 minutes or microwave until just wilted.

Oil an ovenproof dish about the size of two of the lasagna sheets and place 2 lasagna sheets over the base, slightly overlapping. Reserve one-third of the Taleggio for the top, sprinkle a little over the pasta base with one-third of the mushroom sauce and one-third of the spinach leaves. Repeat with two more layers, topping the final layer of lasagna sheets with the remaining mushroom sauce, spinach and Taleggio.

Bake in a preheated 400°F (200°C) oven for 15–20 minutes, until golden and piping hot.

THERE ARE SO MANY ALTERNATIVES TO GROUND BEEF WHEN MAKING LASAGNA — WHY NOT EXPERIMENT?

LEFTOVER TO LUNCH
Open seafood lasagna

Serves 4
Preparation time: 30 minutes
Cooking time: 35 minutes

- 2 tablespoons (30 ml) extra virgin olive oil, plus extra for drizzling
- 1 small onion, finely chopped
- 1 fennel bulb, trimmed and finely chopped
- 2 cloves garlic, crushed
- ¾ cup + 2 tablespoons (200 ml) dry white wine
- 1 cup (250 ml) canned chopped tomatoes
- 1 recipe 1-Egg Pasta Dough (see page 7)
- all-purpose flour, for dusting
- 1 handful of fresh flat-leaf parsley leaves
- 8 ounces (250 g) chunky white fish fillets, such as cod, halibut or monkfish
- 8 ounces (250 g) delicate white fish fillets, such as red mullet, red snapper, sea bass or sea bream
- 12 raw peeled jumbo shrimp
- 6 fresh basil leaves, torn, plus extra to garnish
- salt and pepper

Heat the oil in a large, heavy-bottomed saucepan over low heat. Add the onion and fennel and cook for 8–10 minutes, until softened. Add the garlic and cook, stirring continuously, for 1 minute. Add the wine and boil rapidly for 1 minute. Add the tomatoes and season. Bring to a boil, then simmer gently for 20 minutes.

Meanwhile, roll the pasta dough out into long sheets (see page 7). Scatter half the length of each sheet with parsley, then fold over to cover. Run through the thinnest setting of the pasta machine, then cut into 12 rectangles. Lay on a floured tray, adding a dusting of flour between any that overlap.

Cut the fish fillets into 1½-inch (3.5 cm) pieces. Add the chunky fish to the sauce and simmer gently for 1 minute. Add the delicate fish and shrimp and simmer gently for 1 minute. Remove from the heat, stir in the basil and cover.

Cook the pasta sheets, in batches, in a large saucepan of boiling salted water for 2–3 minutes, until al dente. Drain, drizzle with oil and garnish with basil leaves.

Place a pasta sheet on each plate and top with half the sauce. Repeat, finishing with a pasta sheet. Serve with a drizzle of oil.

Vegetable lasagna

Serves 4
Preparation time: 10 minutes
Cooking time: 1 hour and 15 minutes, plus standing

> 2 tablespoons (30 ml) vegetable oil
> 5 ounces (150 g) slender green beans, chopped
> 1 onion, thinly sliced
> 1 can (14 ounces/398 ml) chopped tomatoes
> ½ cup (125 ml) split red lentils, picked over, rinsed and drained
> 1¼ cups (300 ml) water
> 1 pinch of dried oregano
> 1 pound (500 g) cream cheese
> 2 eggs, beaten
> 4 ounces (125 g) cooked lasagna sheets
> 2 tablespoons (30 ml) freshly grated Parmesan cheese
> salt and pepper

Heat the oil in a saucepan over low heat and fry the beans and onion for 5 minutes, until the onion is soft and translucent.

Sprinkle with salt and pepper, then add the tomatoes, lentils, water and oregano. Bring to a boil. Simmer for about 30 minutes or until the lentils are tender but not mushy.
Mix together the cream cheese and beaten eggs in a bowl.

Spread half the vegetable and lentil mixture over the bottom of a large ovenproof dish, then cover with one-third of the lasagna sheets. Pour over half the cheese mixture, then cover with another layer of lasagna sheets. Make a layer with the remaining vegetable and lentil mixture, cover with the remaining lasagna sheets and, finally, with the rest of the cheese mixture.

Sprinkle with the Parmesan and bake in a preheated 350°F (180°C) oven for 40 minutes. Remove from the oven and leave to stand for 5 minutes before cutting into slices and serving.

WHY NOT TRY... BEEF LASAGNA

Fry the sliced onion in the oil for 5 minutes until soft, omitting the French beans. Increase the heat slightly and add 1 pound (500 g) ground beef. Cook, stirring and breaking up the meat with a wooden spoon, until the mince is browned. Stir in 2 chopped cloves garlic, ½ teaspoon (2 ml) dried oregano and 1 tablespoon (15 ml) all-purpose flour, then mix in the chopped tomatoes and ¾ cup (175 ml) beef stock (see page 9). Simmer gently for 45 minutes, stirring now and then, until the meat is tender. Layer in an ovenproof dish with the lasagna and cream cheese mixture and cook as above.

Wild mushroom lasagna

Serves 6
Preparation time: 20 minutes, plus cooling
Cooking time: 45 minutes

> 7 tablespoons (100 ml) unsalted butter, plus extra for greasing
> 4 tablespoons (60 ml) all-purpose flour
> 4 cups (1 L) milk
> 1 large pinch of freshly grated nutmeg
> 3 tablespoons (45 ml) roughly chopped fresh flat-leaf parsley
> 5 tablespoons (75 ml) freshly grated Parmesan cheese
> 1 tablespoon (15 ml) olive oil
> 1¼ pound (625 g) mixed wild mushrooms, trimmed and thickly sliced
> 1 clove garlic, crushed
> ¾ + 2 tablespoons (100 ml) dry white wine
> 1 ounces (25 g) dried porcini mushrooms, soaked in ¾ + 2 tablespoons (100 ml) hot water for 10 minutes
> 300 g (10 oz) fresh lasagna sheets
> truffle oil, for drizzling
> salt and pepper

Melt half the butter in a saucepan over a low heat. Add the flour and cook, stirring with a wooden spoon, for 1–2 minutes, until a pale biscuity color. Remove from the heat and gradually stir in the milk until smooth. Return to medium heat and cook, stirring constantly, until thick and velvety. Add the nutmeg and season with salt and pepper, then stir in the parsley and 2 tablespoons (30 ml) of the Parmesan. Remove from the heat and leave to cool to room temperature.

Melt the remaining butter with the oil in a large, heavy frying pan. Add the fresh mushrooms and cook over high heat for 2 minutes. Stir in the garlic and cook for 1 minute. Season with salt and pepper. Pour in the wine and porcini with the water they were soaking in. Cook, stirring continuously, until the liquid has evaporated. Stir into the white sauce.

Grease an ovenproof dish, about 8 x 12 inches (20 x 30 cm). Cover the base with a layer of slightly overlapping lasagna sheets. Top with a quarter of the sauce, then continue layering, finishing with a layer of sauce. Scatter with the remaining Parmesan. Bake in a preheated 400°F (200°C) oven for 30 minutes. Drizzle lightly with truffle oil and serve with a green salad, if desired.

9

WATCHING MY WEIGHT
Lean lasagna

Serves 8
Preparation time: 30 minutes
Cooking time: about 1 hour

> 7 ounces (200 g) precooked sheets of lasagna
> pepper
>
> **FOR THE MEAT SAUCE**
> 2 eggplants, peeled and diced
> 2 red onions, chopped
> 2 cloves garlic, crushed
> 1¼ cups (300 ml) vegetable stock (see page 8)
> 4 tablespoons (60 ml) red wine
> 1 pound (500 g) extra-lean ground beef
> 2 cans (each 14 ounces/398 ml) chopped tomatoes
>
> **FOR THE CHEESE SAUCE**
> 3 egg whites
> 8 ounces (250 g) ricotta cheese
> ¾ cup (175 ml) milk
> 6 tablespoons (90 ml) freshly grated Parmesan cheese

Make the meat sauce. Place the eggplants, onions, garlic, stock and wine in a large nonstick saucepan. Cover and simmer briskly for 5 minutes.

Uncover and cook for about 5 minutes, until the eggplant is tender and the liquid is absorbed, adding a little more stock if necessary. Remove from the heat, allow to cool slightly, then purée in a food processor or blender.

Meanwhile, brown the beef in a nonstick frying pan. Skim off any fat. Add the eggplant mixture, tomatoes and pepper to taste. Simmer briskly, uncovered, for about 10 minutes, until thickened.

Make the cheese sauce. Beat the egg whites with the ricotta, then beat in the milk and 4 tablespoons (60 ml) of Parmesan. Season to taste with pepper.

Alternate layers of meat sauce, lasagna and cheese sauce in an ovenproof dish. Start with meat sauce and finish with cheese sauce. Sprinkle the top layer of cheese sauce with the remaining Parmesan. Bake in a preheated 350°F (180°C) oven for 30–40 minutes, until browned.

10

INSPIRE ME
Parma ham lasagna

Serves 8
Preparation time: 25 minutes, plus soaking and infusing
Cooking time: 35–40 minutes

> ¾ ounce (20 g) dried porcini mushrooms
> 3 cups (750 ml) milk
> 1 bay leaf
> 1 small onion, quartered
> ½ cup (125 ml) unsalted butter
> ¼ cup (60 ml) all-purpose flour
> ¾ cup (175 ml) half-and-half (10%) cream
> ¼ teaspoon (1 ml) freshly grated nutmeg
> 7 ounces (200 g) Parma ham, 4 whole slices, remainder torn into
>   strips
> 3 tablespoons (45 ml) olive oil
> 11 ounces (325 g) chestnut or cremini mushrooms, chopped
> ¼ cup (60 ml) dry white wine
> 8 ounces (250 g) dried lasagna sheets
> 5 tablespoons (75 ml) freshly grated Parmesan cheese
> salt and pepper

Soak the porcini in a little boiling water for 30 minutes.

Meanwhile, bring the milk with the bay leaf and onion to a simmer. Take off the heat and infuse for 20 minutes. Strain.

Melt ¼ cup (60 ml) of the butter in a saucepan over very low heat. Add the flour and cook, stirring continuously, for 2 minutes, until a light biscuity color. Remove from the heat and slowly add the infused milk, stirring away any lumps as you go. Return to the heat and simmer, stirring continuously, for 2–3 minutes, until creamy. Add the cream, nutmeg and ham strips. Season with salt and pepper.

Drain the porcini, reserving the soaking water, and chop. Heat the oil in a frying pan over high heat, add all the mushrooms and cook for 1 minute. Add the soaking water and wine. Boil rapidly until absorbed. Season and stir into the sauce.

Cook the pasta sheets, in batches, in boiling salted water according to the package instructions, until just al dente. Refresh in cold water. Drain on a tea towel.

Lightly grease an ovenproof dish. Cover the base with a layer of pasta. Top with a quarter of the sauce. Dot with a quarter of the remaining butter, then scatter with 1 tablespoon (15 ml) Parmesan. Repeat, finishing with a layer of sauce topped with the ham slices and remaining butter and Parmesan. Bake in a preheated 425°F (220°C) oven for 20 minutes, until browned.

10 WAYS WITH RAVIOLI

1

BASIC
Tomato & cream ravioli

Serves 4
Preparation time: 10 minutes
Cooking time: 25 minutes

- 1 tablespoon (15 ml) unsalted butter
- 1 tablespoon (15 ml) olive oil
- ½ onion, finely chopped
- ½ stalk celery, finely chopped
- 1½ cups (375 ml) tomato sauce
- 1 large pinch of granulated sugar
- 8 ounces (250 g) fresh spinach and ricotta ravioli
- ⅓ cup + 2 tablespoons (100 ml) whipping (35%) cream
- 1 large pinch of freshly grated nutmeg
- salt and pepper
- fresh Parmesan cheese shavings, to serve
- fresh basil leaves, to garnish

Melt the butter with the oil in a heavy-bottomed saucepan over low heat. Add the onion and celery and cook, stirring occasionally, for 10 minutes, until softened but not colored. Stir in the tomato sauce and sugar and bring to a boil. Reduce the heat and gently simmer, uncovered, for 10 minutes, until thickened. Season with salt and pepper.

Cook the ravioli in a large saucepan of salted boiling water according to the package instructions, until al dente. Meanwhile, add the cream to the sauce and bring to a boil. Stir in the nutmeg and remove from the heat.

Drain the pasta thoroughly and transfer to a serving dish. Spoon the sauce over and serve immediately with a scattering of Parmesan shavings and garnished with basil leaves.

2

GIVE IT A TWIST
Arugula, potato & lemon ravioli

Serves 4
Preparation time: 25 minutes
Cooking time: 1 hour 5 minutes

- 1 pound (500 g) floury potatoes, such as King Edwards or Maris Piper
- 3 tablespoons (45 ml) freshly grated Parmesan cheese
- 3 ounces (75 g) wild arugula leaves, plus extra to serve
- finely grated zest of 1 unwaxed lemon
- ½ cup (125 ml) butter
- 1 large pinch of freshly grated nutmeg
- 1 recipe 3-Egg Pasta Dough (see page 7)
- all-purpose flour, for dusting
- salt and pepper
- fresh Parmesan cheese shavings, to serve

Prick the potatoes all over with a fork and put on a large baking sheet. Bake in a preheated 425°F (220°C) oven for 1 hour, or until cooked through — to test, pierce the largest potato with a blunt knife.

When cool enough to handle, halve the potatoes and scoop the flesh out into a bowl. Mash in the Parmesan, arugula, lemon zest and half the butter. Add the nutmeg and season with salt and pepper.

Roll the pasta dough out into long sheets (see page 7). Working on one sheet at a time, add a heaped teaspoonful of filling every 2 inches (5 cm) until half the sheet is filled. Lightly brush with water and fold the empty side over the filling. Gently but firmly push down between the filling, sealing the pasta and ensuring there is no trapped air. Cut into squares or rounds using a pastry wheel, crinkle cutter or cookie cutter. Transfer to a floured baking sheet and cover with a tea towel.

Cook the pasta in a large saucepan of salted boiling water for 2–3 minutes, until al dente. Drain, reserving a ladleful of the cooking water.

Meanwhile, melt the remaining butter in a large frying pan over low heat. Add the ravioli and its reserved cooking water and simmer gently until coated in a silky sauce. Serve immediately with a scattering of Parmesan shavings and arugula.

3 🕐

SAVE ME TIME
Spinach & ricotta ravioli

Serves 4
Preparation time: 25 minutes
Cooking time: 2–3 minutes

> 1 pound (500 g) frozen spinach, defrosted and squeezed dry
> 6 ounces (175 g) ricotta or curd cheese
> ½ teaspoon (2 ml) freshly grated nutmeg
> 1 teaspoon (5 ml) salt
> 1 recipe 3-Egg Pasta Dough (see page 7)
> fine all-purpose flour, for dusting
> ½ cup (125 ml) butter, melted
> pepper
> freshly grated Parmesan cheese, to serve

Put the spinach and ricotta or cottage cheese in a food processor with the nutmeg, salt and pepper to taste and process until smooth. Cover and refrigerate while you roll out the pasta dough.

Roll the pasta dough out into long sheets (see page 7). Working on one sheet at a time, add a heaped teaspoonful (5 ml) of filling every 2 inches (5 cm) until half the sheet is filled. Lightly brush with water and fold the empty side over the filling. Gently but firmly push down between the filling, sealing the pasta and ensuring that there is no trapped air. Cut into squares using a pastry wheel, crinkle cutter or sharp knife, or cut into semicircles with the top of a glass. Transfer to a floured baking sheet and cover with a tea towel.

Cook the pasta in a large saucepan of salted boiling water for 2–3 minutes, until al dente. Drain thoroughly, return to the pan and toss with the melted butter. Divide between 4 warmed serving plates and serve immediately with a scattering of grated Parmesan.

4

SAVE ME MONEY
Tortellini with creamy ham & peas

Serves 4
Preparation time: 2 minutes
Cooking time: 8–12 minutes

> 1 tablespoon (15 ml) unsalted butter
> 1¼ cups (300 ml) peas, defrosted if frozen
> 3 ounces (75 g) ham, cut into strips
> 1¼ cups (300 ml) crème fraîche or sour cream
> 1 large pinch of freshly grated nutmeg
> 1 pound (500 g) fresh spinach and ricotta or meat tortellini
> 1½ ounces (40 g) Parmesan cheese, freshly grated, plus extra to serve
> salt and pepper

Melt the butter in a large frying pan over medium heat until it begins to sizzle. Add the peas and ham and cook, stirring continuously, for 3–4 minutes if using fresh peas, or just 1 minute if using defrosted frozen peas.

Stir in the crème fraîche, add the nutmeg and season with salt and pepper. Bring to a boil and boil for 2 minutes, until slightly thickened.

Cook the tortellini in a large saucepan of salted boiling water according to the package instructions until it is al dente. Drain and toss into the creamy sauce with the Parmesan. Gently stir to combine and serve at once with a scattering of Parmesan.

FILLED PASTA SUCH AS RAVIOLI MAKES AN ELEGANT DISH WHEN ENTERTAINING FRIENDS.

5

KIDS WILL LOVE THIS

Duck tortellini

Serves 4
Preparation time: 40 minutes
Cooking time: 1 hour and 30 minutes

2 tablespoons (30 ml) unsalted butter
1 tablespoon (15 ml) olive oil
1 small onion, finely chopped
2 stalks celery, finely chopped
1 carrot, finely chopped
¾ cup (175 ml) dry white wine
finely grated zest and juice of 1 orange
2 tablespoons (30 ml) chopped fresh thyme
1 cup (250 ml) canned chopped tomatoes
2 skinless duck legs, about 6–7 ounces (175–200 g) each
2 tablespoons (30 ml) freshly grated Parmesan cheese, plus extra
   to serve
2 tablespoons (30 ml) fresh white breadcrumbs
1 egg
1 recipe 3-Egg Pasta Dough (see page 7)
fine all-purpose flour, for dusting
salt and pepper
chopped fresh flat-leaf parsley, to serve

Melt the butter with the oil in a large, heavy-bottomed saucepan over low heat. Add the onion, celery and carrot and cook for 10 minutes. Add the wine and boil for 1 minute. Add the orange zest and juice, thyme and tomatoes. Return to a boil.

Season the duck with salt and pepper. Add to the sauce and simmer gently, covered, for 1¼ hours, until the meat flakes off the bone. Remove, then shred the flesh off the bone. Process in a food processor until finely chopped. Mix with the Parmesan, breadcrumbs and egg.

Roll the pasta dough out into long sheets (see page 7). Cut into 3¼-inch (8 cm) squares. Place a small ball of filling in the center of each. Brush the edges with water, then fold the dough over the filling to make triangles. Gently but firmly push down between the filling to seal, ensuring that there is no trapped air. Bring the corners on the longest edge together and pinch tightly. Transfer to a floured baking sheet and cover with a tea towel.

Cook in a large saucepan of salted boiling water for 3–4 minutes, until al dente. Meanwhile, reheat the sauce. Drain the pasta. Serve immediately with the sauce and a scattering of grated Parmesan and parsley.

6 ⊕

LEFTOVER TO LUNCH

Feel-good broth

Serves 4
Preparation time: 2 minutes, plus cooling
Cooking time: 25 minutes

2 boneless skinless chicken breasts, about 10 oz (300 g) in total
3½ cups (875 ml) cold chicken stock (see page 9)
1 slice lemon
2 teaspoons (10 ml) roughly chopped fresh thyme
8 ounces (250 g) fresh meat cappelletti or small tortellini
salt and pepper
freshly grated Parmesan cheese, to serve

Put the chicken breasts, stock, lemon slice and thyme in a large saucepan. Bring to a very gentle simmer — the water should shiver rather than bubble in the pan. Cover and cook for 15–16 minutes, until the chicken is opaque all the way through. Lift the chicken from the liquid with a slotted spoon and transfer to a plate. Remove the lemon slice.

When the chicken is cool enough to handle, shred into large pieces.

Bring the stock to a rapid boil and season with salt and pepper. Add the pasta and cook for 2–3 minutes, adding the shredded chicken for the last minute of the cooking time. Serve immediately with a generous scattering of grated Parmesan.

7

BUT I DON'T LIKE ...
RAVIOLI

Warm ravioli salad with beets

Serves 4
Preparation time: 10 minutes, plus cooling
Cooking time: 12 minutes

> 4 tablespoons (60 ml) extra virgin olive oil
> 2 red onions, thinly sliced
> 2 cloves garlic, thinly sliced
> 1 pound (500 g) fresh spinach and ricotta ravioli
> 1 can (13 ounces/385 ml) beets in natural juices, drained and diced
> 2 tablespoons (30 ml) capers in brine, rinsed and drained
> 2 tablespoons (30 ml) good-quality aged balsamic vinegar
> salt
>
> **TO SERVE**
> mixed bitter salad leaves, such as chicory, radicchio, arugula and frisée
> fresh parsley sprigs
> fresh basil leaves
> fresh pecorino cheese shavings (optional)

Heat 2 tablespoons (30 ml) of the oil in a large frying pan over medium heat, add the onions and garlic and cook, stirring occasionally, for 10 minutes, until golden.

Meanwhile, cook the pasta in a large saucepan of salted boiling water according to the package instructions, until al dente. Drain and gently toss with the remaining oil.

Add the beets, capers and vinegar to the onions and garlic in the pan and heat through. Stir into the pasta. Transfer to a large bowl, including all the juices from the pan, and leave to cool for 5 minutes.

Arrange the ravioli in serving bowls or on plates with the salad leaves and herbs. Serve with a scattering of pecorino shavings, if desired.

WHY NOT TRY... PENNE SALAD WITH BEETS & RICOTTA

Replace the ravioli with 7 ounces (200 g) penne. Cook the pasta and combine with the sauce, as above, then finish with 3½ ounces (100 g) crumbled ricotta cheese.

8

FRIENDS FOR DINNER
Wild mushroom ravioli

Serves 4
Preparation time: 35 minutes
Cooking time: 10–11 minutes

> 2 tablespoons (30 ml) olive oil
> 2 shallots, finely chopped
> 8 ounces (250 g) mixed wild mushrooms, finely chopped
> 1 ounces (25 g) Greek-style black olives, pitted and finely chopped
> 4 sun-dried tomato halves in oil, drained and chopped
> 1 tablespoon (15 ml) dry Marsala
> freshly grated nutmeg
> 1 recipe 2-Egg Pasta Dough (see page 7), with 4 tablespoons (60 ml) mixed chopped fresh tarragon, marjoram and parsley
> fine all-purpose flour, for dusting
> 2 ounces (50 g) butter, melted
> salt and pepper
> fresh herb sprigs, to garnish
>
> **TO SERVE**
> fresh Parmesan shavings
> sautéed wild mushrooms

Heat the oil in a frying pan over medium heat, add the shallots and cook, stirring frequently, for 5 minutes or until soft and golden. Add the mushrooms, olives and tomatoes and cook over high heat, stirring continuously, for 2 minutes. Sprinkle with the Marsala and cook for a further minute. Season well with salt, pepper and nutmeg. Transfer to a bowl and leave to cool.

Roll the pasta dough out into long sheets (see page 7). Working on one sheet at a time, add a heaped teaspoonful (5 ml) of filling every 1½ inches (4 cm) until half the sheet is filled. Lightly brush with water and fold the empty side over the filling. Gently but firmly push down between the filling, sealing the pasta and ensuring that there is no trapped air. Cut into squares using a pastry wheel, crinkle cutter or sharp knife. Transfer to a floured baking sheet and cover with a tea towel.

Cook the pasta in a large pan of salted boiling water for 2–3 minutes, until al dente. Drain thoroughly, return to the pan and toss with the melted butter. Divide between 4 warmed serving plates and serve at once with a scattering of Parmesan shavings and sautéed wild mushrooms, garnished with herb sprigs.

9

WATCHING MY WEIGHT
Italian tortellini in brodo

Serves 6
Preparation time: 10 minutes
Cooking time: about 10 minutes

> 1 pound (500 g) tomatoes
> 6 cups (1.5 L) chicken stock (see page 9)
> ¾ cup (175 ml) dry white wine
> 1 tablespoon (15 ml) sun-dried tomato paste
> 1 small bunch fresh basil, roughly torn into pieces
> 10 ounces (300 g) spinach and ricotta tortellini, or filling
>   of your choice
> 6 tablespoons (90 ml) freshly grated Parmesan cheese, plus extra
>   to serve
> salt and pepper

Make a cross cut in the base of each tomato, put into a bowl and cover with boiling water. Leave to soak for 1 minute, then drain and peel away the skins. Quarter the tomatoes, scoop out the seeds and dice the flesh.

Put the tomatoes into a saucepan, add the stock, wine and tomato paste, season with salt and pepper and bring to a boil. Simmer gently for 5 minutes.

Add half the basil and all the pasta, bring back to a boil and cook for 3–4 minutes, until the pasta is just cooked. Stir in the Parmesan, taste and adjust the seasoning if needed. Ladle into bowls, serve with a little extra grated Parmesan and garnish with the remaining basil leaves.

10

INSPIRE ME
Homemade pasta with squash & sage

Serves 4
Preparation time: 30 minutes
Cooking time: 25 minutes

> 8 ounces (250 g) winter squash flesh, cubed
> 1 clove garlic, crushed
> 2 sprigs fresh sage
> 2 tablespoons (30 ml) extra virgin olive oil
> 3 ounces (75 g) ricotta cheese
> 1 ounces (25 g) Parmesan cheese, grated, plus extra to serve
> 1 recipe 2-Egg Pasta Dough (see page 7)
> fine all-purpose flour, for dusting
> ⅓ cup (75 ml) butter
> 2 tablespoons (30 ml) whole sage leaves
> salt and pepper
> lemon juice, to serve

Put the squash in a small roasting pan with the garlic, sage sprigs and oil. Season with salt and pepper. Cover loosely with foil and roast in a preheated 400°F (200°C) oven for 20 minutes, until soft. Transfer to a bowl, mash well and leave to cool.

Once cold, beat the ricotta and Parmesan into the squash purée and season with salt and pepper to taste.

Roll the pasta dough out into thin sheets (see page 7). Cut into 3¼-inch (8 cm) squares. Place a spoonful of the filling in the center of each. Brush the edges with water, then fold the dough over the filling to make triangles. Gently but firmly push down between the filling to seal, ensuring that there is no trapped air. Transfer to a floured baking sheet and cover with a tea towel.

Cook the pasta in a large saucepan of salted boiling water for 3–4 minutes, until al dente. Meanwhile, melt the butter with the sage leaves and pepper until it just begins to turn a nutty brown color. Drain the pasta and serve immediately, bathed in the sage butter, with a squeeze of lemon juice and a scattering of grated Parmesan.

10 WAYS WITH SPAGHETTI

BASIC
Spaghetti with easy tomato sauce

Serves 4
Preparation time: 5 minutes
Cooking time: 30 minutes

> 13 ounces (400 g) dried spaghetti
> salt and pepper
> 3 tablespoons (45 ml) freshly grated Parmesan cheese, to serve
>
> **FOR THE EASY TOMATO SAUCE**
> 1 can (28 ounces/796 ml) chopped tomatoes
> 2 tablespoons (30 ml) extra virgin olive oil
> 2 large cloves garlic, crushed
> 1 teaspoon (5 ml) granulated sugar
> ¼ teaspoon (1 ml) hot pepper flakes
> 2 tablespoons (30 ml) chopped fresh basil

Start by making the sauce. Place the tomatoes, oil, garlic, sugar, chili and some salt and pepper in a saucepan and bring to a boil. Lower the heat and simmer gently for 20–30 minutes, until thickened and full of flavor.

Stir in the basil and adjust the seasoning. Keep warm.

Meanwhile, plunge the pasta into a saucepan of lightly salted boiling water, bring back to a boil and cook until al dente or according to the package instructions.

Drain the pasta and divide between bowls, spoon on the sauce and serve with grated Parmesan.

GIVE IT A TWIST
Pesto Trapenese

Serves 4
Preparation time: 10 minutes
Cooking time: 10–12 minutes

> 13 ounces (400 g) dried spaghetti
> 2 cloves garlic, peeled
> 1⅓ cups (325 ml) fresh basil leaves, plus extra to garnish
> 2 fresh red chilies, seeded
> 13 ounces (400 g) ripe tomatoes, roughly chopped
> 5 ounces (150 g) almonds with skin on, coarsely ground
> ⅔ cup (150 ml) extra virgin olive oil
> salt
> freshly grated pecorino cheese, to serve (optional)

Cook the pasta in a large saucepan of salted boiling water until al dente or according to the package instructions.

Meanwhile, put the cloves garlic, basil, chilies and tomatoes in a food processor and process until finely chopped but not smooth. Stir in the ground almonds and oil, and season with salt.

Drain the pasta and return to the pan. Add the pesto and stir thoroughly. Serve immediately with a scattering of grated pecorino, if desired, and garnished with basil leaves.

3 🕐

SAVE ME TIME

No-cook tomato spaghetti

Serves 4
Preparation time: 10 minutes, plus infusing
Cooking time: 10–12 minutes

> 1½ pounds (750 g) very ripe tomatoes, quartered
> 2 cloves garlic, peeled
> 10 fresh basil leaves
> 2 teaspoons (10 ml) fennel seeds
> 5 tablespoons (75 ml) extra virgin olive oil
> 13 ounces (400 g) dried spaghetti
> 2 buffalo mozzarella cheese balls, (about 5 ounces/150 g) each, cut into cubes
> salt and pepper

Put the tomatoes, garlic cloves and basil in a food processor and process until the tomatoes are finely chopped but not smooth. Transfer to a large bowl and add the fennel seeds and oil. Season with salt and pepper. Leave the flavors to infuse for at least 15 minutes before cooking the pasta.

Cook the pasta in a large saucepan of salted boiling water until al dente or according to the package instructions. Drain, stir into the prepared tomato sauce, then toss in the mozzarella. Serve immediately.

4

SAVE ME MONEY

Spaghetti puttanesca

Serves 4
Preparation time: 10 minutes
Cooking time: 20 minutes

> 2 tablespoons (30 ml) capers in salt or brine
> 4 tablespoons (60 ml) olive oil
> 1 large pinch of hot pepper flakes
> 1 clove garlic, crushed
> 8 anchovy fillets in oil, drained and roughly chopped
> 1 can (13 ounces/400 g) chopped tomatoes
> 3 ounces (75 g) pitted black olives, roughly chopped
> 13 ounces (400 g) dried spaghetti
> salt

Rinse the capers and, if you are using capers in salt, soak them in cold water for 5 minutes, then drain; if using capers in brine, simply rinse, then drain.

Meanwhile, heat the oil in a large frying pan over low heat. Add the hot pepper, garlic and anchovies and cook, stirring continuously, for 2 minutes, until the anchovies begin to melt into the oil. Increase the heat to high, add the capers and cook, stirring, for 1 minute. Add the tomatoes and olives, season with salt and bring to a boil. Leave the sauce to boil rapidly while you cook the pasta.

Cook the pasta in a large saucepan of salted boiling water until al dente or according to the package instructions. Drain, reserving a ladleful of the cooking water. Stir the pasta into the sauce, tossing until well combined. Add the reserved pasta cooking water and continue stirring until the pasta is well coated and looks silky. Serve immediately.

KIDS WILL LOVE THIS
Spaghetti with meatballs

Serves 4
Preparation time: 20 minutes
Cooking time: 1 hour 20 minutes

> 2 slices stale bread, crusts removed
> ⅓ cup (75 ml) milk
> 4 tablespoons (60 ml) olive oil
> 6 green onions or 1 small onion, chopped
> 1 clove garlic, chopped
> 1½ pound (750 g) lean ground beef
> 2 tablespoons (30 ml) freshly grated Parmesan cheese
> freshly grated nutmeg
> 1¼ cups (300 ml) dry white wine
> 1 can (14 ounces/400 g) chopped tomatoes
> 2 bay leaves
> salt and pepper
> freshly cooked spaghetti, to serve
> fresh basil leaves, to garnish

Put the bread in a large bowl, moisten with the milk and leave to soak for a few minutes.

Heat half the oil in a frying pan over medium heat. Add the green onions or onion and garlic and cook for 5 minutes until soft and just beginning to brown.

Combine the ground beef with the moistened bread, the cooked onions, garlic and Parmesan, and season with nutmeg, salt and pepper. Work together with your hands until the mixture is well mixed and smooth. With clean, wet hands, roll the mixture into 28 even-sized balls.

Heat the remaining oil in a large nonstick frying pan. Add the meatballs, in batches, and cook until browned all over. Transfer to a shallow ovenproof dish.

Add the wine and tomatoes to the pan and bring to a boil, scraping up any sediment from the base. Add the bay leaves, season with salt and pepper and boil rapidly for 5 minutes. Pour over the meatballs, cover with foil and bake in a preheated 350°F (180°C) oven for 1 hour or until tender. Serve with spaghetti, garnished with basil leaves.

SPAGHETTI IS ONE OF THE ULTIMATE COMFORT FOODS – BUT IT'S GOOD TO EAT IT WITH FRIENDS, AS IT CAN BE A BIT MESSY!

LEFTOVER TO LUNCH
Spaghetti & zucchini frittata

Serves 4
Preparation time: 10 minutes, plus cooling
Cooking time: 25 minutes

> 2 tablespoons (30 ml) olive oil
> 1 onion, thinly sliced
> 2 zucchini, thinly sliced
> 1 clove garlic, crushed
> 4 eggs
> 4 ounces (125 g) cooked spaghetti
> 4 tablespoons (60 ml) freshly grated Parmesan cheese
> 10 fresh basil leaves, torn
> salt and pepper

Heat the oil in a heavy, ovenproof nonstick 9-inch (23 cm) frying pan over low heat. Add the onion and cook, stirring occasionally, for 6–8 minutes, until softened. Stir in the zucchini and garlic and cook, stirring continuously, for 2 minutes.

Beat the eggs in a large bowl and season with salt and pepper. Stir in the cooked vegetables, spaghetti and half the Parmesan and basil. Pour the mixture into the frying pan and quickly arrange the ingredients so they are evenly dispersed. Cook over low heat for 8–10 minutes or until all but the top of the frittata is set.

Transfer to a preheated very hot broiler and place about 4 inches (10 cm) from the heat source. Cook until set but not colored.

Give the pan a shake to loosen the frittata, then transfer to a plate. Scatter the top with the remaining Parmesan and basil and leave to cool for 5 minutes before serving.

BUT I DON'T LIKE ...
SPAGHETTI

Chili & lemon shrimp with pasta

Serves 2
Preparation time: 5 minutes, plus marinating
Cooking time: 3 minutes

- 3 tablespoons (45 ml) extra virgin olive oil, plus extra for stir-frying
- 2 large cloves garlic, crushed
- 1 large red chili, seeded and chopped
- grated zest and juice of 1 lemon
- 12 ounces (375 g) large raw peeled shrimp
- 8 ounces (250 g) fresh spaghetti
- 4 green onions, sliced
- 2 tablespoons (30 ml) chopped fresh basil
- salt and pepper

Combine the oil, garlic, chili, lemon zest and salt and pepper to taste in a non-metallic bowl, add the shrimp and stir well. Cover and leave to marinate in the refrigerator for 1 hour.

Cook the pasta in a large saucepan of salted boiling water for about 3 minutes, until al dente, then drain.

Meanwhile, heat a wok or large frying pan until hot and add a drizzle of oil. Tip in the shrimp mixture and the green onions and stir-fry over high heat for 2–3 minutes, until the shrimp are lightly browned. Add the lemon juice and basil and stir well.

Serve the shrimp immediately with the cooked pasta.

WHY NOT TRY... SPICY ASIAN SHRIMP WITH JASMINE RICE

Combine the oil, garlic and chili as above with the grated zest of 1 lime and 2 teaspoons (10 ml) grated gingerroot. Add the shrimp and stir well. Leave to marinate as above. Put ⅔ cup (150 ml) jasmine rice in a small saucepan, cover with 1¼ cups (300 ml) cold water and add a little salt. Bring to a boil, then reduce the heat, cover with a tight-fitting lid and simmer over very low heat for 12 minutes. Remove from the heat and leave to stand for 10 minutes. Meanwhile, stir-fry the shrimp and green onions as above, but add 1 tablespoon (15 ml) light soy sauce just before the shrimp are cooked. Add the juice of the lime and 2 tablespoons (30 ml) chopped fresh coriander and stir well. Fluff up the rice and serve with the shrimp mixture.

FRIENDS FOR DINNER

Spaghetti with lobster sauce

Serves 6
Preparation time: 10 minutes
Cooking time: 25 minutes

- 3 shell-on lobsters, weighing about 13 ounces (400 g) each
- 1 pound 3 ounces (575 g) dried spaghetti
- 3 tablespoons (45 ml) olive oil
- 2–3 cloves garlic, chopped
- 1 large pinch of hot pepper flakes
- ⅔ cup (150 ml) dry white wine
- 1 tablespoon (15 ml) chopped fresh parsley, plus extra to garnish
- salt and pepper

Bring a large saucepan of salted water to a boil, drop in 1 lobster and simmer for 12 minutes. Leave to cool, then remove the lobster flesh from the shell.

Cook the pasta in a large saucepan of salted boiling water until al dente or according to the package instructions.

Meanwhile, split the other 2 lobsters in half lengthwise, remove and discard the stomach sacs, then chop into large pieces, legs, head and all.

Heat the oil in a sauté pan, add the garlic, hot pepper flakes and chopped lobster and cook, stirring continuously, for 2 minutes. Add the wine and bring to a boil. Add the boiled lobster meat and stir in the parsley. Season with salt and pepper.

Drain the pasta and toss with the lobster mixture. Serve immediately, garnished with parsley. Eat the lobster from the shells with your fingers — sucking the shells is part of the enjoyment!

9

WATCHING MY WEIGHT

Broad bean & lemon spaghetti

Serves 4
Preparation time: 10 minutes
Cooking time: 10–12 minutes

> 14½ ounces (450 g) dried spaghetti
> 11½ ounces (350 g) fresh or frozen shelled broad beans
> 4 tablespoons (60 ml) extra virgin olive oil
> 3 cloves garlic, finely chopped
> 1 pinch of hot pepper flakes
> grated zest and juice of 1 lemon
> 2 tablespoons (30 ml) torn fresh basil leaves
> salt and pepper
> freshly grated Parmesan or pecorino cheese, to serve

Cook the pasta in a large saucepan of lightly salted boiling water for 10–12 minutes, or according to the package instructions, until al dente. Drain, reserving 4 tablespoons (60 ml) of the cooking water, and return the pasta to the pan.

Meanwhile, cook the beans in a separate saucepan of salted boiling water for 3–4 minutes. Drain well.

While the pasta and beans are cooking, heat the oil in a frying pan, add the garlic, hot pepper flakes, lemon zest and salt and pepper and cook over low heat, stirring continuously, for 3–4 minutes, until the garlic is soft but not browned.

Scrape the oil mixture onto the pasta with the beans, reserved pasta-cooking water, lemon juice and basil and stir over medium heat until heated through. Serve with grated Parmesan or pecorino.

10

INSPIRE ME

Squid, tomato & chili spaghetti

Serves 4
Preparation time: 20 minutes
Cooking time: 20 minutes

> 2 pounds (1 kg) raw squid
> 4 tablespoons (60 ml) extra virgin olive oil, plus extra to serve
> 1 fresh red chili, thinly sliced into rounds
> 1 pound (500 g) cherry tomatoes, halved
> 7 tablespoons (100 ml) dry vermouth
> 13 ounces (400 g) dried spaghetti
> 1 clove garlic, finely chopped
> grated zest of ½ unwaxed lemon
> ⅓ cup (75 ml) fresh basil leaves
> salt

Wash the squid under cold running water. Pull the tentacles away from the body — the entrails will come out easily. Remove the clear piece of cartilage from the body cavity. Wash the body thoroughly, pulling away the pinkish membrane. Cut between the tentacles and head, discarding the head and entrails. Repeat with the remaining squid. Cut the cleaned squid bodies into rounds, dry thoroughly with paper towels and keep chilled and covered until required.

Heat the oil in a large frying pan over high heat, add the chili and tomatoes and season with salt. Cook, stirring occasionally, for 5–6 minutes, until the tomatoes start to soften and look slightly charred. Pour in the vermouth and boil rapidly for 2 minutes.

Cook the pasta in a saucepan of salted boiling water according to the package instructions, until al dente. Drain. When the pasta is almost ready, bring the tomato sauce to a boil and stir in the squid, garlic and lemon zest. Cook, stirring continuously, for 1 minute, then toss in the pasta and stir until well combined. Scatter the basil leaves over the top and serve immediately.

10 WAYS WITH RICE NOODLES

1

BASIC
Vietnamese rolls

Serves 4
Preparation time: 20 minutes, plus soaking
Cooking time: 5 minutes

2 ounces (50 g) rice vermicelli noodles
12 rice paper rounds
½ cucumber, seeded and shredded
1 carrot, shredded
2 green onions, shredded
⅓ cup (75 ml) mint leaves, left whole
2 ounces (50 g) bean sprouts
2 napa cabbage of Chinese broccoli, shredded
½ cup (125 ml) cashew nuts, chopped and roasted

FOR THE DIPPING SAUCE
2 tablespoons (30 ml) hoisin sauce
2 tablespoons (30 ml) chili sauce
2 tablespoons (30 ml) natural peanuts, chopped and roasted
1 red chili, finely chopped

Cook the noodles according to the instructions on the package. Drain and set aside.

Soak the rice paper rounds in cold water for 3 minutes or until softened. Do not soak for too long or they will fall apart.

Mix together the cucumber, carrot, green onions, mint, bean sprouts, shredded leaves and cashews.

Make the sauce by mixing the hoisin and chili sauces with the peanuts and chili.

Put a generous spoonful of vegetables and cooked noodles in the center of each rice paper round, roll it up tightly and fold over the ends. Serve the rolls immediately with the dipping sauce.

2

GIVE IT A TWIST
Spicy mixed noodles

Serves 4
Preparation time: 10 minutes
Cooking time: 10 minutes

8 ounces (250 g) thin dried rice noodles
2 teaspoons (10 ml) toasted sesame oil
2 tablespoons (30 ml) peanut oil
3 cloves garlic, crushed
1 tablespoon (15 ml) chopped gingerroot
1 red onion, finely sliced
1 red chili, cut into thin strips
3 ounces (75 g) shiitake mushrooms, finely diced
5 ounces (150 g) ham
5 ounces (150 g) peeled cooked shrimp
3 ounces (75 g) fresh or frozen peas, defrosted if frozen
7 ounces (200 g) bean sprouts
4 green onions, finely sliced
1 handful of fresh coriander leaves, roughly chopped

FOR THE SPICY SAUCE
1½ tablespoons (22 ml) Madras curry paste
2 tablespoons (30 ml) light soy sauce
2 tablespoons (30 ml) Chinese rice wine or dry sherry
½ teaspoon (2 ml) salt

Combine all the sauce ingredients and set aside.

Cook the noodles in a large pan of boiling water according to the package instructions. Refresh in cold running water, then drain and toss into a bowl with the sesame oil.

Heat the peanut oil in a wok over high heat until the oil starts to shimmer. Add the garlic, ginger, onion and chili and give the ingredients a good stir. Tip in the mushrooms and stir-fry for 1 minute, then add the ham, shrimp, peas and bean sprouts. Stir for 1 minute.

Pour in the prepared sauce and toss well to combine, then stir in the cooked noodles, green onions and coriander. Stir until the noodles are heated through, then serve.

3 🕐

SAVE ME TIME
Ginger rice noodles

Serves 4
Preparation time: 10 minutes
Cooking time: 5 minutes

- 3½ ounces (100 g) fine rice noodles
- 4 ounces (125 g) green beans, halved
- finely grated zest and juice of 2 limes
- 1 Thai chili, seeded and finely chopped
- 1-inch (2.5 cm) piece gingerroot, peeled and finely chopped
- 2 teaspoons (10 ml) granulated sugar
- 1 small handful of fresh coriander leaves, chopped
- 2 ounces (50 g) dried pineapple pieces, chopped

Place the noodles in a bowl, cover with plenty of boiling water and leave for 4 minutes, until soft.

Meanwhile, cook the beans in boiling water for about 3 minutes, until tender. Drain.

Mix together the lime zest and juice, chili, ginger, sugar and coriander in a small bowl.

Drain the noodles and place in a large serving bowl. Add the cooked beans, pineapple and dressing and toss together lightly before serving.

4 🐷

SAVE ME MONEY
Crispy rice noodles

Serves 6–8
Preparation time: 15 minutes
Cooking time: 30 minutes

- 3 ounces (75 g) rice vermicelli noodles
- sunflower oil, for deep-frying
- 7 ounces (200 g) firm tofu, cut into matchsticks
- 3 ounces (75 g) shallots, finely sliced
- 5 ounces (150 g) raw shrimp, peeled and deveined
- 2 tablespoons (30 ml) fish sauce
- 2 tablespoons (30 ml) pickled garlic juice or water
- 1 tablespoon (15 ml) lemon juice
- 2 tablespoons (30 ml) tomato ketchup
- ⅔ cup (150 ml) granulated or superfine sugar
- ⅓ cup (75 ml) coconut, palm or brown sugar, or 6 tablespoons (90 ml) liquid honey
- ¼ teaspoon (1 ml) cayenne pepper
- 3 small whole pickled garlic, finely sliced
- 4 ounces (125 g) bean sprouts

TO GARNISH
- a few slices of green onions
- a few slices of red chili

Put the rice noodles in a plastic bag and break into 2–3-inch (5–7 cm) pieces.

Heat 3 inches (7 cm) of oil in a wok over medium heat. The oil is ready when a piece of noodle sinks, then immediately floats and puffs. Drop a handful of rice noodles into the oil. Turn them once and remove as soon as they swell and turn an ivory color (it only takes seconds). Drain on paper towels. Fry the remaining noodles. In the same oil, deep-fry the tofu for 7–10 minutes or until crisp. Remove and drain. Deep-fry the shallots until crispy and golden brown. Remove and drain. Deep-fry the shrimp for 1–2 minutes, until pink. Remove and drain.

Remove the oil from the wok. Add the fish sauce, garlic juice or water, lemon juice, ketchup and both types of sugar (or honey). Stir for 4–5 minutes over low heat, until slightly thick. Add the cayenne.

Add half the rice noodles and gently toss with the sauce. Add the remaining noodles, tofu, pickled garlic, shrimp and shallots, tossing for 1–2 minutes, until coated. Serve with the bean sprouts and garnish with green onions and chili.

5

KIDS WILL LOVE THIS
Crab & noodle Asian wraps

Serves 4
Preparation time: 15 minutes, plus standing
Cooking time: 5 minutes

- 7 ounces (200 g) rice noodles
- 1 bunch green onions, finely sliced
- ¾-inch (1.5 cm) piece gingerroot, grated
- 1 clove garlic, finely sliced
- 1 red chili, finely chopped
- 2 tablespoons (30 ml) chopped fresh coriander
- 1 tablespoon (15 ml) chopped fresh mint
- ¼ cucumber, cut into fine matchsticks
- 2 cans (each 6 ounces/170 g) crabmeat, drained, or 10 ounces (300 g) fresh white crabmeat
- 1 tablespoon (15 ml) sesame oil
- 1 tablespoon (15 ml) sweet chili sauce
- 1 teaspoon (5 ml) Thai fish sauce
- 16 Chinese pancakes or Vietnamese rice paper wrappers

Cook the rice noodles according to the package instructions. Drain, then refresh under cold running water.

Mix together all the other ingredients, except the pancakes or rice paper wrappers, in a large bowl. Add the noodles and toss to mix. Cover and set aside for 10 minutes to allow the flavors to develop, then transfer to a serving dish.

To serve, let people take a pancake or rice paper wrapper, top with some of the crab and noodle mixture, roll up and enjoy.

RICE NOODLES ARE USUALLY MADE FROM RICE FLOUR AND WATER AND ARE AN IDEAL ALTERNATIVE TO TRADITIONAL EGG PASTA FOR ANYONE WHO IS ALERGIC TO WHEAT.

6

LEFTOVER TO LUNCH
Glass noodle soup

Serves 2
Preparation time: 30 minutes, plus soaking
Cooking time: 6 minutes

- 3–4 dried shiitake mushrooms
- 2 ounces (50 g) dried sheets bean curd (tofu)
- 1 ounces (25 g) dried lily flowers, soaked, drained, or canned bamboo shoots, drained and thinly sliced
- 4 ounces (125 g) mung bean vermicelli, soaked, drained
- 2½ cups (625 ml) vegetable stock (see page 8)
- 1½–2 tablespoons (22–30 ml) light soy sauce
- chopped celery leaves, to garnish

Soak the shiitake mushrooms in 1¼ cups (300 ml) boiling water for 10 minutes or until soft. Drain the mushrooms, then squeeze any excess water out of them, strain the liquid through a fine sieve into a bowl to remove any grit and reserve the liquid. Remove and discard the hard stalks and thinly slice the mushrooms.

Soak the dried bean curd sheets in boiling water for 6–8 minutes or until tender, drain and roughly tear the bean curd into pieces. Soak the dried lily flowers in boiling water for 8–10 minutes, then drain. Finally, soak the vermicelli in boiling water for 1–2 minutes or until soft, then drain.

Heat the stock and reserved soaking liquid to boiling point in a saucepan. Add the soy sauce, bean curd, lily flowers and mushrooms and cook for 2–3 minutes. Add the noodles and cook for another 2–3 minutes, stirring frequently. Taste and adjust the seasoning if necessary.

Spoon into serving bowls and garnish with chopped celery leaves scattered over the top.

BUT I DON'T LIKE ...
RICE NOODLES
Indonesian shrimp salad

Serves 4
Preparation time: 20 minutes
Cooking time: 5 minutes

4 ounces (125 g) rice noodles
2-inch (5 cm) piece English cucumber, thinly sliced
2 tablespoons (30 ml) rice vinegar
2 tablespoons (30 ml) granulated or superfine sugar
1 egg, beaten
cooking spray
4 shallots, sliced
2 cloves garlic, crushed
1 teaspoon (5 ml) grated gingerroot
1 teaspoon (5 ml) ground coriander
2 bell peppers, chopped
3 red chilies, sliced
1 tablespoon (15 ml) Thai fish sauce
8 ounces (250 g) cooked peeled shrimp
1 tablespoon (15 ml) soy sauce
salt

TO SERVE
fresh coriander leaves
3 tablespoons (45 ml) chopped roasted peanuts
2 green onions, finely sliced
shrimp crackers

Cook the noodles according to the instructions on the package. Drain, rinse well and set aside.

Pickle the cucumber in equal quantities of rice vinegar and sugar for 5 minutes, drain and set aside.

Mix the egg with 3 tablespoons (45 ml) water. Spray a wok or large frying pan with oil and, when it is quite hot, make a thin omelet with the egg mixture. Roll it up, leave to cool and then cut into thin strips.

Combine the shallots, garlic, ginger and ground coriander in a large bowl. Add the peppers, chilies, fish sauce, shrimp and noodles and mix in, using two spoons to lift and stir, until they are thoroughly combined. Add the soy sauce and salt to taste. Transfer to a serving dish and serve with the omelet strips, pickled cucumber, coriander leaves, peanuts and green onions with shrimp crackers on the side.

WHY NOT TRY... HOT & SWEET PORK WITH RICE

Cook 8 ounces (250 g) rice according to the package instructions, instead of the noodles. Meanwhile, stir-fry 8 ounces (250 g) lean boneless pork strips until cooked, then mix with the hot rice and dressed shrimp. Garnish with the omelet and pickled cucumber, as above.

FRIENDS FOR DINNER
Beef & flat noodle soup

Serves 4–6
Preparation time: 30 minutes
Cooking time: about 2 hours

1 tablespoon (15 ml) vegetable oil
1 pound (500 g) stewing beef
7 cups (1.75 L) beef stock (see page 9)
4 whole star anise
1 cinnamon stick
1 teaspoon (5 ml) black peppercorns
4 shallots, thinly sliced
4 cloves garlic, crushed
3-inch (7 cm) piece gingerroot, finely sliced
10 ounces (300 g) flat rice noodles
4 ounces (125 g) bean sprouts
6 green onions, thinly sliced
1 handful of fresh coriander
8 ounces (250 g) beef tenderloin, sliced
2 tablespoons (30 ml) Thai fish sauce
hot red chilies, to garnish

FOR THE NUOC CHAM SAUCE
2 red chilies, chopped
1 clove garlic, chopped
1½ tablespoons (22 ml) granulated or superfine sugar
1 tablespoon (15 ml) lime juice
1 tablespoon (15 ml) rice wine vinegar
3 tablespoons (45 ml) fish sauce

Heat the oil in a large saucepan or casserole and sear the beef well.

Add the stock, star anise, cinnamon, black peppercorns, half the shallots, the garlic and ginger. Bring to a boil, reduce the heat, cover the pan and simmer for about 1½ hours, until tender.

Pound the chili, garlic and sugar until smooth. Add the lime juice, vinegar, fish sauce and 4 tablespoons (60 ml) water and blend well.

When the beef is tender, lift it out and slice thinly. Add the noodles to the broth and cook gently for 2–3 minutes. Add the bean sprouts along with the sliced beef and heat for 1 minute. Strain the broth, noodles and bean sprouts into warmed bowls. Scatter with the beef tenderloin, green onions, coriander and remaining shallots. Garnish with the chilies. Serve with the sauce.

9

WATCHING MY WEIGHT
Lime- & chili-marinated chicken

Serves 4
Preparation time: 15–20 minutes, plus marinating
Cooking time: 10 minutes

> 4 boneless skinless chicken breasts, about 4 ounces (125 g) each
> 4 limes
> 2 cloves garlic, chopped
> 2 tablespoons (30 ml) chopped dried or fresh red chili
> ¼ cup (60 ml) sunflower oil
> 7 ounces (200 g) rice noodles
> 2 tablespoons (30 ml) chopped fresh coriander, to garnish
> salt and pepper

Presoak about 12 wooden skewers in warm water. Cut the chicken into strips.

Grate the zest and squeeze the juice from 2 limes and mix with the garlic, chili and oil. Toss the chicken in the lime and chili mix, season with salt and pepper and set aside for 1 hour.

Thread pieces of chicken onto skewers, not overloading each one. Halve the remaining limes. Cook the chicken and lime halves under a preheated hot broiler or on a preheated grill for about 10 minutes. Meanwhile, cook the noodles according to the instructions on the package.

Serve the chicken with the noodles, garnished with coriander and the caramelized lime halves.

10

INSPIRE ME
Northern Thai salad

Serves 4
Preparation time: 10 minutes, plus soaking
Cooking time: 8–10 minutes

> 8 ounces (250 g) mung bean vermicelli
> 2 tablespoons (30 ml) sunflower oil
> 4 cloves garlic, crushed
> 6 ounces (175 g) ground pork
> 2 teaspoons (10 ml) granulated or superfine sugar
> 4 ounces (125 g) cooked, peeled shrimp
> 2 shallots, finely sliced
> 2 tablespoons (30 ml) Thai fish sauce
> 1 tablespoon (15 ml) lime juice
> 2 small red chilies, finely chopped
> 2 small green chilies, finely chopped
> 3 tablespoons (45 ml) roasted peanuts, chopped, plus extra to serve
> 2 tablespoons (30 ml) chopped fresh coriander leaves
>
> **TO GARNISH**
> 2 green onions, diagonally sliced
> 1 large red chili, sliced diagonally
> fresh coriander leaves

Soak the vermicelli in warm water for about 6–7 minutes. Drain well and, using a pair of scissors, snip them into shorter lengths.

Heat the oil in a frying pan and lightly brown the garlic. Add the pork, crumbling and breaking up the meat until it has separated and is cooked through. Add 1 teaspoon (5 ml) of the sugar and mix together.

Remove from the heat and stir in the noodles, shrimp, shallots, fish sauce, lime juice, the remainder of the sugar, chilies, peanuts and coriander.

Toss the ingredients together and serve in heaped portions, garnished with green onions, red chili, coriander leaves and the extra chopped roasted peanuts.

RICE, DRIED BEANS & GRAINS

A versatile selection of recipes using long-grain rice, risotto, couscous, lentils and chickpeas — all classic kitchen staples that can be combined with other ingredients for tasty and nutritious meals.

RICE, DRIED BEANS & GRAINS

1	**2**	**3**	**4**	**5**
BASIC	**GIVE IT A TWIST**	**SAVE ME TIME**	**SAVE ME MONEY**	**KIDS WILL LOVE THESE**

LONG-GRAIN RICE PAGE 184

Chinese fried rice	Japanese rice with nori	Swordfish brochettes & lemon rice	Mixed bean kedgeree	Chicken rice salad

RISOTTO PAGE 190

Saffron risotto	Asparagus, pea & mint risotto	Parma ham & sweet potato risotto	Carrot, pea & broad bean risotto	Tomatoes stuffed with rice

COUSCOUS PAGE 196

Roast vegetable & herb couscous	Curried couscous salad	Swordfish with couscous & salsa	Chicken skewers with couscous	Jeweled couscous

LENTILS PAGE 202

Cumin lentils	Scallops with spiced lentils	Braised lentils with gremolata	Chicken, vegetable & lentil stew	Sausages & lentils in tomato sauce

CHICKPEAS PAGE 208

Chickpea tagine	Chorizo & chickpea stew	Baked tortillas with hummus	Curried cauliflower with chickpeas	Falafel cakes

6 LEFTOVER TO LUNCH

7 BUT I DON'T LIKE...

8 FRIENDS FOR DINNER

9 WATCHING MY WEIGHT

10 INSPIRE ME

Smoked salmon & shrimp sushi

Mediterranean rice salad

Tamarind rice

Rice soup with fish

Fragrant Persian herbed rice

Chestnut, rice & pancetta soup

Creamy pea & mint risotto with Brie

Cod & olive risotto

Red rice & squash risotto

Iced fig risotto

Chicken couscous salad

Roasted vegetable couscous

Lamb with pomegranate couscous

Pilaf with nuts, lemon & herbs

Curried chicken & couscous salad

Warm lentil & goat cheese salad

Lentil & pea soup

Braised pollock with lentils

Lentil, chorizo & scallop salad

Chicken pimenton with Puy lentils

Chickpea & pepper salad

Chickpea & parsley soup

Lamb with orange & chickpeas

Chickpea & tomato casserole

Herby chickpea crab cakes

10 WAYS WITH LONG-GRAIN RICE

BASIC
Chinese fried rice

Serves 4
Preparation time: 10 minutes, plus chilling
Cooking time: 10 minutes

>   2 tablespoons (30 ml) vegetable oil
>   2 eggs, beaten
>   1 carrot, finely diced
>   ⅔ cup (150 ml) frozen peas
>   7 ounces (200 g) cooked peeled shrimp, defrosted if frozen
>   3 cups (750 ml) cooked basmati rice
>   2 tablespoons (30 ml) light soy sauce
>   6 green onions, trimmed and sliced
>   2 teaspoons (10 ml) sesame oil
>   green onion curls, to garnish

First make the spring onion curls for garnishing. Cut 2 green onions into 1½-inch (3.5 cm) lengths, then cut each piece into very thin strips, add to a bowl of cold water with 2–3 ice cubes and leave for 15 minutes, until curled.

Heat a wok over high heat until smoking. Add half the oil, heat again, then add the eggs and cook until a thin omelet forms. Loosen and slide out of the pan, roll up and leave to cool.

Heat the remaining oil, add the carrot and stir-fry together for 2 minutes, then add the peas, shrimp and rice and stir-fry for a further 2 minutes.

Add the soy sauce, green onions and sesame oil and take off the heat. Mix all together thoroughly and top with strips of the egg rolls.

Drain the green onions and serve on top of the rice.

GIVE IT A TWIST
Japanese rice with nori

Serves 4
Preparation time: 10 minutes
Cooking time: 15 minutes

>   1 cup (250 ml) Japanese sushi or glutinous rice
>   1⅔ cups (400 ml) water
>   2 tablespoons (30 ml) black or white sesame seeds
>   1 teaspoon (5 ml) coarse salt
>   1 tablespoon (15 ml) peanut or vegetable oil
>   2 eggs, beaten
>   4 green onions, finely sliced
>   1 red chili, seeded and sliced
>   4 tablespoons (60 ml) seasoned rice vinegar
>   2 teaspoons (10 ml) granulated or superfine sugar
>   1 tablespoon (15 ml) light soy sauce
>   1 ounce (30 g) pickled Japanese ginger
>   2 sheets roasted nori (seaweed)

Put the rice in a saucepan with the water. Bring to a boil, then reduce the heat and simmer, uncovered, for about 5 minutes, until all the water is absorbed. Cover the pan and set aside for a further 5 minutes, until the rice is cooked.

Meanwhile, put the sesame seeds and salt in a frying pan and heat gently for about 2 minutes, until the seeds are toasted. Remove and set aside.

Heat the oil in the pan, add the eggs and cook gently until just firm. Slide the omelet onto a plate, roll it up and cut it across into shreds.

Transfer the cooked rice to a bowl and stir in the green onions, chili, rice vinegar, sugar, soy sauce, ginger and half the toasted sesame seeds. Crumble one sheet of nori over the rice and stir in with the omelet shreds.

Transfer to a serving dish. Crumble the remaining nori over the rice, scatter with the remaining toasted sesame seeds and serve immediately.

3

SAVE ME TIME
Swordfish brochettes & lemon rice

Serves 4
Preparation time: 10 minutes, plus standing
Cooking time: 20 minutes

3 tablespoons (45 ml) extra virgin olive oil
1 large onion, finely chopped
2 teaspoons (10 ml) ground turmeric
1 teaspoon (5 ml) ground cinnamon
grated zest and juice of 1 lemon
1¼ cups (300 ml) jasmine rice
3 cups (750 ml) chicken stock (see page 9)
2 tablespoons (30 ml) chopped fresh coriander
1½ pounds (750 g) swordfish steaks, cut into 1-inch (2.5 cm) cubes
salt and pepper
cooking spray, for oiling

Heat 2 tablespoons (30 ml) of the oil in a saucepan and add the onion, spices, lemon zest and salt and pepper to taste and cook gently for 5 minutes, until softened.

Add the rice and stir well. Pour in the stock and bring to a boil. Reduce the heat, cover and simmer gently for 10 minutes. Stir in the lemon juice, remove the pan from the heat and leave to stand, covered, for 10 minutes. Stir in the coriander.

While the rice is standing, thread the swordfish cubes onto 8 bamboo skewers, presoaked in boiling water for 10 minutes. Brush with the remaining oil and season well with salt and pepper. Spray a preheated ridged grill pan with oil and cook the brochettes for 2 minutes on each side, until evenly browned. Serve the rice and kebabs with an arugula salad, if desired.

4

SAVE ME MONEY
Mixed bean kedgeree

Serves 4
Preparation time: 10 minutes
Cooking time: 15–20 minutes

2 tablespoons (30 ml) olive oil
1 onion, chopped
2 tablespoons (30 ml) mild curry powder
1 cup (250 ml) long-grain rice
3 cups (750 ml) vegetable stock (see page 8)
4 eggs
2 cans (each 14 ounces/398 ml) mixed beans, drained and rinsed
⅔ cup (150 ml) sour cream
salt and pepper
2 tomatoes, finely chopped, to garnish
flat-leaf fresh parsley, to garnish

Heat the oil in a saucepan, add the onion and cook until soft. Stir in the curry powder and rice. Add the stock and season to taste with salt and pepper. Bring to a boil, then reduce the heat, cover and simmer, stirring occasionally, for 10–15 minutes, until all the stock has been absorbed and the rice is tender.

Meanwhile, put the eggs in a saucepan of cold water and bring to a boil. Cook for 10 minutes, then plunge into cold water to cool. Shell the eggs, then cut them into wedges.

Stir the beans and sour cream into the rice and cook briefly over low heat to heat through. Serve garnished with the eggs, tomatoes and parsley.

5

KIDS WILL LOVE THIS
Chicken rice salad

Serves 4
Preparation time: 10 minutes, plus cooling
Cooking time: about 15 minutes

- 4 chicken thighs, skinned and boned
- ¾ cup (175 ml) long-grain rice
- 2 teaspoons (10 ml) lemon juice
- 2 tablespoons (30 ml) peanut butter (optional)
- 2 tablespoons (30 ml) olive oil
- 2 pineapple rings, chopped
- 1 red bell pepper, cored, seeded and chopped
- 3 ounces (75 g) sugar snap peas, sliced
- 4 tablespoons (60 ml) peanuts (optional)

Place the chicken thighs in a steamer set over boiling water for 10–12 minutes, until cooked through. Alternatively, simmer them in shallow water in a frying pan for 10 minutes. Remove from the steamer or pan and set aside to cool.

Meanwhile, cook the rice according to the package instructions. Drain and rinse under cold water to cool the rice completely, then tip it into a large bowl.

Make the dressing. Mix together the lemon juice and peanut butter, if using, until well combined, then whisk in the oil.

Dice the chicken thighs into bite-size pieces and stir into the rice. Add the pineapple, red pepper, sugar snap peas and peanuts, if using. Pour the dressing over the chicken rice salad and serve.

THE GRAINS IN LONG-GRAIN RICE ARE USUALLY FOUR OR FIVE TIMES AS LONG AS THEY ARE WIDE. IT TENDS TO BE LESS STICKY THAN SHORTER-GRAINED VARIETIES, WHICH MEANS THAT, WHEN COOKED, IT IS LESS LIKELY TO STICK TOGETHER.

6

LEFTOVER TO LUNCH
Smoked salmon & shrimp sushi

Serves 4–6
Preparation time: 45 minutes, plus cooling
Cooking time: 20–25 minutes

- 1¾ cups (425 ml) water
- 1 cup (250 ml) sushi rice
- 4 tablespoons (60 ml) rice vinegar
- 1 teaspoon (5 ml) wasabi paste, plus extra to serve
- 8 ounces (250 g) cooked tiger shrimp
- grated zest and juice of 2 limes
- 5 sheets nori (seaweed)
- 7 ounces (200 g) sliced smoked salmon
- 1½ ounces (45 g) pickled Japanese ginger, drained
- 1 jar (11 ounces/325 ml) of red pimentos, drained and cut into long strips
- 3 green onions, cut into long thin strips

Bring the water to a boil in a saucepan, add the rice, cover and simmer gently for 20–25 minutes, until very soft. Drain off any excess water. Mix the vinegar and wasabi and stir into the rice. Leave to cool. Toss the shrimp with the lime zest and juice and set aside.

Place one nori sheet on a bamboo rolling mat, spoon over one-fifth of the rice and spread into an even layer, leaving a small border of nori showing. Arrange one-fifth of the smoked salmon in a long line in the centre of the rice. Next to that add one-fifth of the shrimp, and on top some ginger, pimentos and green onions.

Using the mat to help, roll up the nori sheet so the rice wraps around the filling and the edges of nori overlap slightly. Rock back and forth for an even shape. Repeat to make the remaining rolls. Wrap them individually in plastic wrap and chill until required. When ready to serve, cut the rolls into thick slices and arrange with cut edges uppermost on a plate. Serve with extra wasabi.

7

BUT I DON'T LIKE ...
LONG-GRAIN RICE
Mediterranean rice salad

Serves 4
Preparation time: 10 minutes, plus cooling
Cooking time: 5 minutes

> 3 ounces (75 g) broccoli, finely chopped
> 3 ounces (75 g) zucchini, finely chopped
> 3 ounces (75 g) mixed red and yellow bell peppers, finely chopped
> 1 ounce (30 g) green onions, finely chopped
> 1½ ounces (45 g) mushrooms, finely sliced
> 2 tablespoons (30 ml) water
> 2 tablespoons (30 ml) pesto
> ⅓–½ cup (75–125 ml) cooked brown rice
> ⅓–½ cup (75–125 ml) cooked wild rice
> salt and pepper

Heat a large frying pan or wok, add the vegetables and water and cook over high heat for 3–5 minutes, until the vegetables have softened. Remove from the heat and allow to cool.

Mix the cooled vegetables with the pesto and cooked rices, season well and stir to combine. Cover and chill until required. Serve topped with a few Parmesan shavings and some basil leaves, if desired.

WHY NOT TRY... MEDITERRANEAN PASTA SALAD

Cook the vegetables as above. Meanwhile, cook 5 ounces (150 g) macaroni in lightly salted boiling water until just tender. Mix 4 tablespoons (60 ml) olive oil with 1 tablespoon (15 ml) red wine vinegar, 1 finely chopped clove garlic, 2 teaspoons (10 ml) sun-dried tomato paste and a small bunch torn basil leaves. Season well and toss with the pasta and the vegetables.

8

FRIENDS FOR DINNER
Tamarind rice

Serves 4
Preparation time: 10 minutes
Cooking time: about 20 minutes

> 1 tablespoon (15 ml) sunflower oil
> 1 large red onion, thinly sliced
> 2 Japanese eggplants, cut into cubes
> 1 red chili, seeded and thinly sliced
> 2 tablespoons (30 ml) tamarind paste
> 1 tablespoon (15 ml) dark brown or muscovado sugar
> 4 cups (1 L) cooked basmati rice
> ½ cup (125 ml) fresh mint leaves, roughly chopped
> 7 ounces (200 g) baby spinach leaves
> salt and pepper

Warm the oil in a large frying pan over medium heat. Add the sliced onion and cook for 10 minutes or until lightly browned.

Increase the heat to high. Add the cubed eggplant, half the sliced chili, a tablespoon (15 ml) of tamarind and the brown sugar. Stir-fry for 5 minutes, until the eggplant is golden and beginning to soften.

Add the cooked rice, mint, spinach and the remaining tamarind to the eggplant and onion mixture. Continue to stir-fry for 5–6 minutes or until piping hot.

Sprinkle with the remaining chili slices. Season with salt and pepper and serve immediately.

THE LONGER THE GRAIN, THE BETTER QUALITY THE RICE. BASMATI RICE IS ONE OF THE BEST LONG-GRAIN RICES AVAILABLE.

WATCHING MY WEIGHT
Rice soup with fish

Serves 4
Preparation time: 10 minutes
Cooking time: 15 minutes

> 1½ tablespoons (22 ml) sunflower oil
> 3–4 cloves garlic, finely chopped
> 7 cups (1.75 L) vegetable or fish stock (see page 8)
> 30 sun-dried goji berries (optional)
> 3 cups (750 ml) cooked rice
> 2 tablespoons (30 ml) preserved radish
> 3½ tablespoons (52 ml) light soy sauce
> 12 ounces (375 g) skinless fish fillets, fine bones removed,
>   cut into 1½-inch (4 cm) pieces
> handful of Chinese (napa) cabbage or chard, roughly chopped
> 1-inch (2.5 cm) piece gingerroot, peeled, finely shredded

> **TO GARNISH**
> 2 green onions, finely sliced
> fresh coriander leaves
> 1 pinch of ground white pepper

Heat the oil in a small saucepan and stir-fry the garlic over medium heat for 1–2 minutes or until lightly browned. Spoon into a small serving bowl.

Heat the stock, goji berries (if using), rice (crumbled apart if necessary) and preserved radish in a saucepan over medium heat for 6–8 minutes. Add the soy sauce, fish, Chinese cabbage or chard and ginger and cook for another 4–5 minutes or until the fish is cooked, stirring gently from time to time. Taste and adjust the seasoning if necessary.

Spoon into 4 serving bowls; garnish with green onions, coriander leaves and pepper. Drizzle with the garlic oil.

INSPIRE ME
Fragrant Persian herbed rice

Serves 4
Preparation time: 20 minutes, plus soaking
Cooking time: 30–35 minutes

> 2 cups (500 ml) basmati rice
> ¼ cup (60 ml) butter, plus extra to serve (optional)
> ⅓ cup (75 ml) sunflower oil
> 1 cinnamon stick
> 2 cardamom pods, lightly crushed
> 2 cloves
> 3½ ounces (100 g) mixture of fresh dill, coriander and mint,
>   roughly chopped
> salt and pepper

Wash the rice well until the water runs clear. Put the rice in a bowl, cover with water and leave to soak for 2 hours. Wash again.

Bring a saucepan of water to a boil, then add the rice. Cook the rice for about 6 minutes, until it begins to soften on the outside. Drain and rinse in lukewarm water.

Heat the butter and oil in a heavy saucepan until foaming, then add the spices and half the rice. Cover the rice with half the herbs. Add the remaining rice, then finish with the remaining herbs. Season each layer with salt and pepper.

Turn the heat down to low and make 3 steam holes in the rice with the handle of a wooden spoon. Wrap the lid of the saucepan in a clean tea towel and place it on the saucepan — the tea towel stops condensation from falling into the rice. Leave the rice to cook for 20–25 minutes.

Empty the rice into a bowl. Scrape off and break up the lovely crisp bits at the bottom of the saucepan and add them to the rice. Add additional butter, if desired. Serve immediately with a curry of your choice.

10 WAYS WITH RISOTTO

1

BASIC
Saffron risotto

Serves 4
Preparation time: 5 minutes
Cooking time: 35 minutes

- ¼ cup (60 ml) butter
- 1 onion, finely chopped
- 1¼ cups (300 ml) Arborio, carnaroli or vialone nano rice
- ⅔ cup (150 ml) dry white wine
- 4 cups (1 L) vegetable or beef stock (see pages 8–9), simmering
- ½ teaspoon (2 ml) saffron threads
- 4 tablespoons (60 ml) freshly grated Parmesan cheese, plus extra to serve

Melt half the butter in a heavy-bottomed saucepan over low heat. Add the onion and cook for 10 minutes, until softened. Add the rice and cook, stirring continuously, for 1 minute. Pour in the wine and cook, stirring continuously, until absorbed.

Add 2 ladlefuls of the simmering stock and the saffron. Slowly simmer, stirring constantly, until the stock has been absorbed and the rice parts when a wooden spoon is run through it. Add another ladleful of stock and continue to cook, stirring and adding the stock in ladlefuls, for 18–20 minutes, until the rice is creamy and almost tender to the bite.

Remove from the heat and stir in the Parmesan and remaining butter. Stir vigorously for 15 seconds. Cover with a tight-fitting lid and leave to stand for 1 minute. Serve immediately with extra Parmesan on the side.

2

GIVE IT A TWIST
Asparagus, pea & mint risotto

Serves 4
Preparation time: 10 minutes, plus standing
Cooking time: 45 minutes

- 1 pound (500 g) asparagus spears
- 4 cups (1 L) vegetable or fish stock (see page 8)
- ¼ cup (60 ml) butter
- 1 onion, finely chopped
- 1¼ cups (300 ml) Arborio, carnaroli or vialone nano rice
- ⅔ cup (150 ml) dry white wine
- ¾ cup (175 ml) shelled fresh or frozen peas
- 4 tablespoons (60 ml) freshly grated Parmesan cheese, plus extra to serve
- 1 handful of fresh mint leaves, roughly chopped

Cut the asparagus in half, at an angle, separating the tips from the thicker stalks. Reserve the tips. Put the stalks in a saucepan with the stock and bring to a boil. Boil for 5 minutes, then reduce the heat to a simmer. Remove the asparagus with a slotted spoon and process in a food processor or blender until puréed.

Melt half the butter in a heavy-bottomed saucepan over low heat. Add the onion and cook for 10 minutes, until softened. Add the rice and cook, stirring continuously, for 1 minute. Add the wine and cook, stirring continuously, until absorbed. Stir in the puréed asparagus.

Add 2 ladlefuls of the simmering stock. Slowly simmer, stirring constantly, until the stock has been absorbed and the rice parts when a wooden spoon is run through it. Add another ladleful of stock and continue to cook, stirring and adding the stock in ladlefuls, reserving 2 ladlefuls, for 16–18 minutes, until the rice is creamy and almost tender to the bite.

Add the peas and the reserved asparagus tips and stock and continue cooking until the stock is almost absorbed. Remove from the heat and stir in the Parmesan, mint and remaining butter. Stir vigorously for 15 seconds. Cover with a tight-fitting lid and leave to stand for 2 minutes. Serve immediately with extra Parmesan.

3

Parma ham & sweet potato risotto

Serves 4
Preparation time: 5 minutes
Cooking time: 25 minutes

- 2 medium sweet potatoes, scrubbed and cut into ½-inch (1 cm) chunks
- ¼ cup (60 ml) butter
- 1 bunch green onions, finely sliced
- 1½ cups (375 ml) risotto rice
- 2 bay leaves
- 5 cups (1.25 L) hot vegetable or chicken stock (see pages 8–9)
- 3 tablespoons (45 ml) olive oil
- 3 ounces (75 g) Parma ham, torn into pieces
- ⅔ cup (150 ml) mixed fresh herbs, such as parsley, chervil, tarragon and chives, chopped
- salt and pepper

Cook the sweet potatoes in lightly salted boiling water for 2–3 minutes to soften. Drain and set aside.

Meanwhile, melt the butter in a large, heavy-bottomed saucepan. Add the green onions and sauté for 1 minute. Add the rice and stir well to coat the grains with the butter.

Add the bay leaves to the rice. Add the hot stock, a large ladleful at a time, stirring until each addition is absorbed into the rice. Continue adding stock in this way, cooking until the rice is creamy but the grains are still firm. This should take about 20 minutes.

Meanwhile, heat 1 tablespoon (15 ml) of the oil in a frying pan and cook the ham until golden. Drain and keep warm. Add the remaining oil and fry the sweet potatoes, turning frequently, for 6–8 minutes, until golden.

Add the herbs to the risotto and season to taste with salt and pepper, then add the ham and sweet potatoes, folding in gently. Cover and leave the risotto to rest for a few minutes before serving.

4

Carrot, pea & broad bean risotto

Serves 4
Preparation time: 15 minutes
Cooking time: about 25 minutes

- ¼ cup (60 ml) butter
- 2 tablespoons (30 ml) olive oil
- 1 large onion, finely chopped
- 2 carrots, finely chopped
- 2 cloves garlic, finely chopped
- 1½ cups (375 ml) risotto rice
- ¾ cup (175 ml) white wine
- 6 cups (1.5 L) vegetable stock (see page 8), simmering
- 7 ounces (200 g) frozen peas, defrosted
- 3½ ounces (100 g) frozen broad fava or lima beans, defrosted and peeled
- 2 ounces (50 g) Parmesan cheese, finely grated
- 1 handful of fresh flat-leaf parsley, roughly chopped
- salt and pepper

Melt the butter with the oil in a saucepan, add the onion, carrots and garlic and cook for about 3 minutes, until soft. Add the rice and stir until coated with the butter mixture. Add the wine and cook rapidly, stirring continuously, until it has evaporated.

Add the hot stock, a ladleful at a time, and cook, stirring constantly, until each addition has been absorbed before adding the next. Continue until all the stock has been absorbed and the rice is creamy and cooked but still retains a little bite — this will take around 15 minutes.

Add the peas and broad beans and heat through for 3–5 minutes. Remove from the heat and stir in the Parmesan and parsley. Season to taste with salt and pepper and serve immediately.

5 😊

KIDS WILL LOVE THIS
Tomatoes stuffed with rice

Serves 4
Preparation time: 15 minutes, plus standing
Cooking time: 35 minutes

> 4 large or 8 small tomatoes, about 1¼ pounds (625 g) in total
> 2 cloves garlic, crushed
> ⅓ cup (75 ml) Arborio, carnaroli or vialone nano rice
> 6 fresh basil leaves, torn
> 2 tablespoons (30 ml) extra virgin olive oil, plus extra for oiling and drizzling
> salt and pepper

Cut a slice off the stalk end of each tomato and set aside to use as lids. Scoop the pulp out of the tomatoes and chop. Transfer to a large bowl, taking care not to lose any of the tomato juices, and add the garlic, rice and basil. Season with salt and pepper and stir in 1 tablespoon (15 ml) of the oil. Cover and leave to stand at room temperature for 1 hour, for the rice to soak up all the juices.

Stuff the tomatoes with the rice mixture, then transfer to an oiled baking dish. Top with their reserved lids and drizzle with the remaining oil. Bake in a preheated 350°F (180°C) oven for 35 minutes, until the tomatoes are soft and the rice is cooked through. Serve warm or at room temperature.

6

LEFTOVER TO LUNCH
Chestnut, rice & pancetta soup

Serves 4
Preparation time: 10 minutes, plus standing
Cooking time: 35 minutes

> ¼ cup (60 ml) butter
> 5 ounces (150 g) pancetta, cubed
> 1 onion, finely chopped
> 7 ounces (200 g) package vacuum-packed cooked chestnuts
> ⅔ cup (150 ml) Arborio, carnaroli or vialone nano rice
> 2 cups (500 ml) chicken stock (see page 9)
> ⅔ cup (150 ml) 1% or 2% milk
> salt and pepper

Melt half the butter in a saucepan over medium heat. Add the pancetta and onion and cook for 10 minutes. Cut the chestnuts in half and add to the pan with the rice and stock. Bring to a boil, then reduce the heat and simmer for 20 minutes or until most of the liquid has been absorbed and the rice is tender.

Heat the milk in a small saucepan until tepid, then stir into the rice with the remaining butter and season the dish with salt and pepper. Cover and leave to stand for 5 minutes before serving.

MEDIUM-GRAINED RICE IS USED TO MAKE RISOTTO AS IT HELPS TO GIVE IT ITS CREAMY CONSISTENCY.

BUT I DON'T LIKE . . . RISOTTO

Creamy pea & mint risotto with Brie

Serves 4
Preparation time: 15 minutes
Cooking time: 35 minutes

> 5 cups (1.25 L) vegetable stock (see page 8)
> ¼ cup (60 ml) butter
> 1 large onion, finely chopped
> 2 cloves garlic, crushed
> 1¼ cups (300 ml) Arborio rice
> ⅔ cup (150 ml) dry white wine
> 11½ ounces (350 g) fresh or frozen shelled peas
> ½ bunch fresh mint leaves, torn
> 2 ounces (50 g) Brie, diced
> salt and pepper
> freshly grated Parmesan cheese, to serve

Put the stock in a saucepan and bring to a very gentle simmer.

Meanwhile, melt the butter in a saucepan, add the onion, garlic and salt and pepper and cook over low heat, stirring occasionally, for 10 minutes, until the onion is softened but not browned. Add the rice and cook, stirring continuously, for 1 minute, until all the grains are glossy. Stir in the wine, bring to a boil and continue to boil for 1–2 minutes, until absorbed. Stir in the peas.

Stir about ⅔ cup (150 ml) of the stock into the rice. Cook over medium heat, stirring constantly, until absorbed. Continue to add the stock, a little at a time, and cook, stirring constantly, for about 20 minutes, until the rice is al dente and the stock has all been absorbed.

Remove the pan from the heat. Stir in the mint and Brie, cover and leave to stand for 5 minutes, until the cheese has melted. Serve with grated Parmesan.

WHY NOT TRY... RICE PATTIES

Leave the risotto until completely cold, then stir in 1 beaten egg. Divide the mixture into small patties and coat with dried breadcrumbs. Heat a little vegetable oil in a frying pan, add the patties and fry for 2–3 minutes on each side, until golden and cooked through. Serve with a green salad.

FRIENDS FOR DINNER

Cod & olive risotto

Serves 4
Preparation time: 10 minutes
Cooking time: 25 minutes

> 1 pound (500 g) cod fillet, skinned
> 2¼ cups (550 ml) white wine
> 2½ cups (625 ml) hot fish stock (see page 8)
> ¼ cup (60 ml) butter
> 2 onions, chopped
> 1½ cups (375 ml) risotto rice
> 2 ounces (50 g) sun-dried tomatoes in oil, drained and sliced
> ¼ cup (60 ml) olive oil
> 2 tablespoons (30 ml) chopped fresh oregano
> 7 ounces (200 g) cherry tomatoes, halved
> 2 ounces (50 g) Parmesan cheese, freshly grated
> 2 ounces (50 g) pitted black olives, chopped
> 1 tablespoon (15 ml) white wine vinegar
> salt and pepper

Pat the fish dry on paper towels and cut into 4 pieces. Season with salt and pepper. Put the wine and stock in a saucepan and bring almost to a boil. Set aside.

Melt the butter in a large, heavy-bottomed saucepan and sauté the onions for 5 minutes, until softened. Add the rice and sun-dried tomatoes and stir well to coat the grains with the butter. Add the hot stock mixture, a large ladleful at a time, stirring until each addition is absorbed into the rice. Continue adding stock in this way, cooking until the rice is creamy but the grains are still firm. This should take about 20 minutes.

Meanwhile, heat 2 tablespoons (30 ml) of the oil in a large frying pan and cook the fish for 3 minutes on each side, until cooked through. Remove with a spatula and keep warm.

Add the oregano and cherry tomatoes to the pan and cook for 1 minute. Season lightly with salt and pepper.

Stir the Parmesan into the risotto and pile onto plates. Top with the fish and tomatoes. Add the olives, the remaining oil and the vinegar to the frying pan, stirring for a few seconds, then pour over the fish to serve.

9

WATCHING MY WEIGHT
Red rice & squash risotto

Serves 4
Preparation time: 20 minutes
Cooking time: 35 minutes

> 4 cups (1 L) vegetable stock (see page 8)
> 1 cup (250 g) Camargue red rice
> 1 tablespoon (15 ml) olive oil
> 1 onion, finely chopped
> 2 cloves garlic, finely chopped
> 1½ pounds (750 g) winter squash, peeled, seeded and diced
> 5 tablespoons (75 ml) finely chopped fresh basil or oregano, plus extra leaves to garnish
> 2 ounces (50 g) Parmesan cheese, coarsely grated, plus shavings to garnish
> salt and pepper

Put the stock in a large saucepan, add the rice and simmer for 35 minutes.

Meanwhile, heat the oil in a frying pan, add the onion and cook, stirring occasionally, for 5 minutes or until softened. Add the garlic, squash and a little salt and pepper, mix together, then cover and cook over medium heat for 10 minutes, stirring occasionally.

Drain the rice and reserve the cooking liquid. Stir the chopped herbs into the frying pan with the drained rice and grated Parmesan. Adjust the seasoning and moisten with the reserved rice liquid if necessary.

Spoon into shallow dishes and serve garnished with extra herbs and Parmesan shavings.

10

INSPIRE ME
Iced fig risotto

Serves 4
Preparation time: 15 minutes, plus cooling
Cooking time: 40 minutes

> 2½ cups (625 ml) 1% or 2% milk
> 3 tablespoons (45 ml) granulated or superfine sugar
> finely grated zest of 1 orange
> ½ cup (125 ml) risotto rice
> 8 fresh figs
> butter, for greasing
> 2 tablespoons (30 ml) liquid honey
> 2 tablespoons (30 ml) orange juice
> 200 grams (7 ounces) vanilla ice cream
> thin slices orange zest, to garnish (optional)

Put the milk, sugar and orange zest in a large saucepan and bring almost to a boil. Add the rice and cook on the lowest possible heat, stirring frequently, for 25–35 minutes or until the rice is creamy but the grains are still firm. Remove from the heat and set aside to cool. Chill until required.

Meanwhile, halve the figs and place in a lightly buttered shallow ovenproof dish. Drizzle with the honey and orange juice and bake in a preheated 400°F (200°C) oven for 20 minutes or until beginning to colour. Allow to cool, then chill until required.

When ready to serve, scoop the ice cream into the rice mixture and stir until it has just melted to make a creamy sauce. Spoon into bowls with the figs and cooking juices and garnish with thin slices of orange zest, if desired, and serve immediately.

10 WAYS WITH COUSCOUS

BASIC
Roast vegetable & herb couscous

Serves 6
Preparation time: 15 minutes, plus soaking
Cooking time: 25 minutes

- 1 pound (500 g) winter squash, peeled, seeded and diced
- 4 zucchini, diced
- 1 red onion, cut into wedges
- ⅓ cup (75 ml) extra virgin olive oil
- 1 cup (250 ml) couscous
- 1 cup (250 ml) boiling water
- 8 ounces (250 g) cherry tomatoes, halved
- 2 tablespoons (30 ml) each chopped fresh coriander, mint and parsley
- juice of 1 large lemon
- salt and pepper

Put the squash, zucchini and onion in a roasting pan with 2 tablespoons (30 ml) of the oil, season to taste with salt and pepper and stir to combine.

Roast in a preheated 425°F (220°C) oven for 25 minutes, until all the vegetables are cooked.

Meanwhile, put the couscous in an ovenproof bowl and pour in the boiling water. Cover the bowl with a clean tea towel and leave to stand for 5 minutes or until the grains are swollen and all the liquid has been absorbed.

Fork through the couscous to fluff up the grains, then stir in the roasted vegetables, cherry tomatoes and herbs.

Whisk together the remaining oil, lemon juice and salt and pepper to taste in a small bowl and stir through the salad.

GIVE IT A TWIST
Curried couscous salad

Serves 4
Preparation time: 15 minutes

- juice of 1 orange
- 2 teaspoons (10 ml) mild curry paste
- 1¼ cups (300 ml) couscous
- ⅓ cups (75 ml) sultanas
- ¼ cups (300 ml) boiling water
- 8 ounces (250 g) smoked mackerel fillets
- 1 small red onion, finely chopped
- ½ red bell pepper, cored, seeded and diced
- 2 tomatoes, chopped
- 1 small bunch fresh coriander, roughly chopped
- pepper

Put the orange juice and curry paste into a bowl and stir together. Add the couscous, sultanas and a little pepper, then pour in the boiling water and fork together. Leave to stand for 5 minutes.

Meanwhile, peel the skin off the mackerel fillets and break the flesh into large flakes, discarding any bones.

Add the mackerel, onion, red pepper and tomatoes to the couscous and mix together lightly. Sprinkle roughly chopped coriander over the top, spoon onto plates and serve immediately.

SAVE ME TIME
Swordfish
with couscous & salsa

Serves 4
Preparation time: 10 minutes
Cooking time: 10 minutes

> **4 swordfish steaks, about 5 ounces (150 g) each**
> **4–5 small ripe tomatoes**
> **16 Kalamata olives in brine, drained**
> **2 tablespoons (30 ml) chopped fresh flat-leaf parsley**
> **salt and pepper**
> **7 ounces (200 g) couscous**

Season the swordfish steaks with salt and pepper.

Dice or quarter the tomatoes and transfer them to a bowl with all the juices. Remove the pits from the olives and chop the flesh if the pieces are still large. Stir them into the tomatoes with parsley, season to taste and set aside.

Cook the couscous according to the instructions on the package and set aside.

Meanwhile, cook the swordfish steaks, 2 at a time, in a preheated hot grill pan. Cook on the first side for 4 minutes, without disturbing them, then turn and cook for a further minute. Serve the swordfish and couscous immediately, topped with the olive and tomato salsa, accompanied with a green salad, if desired.

SAVE ME MONEY
Chicken skewers
with couscous

Serves 4
Preparation time: 25 minutes, plus marinating
Cooking time: 15 minutes

> **1 pound (500 g) boneless skinless chicken breasts**
> **2 tablespoons (30 ml) olive oil**
> **2 cloves garlic, crushed**
> **½ teaspoon (2 ml) each ground cumin, turmeric and paprika**
> **2 teaspoons (10 ml) lemon juice**
>
> **FOR THE COUSCOUS**
> **4 tablespoons (60 ml) olive oil**
> **1 small onion, finely chopped**
> **1 clove garlic, crushed**
> **1 teaspoon (5 ml) each ground cumin, cinnamon, pepper and ginger**
> **2 ounces (50 g) dried dates**
> **2 ounces (50 g) dried apricots**
> **2 ounces (50 g) blanched almonds, toasted**
> **2⅓ cups (575 ml) boiling vegetable stock (see page 8)**
> **¾ cup (175 ml) couscous**
> **1 tablespoon (15 ml) lemon juice**
> **2 tablespoons (30 ml) chopped fresh coriander leaves**
> **salt and pepper**

Cut the chicken into long, thin strips, place them in a shallow dish and add the olive oil, garlic, spices and lemon juice. Stir well, then cover and leave to marinate for 2 hours. Thread the chicken strips onto 8 small, presoaked wooden skewers.

Prepare the couscous by heating half the oil in a saucepan and frying the onion, garlic and spices for 5 minutes. Chop and stir in the dried fruits and almonds and remove from the heat.

Meanwhile, put the couscous in an ovenproof bowl, add the boiling stock and cover with a tea towel and steam for 8–10 minutes, until the grains are fluffed up and the liquid absorbed. Stir in the remaining oil and the fruit and nut mixture, add the lemon juice and coriander and season to taste.

While the couscous is steaming, grill or grill the chicken skewers for 4–5 minutes on each side, until charred and cooked through. Serve with the couscous, garnished with pomegranate seeds, lemon wedges and coriander sprigs, if desired.

5

KIDS WILL LOVE THIS
Jeweled couscous

Serves 2–3
Preparation time: 20 minutes
Cooking time: 2 minutes

⅔ cups (150 ml) couscous
¾ cup (175 ml) hot vegetable stock (see page 8)
2 ounces (50 g) green beans, trimmed and cut into ½-inch
    (1 cm) lengths
1 small orange
2 tablespoons (30 ml) olive oil
1 tablespoon (15 ml) liquid honey
1 pomegranate
½ small pineapple, chopped into small pieces
1 small red bell pepper, cored, seeded and finely diced

Put the couscous in an ovenproof bowl and add the stock. Cover and leave to stand for 20 minutes.

Meanwhile, bring a small pan of water to a boil and add the beans. Cook for 2 minutes. Drain the beans through a colander and rinse in cold water.

Finely grate the zest of half of the orange and mix it in a small bowl with 3 tablespoons (45 ml) of orange juice, the oil and the honey. Whisk lightly with a fork.

Cut the pomegranate in half. Pull the fruit apart with your hands and ease out the clusters of seeds. Separate the seeds, discarding any white parts of the fruit, which are bitter. Add the pomegranate seeds, beans, pineapple and red pepper to the couscous along with the orange and honey dressing. Mix well and chill in the refrigerator until ready to serve.

COUSCOUS IS MADE UP OF TINY GRANULES OF STEAMED AND DRIED DURUM WHEAT, WHICH, WHEN BOILING WATER OR STOCK IS ADDED, QUICKLY BECOME LIGHT AND FLUFFY, CREATING A GREAT ALTERNATIVE TO RICE OR PASTA.

6

LEFTOVER TO LUNCH
Chicken couscous salad

Serves 4
Preparation time: 20 minutes, plus marinating
Cooking time: 8–9 minutes

4 boneless skinless chicken breasts, each about 4 ounces (125 g)
1¼ cups (300 ml) couscous
1¼ cups (300 ml) hot chicken stock (see page 9)
1 pomegranate
zest and juice of 1 orange
1 small bunch fresh coriander
1 small bunch fresh mint

FOR THE MARINADE
1½ tablespoons (22 ml) curry paste (tikka masala)
5 tablespoons (75 ml) natural yogurt
1 teaspoon (5 ml) olive oil
2 tablespoons (30 ml) lemon juice

Make a marinade by mixing the curry paste, yogurt and oil. Put the chicken in a non-metallic dish, cover with half the marinade and leave for at least 1 hour.

Put the couscous in a bowl, add the hot stock, cover and leave for 8 minutes.

Meanwhile, cut the pomegranate in half and remove the seeds. Add them to the couscous with the orange zest and juice.

Remove the chicken from the marinade, reserving the marinade, and transfer to a foil-lined baking sheet. Cook in a preheated 375°F (190°C) oven for 6–7 minutes, then transfer to a preheated hot broiler or barbecue and cook for 2 minutes, until caramelized. Cover with foil and leave to rest for 5 minutes.

Roughly chop the coriander and mint, reserving some whole coriander leaves for garnish, and add to the couscous. Thinly slice the chicken. Spoon the couscous onto plates and add the chicken. Mix the reserved marinade with the lemon juice and drizzle over the couscous. Garnish with the reserved coriander leaves and serve immediately.

BUT I DON'T LIKE ...
COUSCOUS
Roasted vegetable couscous

Serves 6
Preparation time: 15 minutes, plus soaking
Cooking time: 30–35 minutes

- ¾ cup (175 ml) couscous
- 1 chicken stock cube
- 1¾ cups (425 ml) hot water
- 2 zucchini, cut into chunks
- 1 red bell pepper, cored, seeded and cut into chunks
- 1 yellow bell pepper, cored, seeded and cut into chunks
- 12 ounces (375 g) butternut squash, peeled, seeded and cut into chunks
- 1 red onion, chopped
- 5 tablespoons (75 ml) olive oil
- 3 tablespoons (45 ml) chopped fresh parsley or basil
- 5 tablespoons (75 ml) pine nuts, toasted

Place the couscous in a bowl, crumble in the stock cube and stir well. Add the water, stir, then cover and set aside, while preparing and cooking the vegetables, to soak and swell.

Put all the prepared vegetables into a large roasting pan, drizzle over 3 tablespoons (45 ml) of the oil and toss to coat lightly. Roast in a preheated 400°F (200°C) oven for 30–35 minutes, until the vegetables are soft and lightly charred.

Lightly fork the soaked couscous to fluff it up, then drizzle with the remaining oil and toss well. Add the warm vegetables, parsley or basil and pine nuts and toss well before serving.

WHY NOT TRY... ROASTED VEGETABLE QUINOA WITH TOASTED CASHEWS

Replace the couscous with quinoa. Wash ¾ cup (175 ml) quinoa in a sieve, then drain. Place in a large, heavy-bottomed nonstick frying pan and lightly toast over medium heat for 2–3 minutes, until the grain turns a shade darker. Add 1¾ cups (425 ml) water and 1 chicken stock cube and cook over medium heat for 8–10 minutes, until the grain is tender and cooked. Drain and set aside. Add the roasted vegetables and parsley as above and replace the pine nuts with ⅔–1 cup (150–250 ml) roughly chopped toasted cashews.

FRIENDS FOR DINNER
Lamb with pomegranate couscous

Serves 4
Preparation time: 40 minutes, plus cooling and chilling
Cooking time: 20–35 minutes

- 2½ pounds (1.25 kg) leg of lamb
- 1 large pomegranate
- 2 cloves garlic
- 1 small bunch fresh mint, torn
- 6 tablespoons (90 ml) olive oil
- 1 tablespoon (15 ml) liquid honey
- finely grated zest and juice of 1 lemon
- ¾ cup (175 ml) couscous
- ⅓ cup (75 ml) sultanas
- 3 ounces (75 g) pitted dates, sliced
- ½ red onion, finely chopped
- 1¾ cups (425 ml) boiling water
- ½ cup (125 ml) pistachio nuts, cut into slivers
- 2 teaspoons (10 ml) harissa (optional)
- salt and pepper

Remove bones from the lamb, make a horizontal cut through the thickest part of the meat, then open out so it is about 1½ inches (4 cm) thick. Place in a non-metallic dish. Seed the pomegranate. Place half the seeds in a pestle and mortar with the garlic and crush. Mix with half the mint, half the oil, the honey and half the lemon zest and juice. Season and spoon over the lamb. Cover and chill for 3 hours.

Put the couscous in a bowl with the dried fruit, onion and remaining lemon, then add the water. Cool, cover with plastic wrap and chill. When ready, transfer the lamb to a roasting pan with some of the marinade. Roast in a preheated 425°F (220°C) oven, for 20–25 minutes for medium rare, or 30–35 minutes for well done. Lift out the lamb, add the remaining marinade to the hot pan and mix with the pan juices. Pour over the lamb, cover tightly with foil and leave to stand for 10 minutes.

Add the pomegranate seeds and pistachios to the couscous. Mix the remaining oil with the harissa, if using, drizzle over the couscous, then replace the plastic wrap and microwave on full power for 1½–2 minutes, until piping hot. Sprinkle the remaining mint over the top and fluff up with a fork. Spoon onto serving plates, top with thickly sliced lamb and drizzle with pan juices.

9

Pilaf with nuts, lemon & herbs

Serves 4
Preparation time: 15 minutes
Cooking time: 10 minutes

> 2 tablespoons (30 ml) olive oil
> 1 mild onion, chopped
> 2 cloves garlic, crushed
> 1⅔ cups (400 ml) vegetable stock (see page 8)
> 2 cups (500 ml) couscous
> 1 pomegranate
> ⅓ cup (75 ml) pine nuts, toasted
> 3 tablespoons (45 ml) chopped fresh flat-leaf parsley
> 3 tablespoons (45 ml) chopped fresh dill
> 3 tablespoons (45 ml) chopped fresh coriander
> grated zest and juice of 1 lemon
> salt and pepper

Heat the oil in a large frying pan and cook the onion and garlic for about 5 minutes or until soft. Add the stock and heat, then add the couscous. Stir, cover and leave to steam over gentle heat for 5 minutes.

Meanwhile, take the seeds from the pomegranate, working over a bowl to catch any juice.

When the couscous is cooked, stir in the nuts and herbs and a little salt and pepper.

Mix together the pomegranate seeds and juice and lemon zest and juice. Spoon over the couscous just before serving.

10

Curried chicken & couscous salad

Serves 4
Preparation time: 15 minutes, plus standing

> ¾–1 cup (175–250 ml) couscous
> ⅓ cup (75 ml) sultanas
> 2 teaspoons (10 ml) mild curry paste
> 1 ¾ cups (425 ml) boiling water
> 2 tomatoes, diced
> ½ green, red or yellow bell pepper, cored, seeded, diced
> ½ red onion, finely chopped
> 1 small bunch fresh coriander, finely chopped
> ⅔ cup (150 ml) lightly toasted shredded coconut
> 4–6 ounces (125–175 g) cooked chicken, diced
> grated zest and juice of 1 lime
> 3 tablespoons (45 ml) sunflower oil
> salt and pepper

Put the couscous, sultanas and curry paste into a large bowl, add the boiling water and mix together. Leave to stand for 5 minutes.

Fluff up the couscous with a fork, then mix in the tomatoes, pepper, onion, coriander, coconut and chicken.

Mix the lime zest and juice with the oil and a little seasoning. Add to the couscous and toss together. Spoon into bowls and serve.

10 WAYS WITH LENTILS

BASIC
Cumin lentils

Serves 4
Preparation time: 10 minutes
Cooking time: 13 minutes

4 tablespoons (60 ml) olive oil
2 red onions, thinly sliced
2 cloves garlic, chopped
2 teaspoons (10 ml) cumin seeds
1 pound (500 g) cooked Puy lentils
4 ounces (125 g) peppery leaves, such as beets or arugula
1 large raw beet, peeled and coarsely grated
1 Granny Smith apple, peeled and coarsely grated (optional)
lemon juice, to serve
salt and pepper

FOR THE YOGURT DRESSING
1¼ cups (300 ml) Greek yogurt
2 tablespoons (30 ml) lemon juice
½ teaspoon (2 ml) ground cumin
⅓ cup (75 ml) fresh mint leaves, chopped

Heat the oil in a frying pan and fry the red onions over medium heat for about 8 minutes, until soft and golden. Add the garlic and cumin seeds and cook for a further 5 minutes.

Mix the onion mixture into the lentils, season well and leave to cool.

Make the dressing by mixing together the ingredients in a small bowl.

Serve the cooled lentils on a bed of leaves, with the grated beet and apple (if using), a couple of spoonfuls of yogurt dressing and a generous squeeze of lemon juice.

GIVE IT A TWIST
Scallops with spiced lentils

Serves 4
Preparation time: 10 minutes
Cooking time: 20–25 minutes

1 cup (250 ml) split red lentils
5 tablespoons (75 ml) olive oil
2 tablespoons (30 ml) butter
1 onion, finely chopped
1 eggplant, cut into ½-inch (1 cm) cubes
1 clove garlic, crushed
1 tablespoon (15 ml) curry powder
1 tablespoon (15 ml) chopped fresh parsley
12 cleaned king scallops, corals removed (optional)
4 tablespoons (60 ml) Greek yogurt
salt and pepper

Cook the lentils in water according to the instructions on the package. Drain and set aside.

Heat 1 tablespoon (15 ml) of the oil and the butter in a frying pan over medium heat. Add the onion and cook slowly until golden brown, about 10 minutes. When the onion has browned, remove it from the pan and turn the heat up to high. Add another 2 tablespoons (30 ml) of the oil to the pan and fry the eggplant in batches until colored and softened.

Return the onion to the pan along with the garlic, curry powder and cooked lentils. Fry for a further minute to warm everything through. Season with salt and pepper and finally stir in the parsley.

Heat a frying pan over high heat and add the remaining oil. Season the scallops with salt and pepper. Place them in the frying pan and cook for 1 minute on each side.

Serve the scallops immediately with the spiced lentils and Greek yogurt.

3 🕐

SAVE ME TIME

Braised lentils with gremolata

Serves 4
Preparation time: 5 minutes
Cooking time: 25 minutes

¼ cup (60 ml) butter
1 onion, chopped
2 stalks celery, sliced
2 carrots, sliced
¾ cup (175 ml) Puy lentils, rinsed
2½ cups (625 ml) vegetable stock (see page 8)
1 cup (250 ml) dry white wine
2 bay leaves
2 tablespoons (30 ml) chopped fresh thyme
3 tablespoons (45 ml) olive oil
11 ounces (325 g) mushrooms, sliced
salt and pepper

FOR THE GREMOLATA
2 tablespoons (30 ml) chopped fresh parsley
finely grated zest of 1 lemon
2 cloves garlic, chopped

Melt the butter in a saucepan and fry the onion, celery and carrots for 3 minutes. Add the lentils, stock, wine, herbs and a little salt and pepper. Bring to a boil, then reduce the heat and simmer gently, uncovered, for about 20 minutes or until the lentils are tender.

Meanwhile, mix together the ingredients for the gremolata.

Heat the oil in a frying pan. Add the mushrooms and fry for about 2 minutes until golden. Season lightly.

Ladle the lentils onto plates, top with the mushrooms and serve scattered with the gremolata.

4

SAVE ME MONEY

Chicken, vegetable & lentil stew

Serves 6
Preparation time: 15 minutes
Cooking time: 2 hours

2 pounds (1 kg) boneless skinless chicken thighs cut into large pieces
2 tablespoons (30 ml) all-purpose, seasoned with salt and pepper
3 tablespoons (45 ml) olive oil
1 large onion, chopped
2 carrots, chopped
2 stalks celery, chopped
2 cloves garlic, crushed
⅔ cup (150 ml) dry white wine
4 cups (1 L) chicken stock (see page 9)
1 tablespoon (15 ml) chopped rosemary
⅔ cup (150 ml) Puy lentils
salt and pepper

Dust the chicken thighs with the seasoned flour to coat lightly. Heat half the oil in an ovenproof casserole dish, add the chicken, in two batches, and cook over medium-high heat for 5 minutes, until browned on both sides. Remove from the pan with a slotted spoon.

Reduce the heat to medium and add the remaining oil to the pan. Add the onion, carrots, celery, garlic and salt and pepper to taste and cook, stirring frequently, for 5 minutes. Add the wine, stock, rosemary and lentils and return the chicken thighs to the pan.

Bring to a boil, stirring continuously, then reduce the heat, cover and simmer gently for 1½ hours, until tender.

5

KIDS WILL LOVE THIS
Sausages & lentils in tomato sauce

Serves 4
Preparation time: 10 minutes
Cooking time: 1 hour 10 minutes

> **3 tablespoons (45 ml) olive oil**
> **8 Italian sausages**
> **1 onion, roughly chopped**
> **1 stalk celery, roughly chopped**
> **3 cloves garlic, crushed**
> **1¾ cups (175 ml) full-bodied red wine**
> **1 can (14 ounces/398 ml) chopped tomatoes**
> **5 cups (1.25 L) chicken stock (see page 9)**
> **1 bay leaf**
> **1 dried red chili**
> **½ cup (125 ml) green lentils**
> **salt and pepper**
> **extra virgin olive oil, for drizzling**

Heat the oil in a large, heavy-bottomed saucepan in which the sausages fit in a single layer. Add the sausages and cook over medium heat for 10–12 minutes, until golden brown all over. Remove and set aside.

Add the onion and celery to the pan and cook over low heat for 8–10 minutes, until softened. Stir in the garlic and cook for a further 2 minutes.

Increase the heat to high, pour in the wine and boil vigorously for 2 minutes, scraping any sediment from the base of the pan. Stir in the tomatoes, stock, bay leaf and chili and bring to a boil. Add the lentils and return the sausages to the pan. Simmer gently for 40 minutes, or until the sausages and lentils are cooked through. Season with salt and pepper. Serve with a drizzle of extra virgin olive oil, accompanied by some crusty bread.

6

LEFTOVER TO LUNCH
Warm lentil & goat cheese salad

Serves 4
Preparation time: 10 minutes
Cooking time: 20–30 minutes

> **2 teaspoons (10 ml) olive oil**
> **2 teaspoons (10 ml) cumin seeds**
> **2 cloves garlic, crushed**
> **2 teaspoons (10 ml) grated gingerroot**
> **½ cup (125 ml) Puy lentils**
> **3 cups (750 ml) vegetable stock (see page 8)**
> **2 tablespoons (30 ml) chopped fresh mint**
> **2 tablespoons (30 ml) chopped fresh coriander**
> **½ lime**
> **5 ounces (150 g) baby spinach leaves**
> **4 ounces (125 g) goat cheese, crumbled**
> **pepper**

Heat the oil in a saucepan, add the cumin seeds, garlic and ginger and cook over medium heat, stirring continuously, for 1 minute.

Add the lentils and cook for a further minute. Add the stock, a large ladleful at a time, and cook until each addition has been absorbed before adding the next. Continue in this way until all the stock has been absorbed. This should take about 20–30 minutes. Remove from the heat and stir in the mint and coriander with a squeeze of lime juice.

To serve, divide the spinach leaves between individual bowls, top with a quarter of the lentils and the goat cheese and sprinkle with pepper.

7

BUT I DON'T LIKE ...
LENTILS
Lentil & pea soup

Serves 4
Preparation time: 10 minutes
Cooking time: 25 minutes

> 1 teaspoon (5 ml) olive oil
> 1 leek, finely sliced
> 1 clove garlic, crushed
> 1 can (14 ounces/398 ml) Puy lentils, drained
> 3½ cups (875 ml) vegetable stock (see page 8)
> 2 tablespoons (30 ml) chopped fresh mixed herbs, such as thyme
>   and parsley
> 1½ cups (375 ml) frozen peas
> 2 tablespoons (30 ml) crème fraîche or sour cream
> 1 tablespoon (15 ml) chopped fresh mint
> pepper

Heat the oil in a medium saucepan, add the leek and garlic and fry over gentle heat for 5–6 minutes, until the leek is softened.

Add the lentils, vegetable stock and herbs, bring to a boil and simmer for 10 minutes. Add the peas and continue to cook for 5 minutes.

Transfer half the soup to a blender or food processor and blend until smooth. Return to the pan, stir to combine with the unblended soup, then heat through and season with plenty of pepper.

Stir together the crème fraîche and mint and serve on top of each bowl of soup.

WHY NOT TRY... HAM, LENTIL & PEA SOUP

To serve as a more substantial meal, add a 7-ounce (200 g) piece of cooked ham to the soup when adding the stock. Cook as above, but before liquidizing the soup roughly shred the ham. Blend half the ham with half the soup, then return to the pan as above. Stir in the remaining shredded ham, heat through and complete the recipe as above.

8

FRIENDS FOR DINNER
Braised pollock with lentils

Serves 4
Preparation time: 15 minutes
Cooking time: 50 minutes

> ⅔ cup (150 ml) Puy lentils
> 3 tablespoons (45 ml) extra virgin olive oil
> 1 large onion, finely chopped
> 3 cloves garlic, sliced
> several sprigs fresh rosemary or thyme
> ¾ cup (175 ml) fish stock (see page 8)
> 4 chunky pieces pollock fillet, skinned
> 8 small tomatoes
> salt and pepper
> 2 tablespoons (30 ml) chopped fresh flat-leaf parsley, to serve

Boil the lentils in plenty of water for 15 minutes. Drain. Meanwhile, heat 1 tablespoon (15 ml) of the oil in a frying pan and fry the onion for 5 minutes. Stir in the garlic and fry for a further 2 minutes.

Add the lentils, rosemary or thyme, stock and a little salt and pepper to the frying pan and bring to a boil.

Pour into a shallow baking dish and arrange the fish on top. Score the tops of the tomatoes and tuck them around the fish. Drizzle with the remaining oil.

Bake, uncovered, in a preheated 350°F (180°C) oven for 25 minutes or until the fish is cooked through. Serve sprinkled with the parsley.

LENTILS COME IN MANY VARIETIES, SIZES AND COLOURS, BUT ALL ARE HIGHLY NUTRITIOUS.

9

WATCHING MY WEIGHT
Lentil, chorizo & scallop salad

Serves 4
Preparation time: 10 minutes
Cooking time: 20–25 minutes

> 1 cup (250 ml) Puy lentils
> 2 red bell peppers, quartered, cored and seeded
> 6 tablespoons (90 ml) olive oil
> 3 tablespoons (45 ml) balsamic vinegar
> 5 ounces (150 g) chorizo sausage, thinly sliced or diced
> 12 ounces (375 g) scallops, rinsed and patted dry
> 3 ounces (75 g) arugula leaves
> salt and pepper

Cook the lentils in a saucepan of simmering water for 15–20 minutes, until just tender but still holding their shape. Drain the lentils, rinse in cold water and drain again.

Meanwhile, arrange the peppers, cut sides down, on a piece of foil on a broiler pan, brush with 1 tablespoon (15 ml) of the oil and grill for 10–15 minutes, until softened and lightly charred. Wrap in foil while hot. When cool enough to handle, remove the skins and slice the flesh.

Mix 4 tablespoons (60 ml) of the oil in a bowl with the vinegar and a little seasoning. Add the lentils and toss well, then stir in the pepper strips. Cover and set aside.

When ready to serve, heat the remaining 1 tablespoon (15 ml) of oil in a frying pan, add the chorizo and fry for 2 minutes. Add the scallops and cook for 3–4 minutes, turning once, until browned and just cooked. Divide the arugula leaves between 4 serving plates. Spoon the lentils on top, then add the chorizo and scallops and serve immediately.

10

INSPIRE ME
Chicken pimenton with Puy lentils

Serves 4
Preparation time: 20 minutes
Cooking time: 20 minutes

> ¾ cup + 2 tablespoons (200 ml) Puy lentils
> 3 tablespoons (45 ml) olive oil
> 6 chicken thighs, skinned, boned, cut into cubes
> 1 red onion, halved, sliced
> 1 tablespoon (15 ml) chopped fresh rosemary
> ¼ teaspoon (1 ml) smoked paprika (pimenton)
> 8 ounces (250 g) cherry tomatoes, halved
> 2 tablespoons (30 ml) balsamic vinegar, plus a little extra
> 4 ounces (125 g) baby spinach leaves, rinsed, drained
> salt and pepper

Add the lentils to a saucepan of boiling water and simmer for 15–20 minutes, until just tender. Meanwhile, heat 1 tablespoon (15 ml) of the oil in a large frying pan, add the chicken and onion and fry for 10 minutes, stirring until the chicken is browned.

Stir in the rosemary and paprika and cook for 1 minute, then mix in the tomatoes and seasoning and cook for 3–4 minutes, stirring continuously, until the tomatoes are just beginning to soften.

Drain the lentils into a sieve, add the remaining oil, vinegar and seasoning to the base of the dry pan and mix together. Return the lentils to the pan and mix in the spinach. Cook for 1 minute, stirring continuously, until the spinach is just beginning to wilt.

Spoon the lentil and spinach mixture onto serving plates and top with the chicken mix. Drizzle with a little extra balsamic vinegar, if desired. Serve immediately.

10 WAYS WITH CHICKPEAS

1

BASIC
Chickpea tagine

Serves 4
Preparation time: 15 minutes
Cooking time: 40 minutes

- 7 tablespoons (100 ml) extra virgin olive oil
- 1 large onion, finely chopped
- 2 cloves garlic, crushed
- 2 teaspoons (10 ml) ground coriander
- 1 teaspoon (5 ml) each ground cumin, ground turmeric and ground cinnamon
- 1 large eggplant, about 12 ounces (375 g), diced
- 1 can (14 ounces/398 ml) chickpeas, drained
- 1 can (14 ounces/398 ml) chopped tomatoes
- 1¼ cups (300 ml) vegetable stock (see page 8)
- 8 ounces (250 g) button mushrooms
- 3 ounces (75 g) dried figs, chopped
- 2 tablespoons (30 ml) chopped fresh coriander
- salt and pepper
- preserved lemon, chopped, to serve

Heat 2 tablespoons (30 ml) of the oil in a saucepan, add the onion, garlic and spices and cook over medium heat, stirring frequently, for 5 minutes until lightly golden.

Heat a further 2 tablespoons (30 ml) of the oil in the pan, add the eggplant and cook, stirring continuously, for 4–5 minutes, until browned. Add the chickpeas, tomatoes and stock and bring to a boil. Reduce the heat, cover and simmer gently for 20 minutes.

Meanwhile, heat the remaining oil in a frying pan, add the mushrooms and cook over medium heat for 4–5 minutes, until browned.

Add the mushrooms to the tagine with the figs and cook for a further 10 minutes. Stir in the coriander. Garnish with chopped preserved lemon and serve with couscous.

2

GIVE IT A TWIST
Chorizo & chickpea stew

Serves 4
Preparation time: 5 minutes
Cooking time: 25 minutes

- 1 pound (500 g) new potatoes
- 1 teaspoon (5 ml) olive oil
- 2 red onions, chopped
- 2 red bell peppers, cored, seeded and chopped
- 3½ ounces (100 g) chorizo sausage, thinly sliced
- 1 pound (500 g) plum tomatoes, chopped, or 1 can (14 ounces/398 ml) chopped tomatoes, drained
- 1 can (14 ounces/398 ml) chickpeas, drained and rinsed
- 2 tablespoons (30 ml) chopped fresh parsley, to garnish
- garlic bread, to serve

Bring a saucepan of water to a boil. Add the potatoes and cook for 12–15 minutes, until tender. Drain, then slice.

Meanwhile, heat the oil in a large frying pan, add the onions and red peppers and cook for 3–4 minutes. Add the chorizo and cook for 2 minutes.

Add the potato slices, tomatoes and chickpeas and bring to a boil. Reduce the heat and simmer for 10 minutes. Scatter with the parsley and serve with hot garlic bread to mop up all the juices.

3

Baked tortillas with hummus

Serves 4
Preparation time: 5 minutes
Cooking time: 10–12 minutes

4 small wheat tortillas
1 tablespoon (15 ml) olive oil

FOR THE HUMMUS
1 can (14 ounces/398 ml) chickpeas, drained and rinsed
1 clove garlic, chopped
4–6 tablespoons (60–90 ml) natural yogurt
2 tablespoons (30 ml) lemon juice
1 tablespoon (15 ml) fresh coriander leaves, chopped
salt and pepper
paprika, to sprinkle

TO SERVE
lemon wedges
olives

Cut each tortilla into 8 triangles, put on a baking sheet and brush with a little oil. Cook in a preheated 400°F (200°C) oven for 10–12 minutes, until golden and crisp. Remove from the oven.

Meanwhile, put the chickpeas, garlic, yogurt and lemon juice in a bowl and mix really well until smooth and mushy. Sprinkle with salt and pepper, stir in the coriander and sprinkle with paprika. Serve with the warm tortillas, lemon wedges and olives.

4

Curried cauliflower with chickpeas

Serves 4
Preparation time: 10 minutes
Cooking time: 25 minutes

2 tablespoons (30 ml) olive oil
1 onion, chopped
2 cloves garlic, crushed
4 tablespoons (60 ml) medium curry paste
1 small cauliflower, divided into florets
1½ cups (375 ml) vegetable stock, made with 1 vegetable stock cube and boiling water
4 tomatoes, roughly chopped
1 can (14 ounces/398 ml) chickpeas, drained and rinsed
2 tablespoons (30 ml) mango chutney
salt and pepper
4 tablespoons (60 ml) chopped fresh coriander, to garnish
whisked natural yogurt, to serve (optional)

Heat the oil in a saucepan, add the onion and garlic and cook until the onion is soft and starting to brown. Stir in the curry paste, add the cauliflower and stock and bring to a boil. Reduce the heat, cover tightly and simmer for 10 minutes.

Add the tomatoes, chickpeas and chutney and continue to cook, uncovered, for 10 minutes. Season to taste with salt and pepper. Serve garnished with coriander and drizzled with a little whisked yogurt, if desired.

5

KIDS WILL LOVE THIS
Falafel cakes

Serves 4
Preparation time: 10 minutes
Cooking time: 6 minutes

1 can (14 ounces/398 ml) chickpeas, drained and rinsed
1 onion, roughly chopped
3 cloves garlic, roughly chopped
2 teaspoons (10 ml) cumin seeds
1 teaspoon (5 ml) mild chili powder
2 tablespoons (30 ml) chopped fresh mint
3 tablespoons (45 ml) chopped fresh coriander leaves, plus extra
 leaves to serve
¾ cup (175 ml) fresh breadcrumbs
oil, for shallow frying
salt and pepper

TO SERVE
4 pita breads
2 Little Gem lettuces or romaine hearts, torn into pieces
minted cucumber and yogurt salad

Place the chickpeas in a food processor or blender with the onion, garlic, spices, herbs, breadcrumbs and a little salt and pepper. Blend briefly to make a chunky paste.

Take dessert spoonfuls of the mixture and flatten into cakes. Heat a ½-inch (1 cm) depth of oil in a frying pan and fry half the falafels for about 3 minutes, turning once, until crisp and golden. Drain on paper towels and keep warm while cooking the remainder. Serve the falafels in warmed split pita breads filled with the lettuce, coriander leaves and spoonfuls of minted cucumber and yogurt salad.

CHICKPEAS ARE PERHAPS BEST KNOWN AS BEING THE MAIN INGREDIENT IN HUMMUS, BUT THEIR CREAMY TEXTURE WHEN PURÉED AND NUTTY TEXTURE WHEN WHOLE MAKE THEM A HIGHLY VERSATILE INGREDIENT.

6

LEFTOVER TO LUNCH
Chickpea & pepper salad

Serves 4
Preparation time: 25 minutes
Cooking time: 30 minutes

2 red bell peppers, cored, seeded and halved
1 yellow bell pepper, cored, seeded and halved
1 red onion
4 plum tomatoes, cut into wedges
olive oil
2 tablespoons (30 ml) fennel seeds
2 cans (each 14 ounces/398 ml) chickpeas, rinsed and drained
1 small bunch fresh parsley, chopped
salt and pepper

FOR THE DRESSING
4 tablespoons (60 ml) sherry vinegar
3 tablespoons (45 ml) olive oil
1 clove garlic, crushed
½ teaspoon (2 ml) ground cumin

Cut the peppers into ¾-inch (2 cm) strips. Cut the onion in half and then cut each half into quarters, leaving the root on so the wedges stay together.

Drizzle the peppers, onions and tomatoes with olive oil and add salt and pepper. Heat a grill pan over high heat and cook the peppers for 2 minutes on each side. Slice the peppers and place in an ovenproof dish. Cook the onion in the same way. Place the onion and tomatoes with the peppers, sprinkle with fennel seeds and cook in a preheated 350°F (180°C) oven for 20 minutes, until done.

Meanwhile, make the dressing. Whisk together the vinegar and oil with the crushed garlic and cumin.

Transfer the drained chickpeas to a large salad bowl and mix in the hot vegetables and chopped parsley. Season to taste with salt and pepper, drizzle over the dressing and stir to combine.

BUT I DON'T LIKE ...
CHICKPEAS

Chickpea & parsley soup

Serves 6
Preparation time: 15 minutes, plus cooling
Cooking time: 30 minutes

> 1 small onion
> 3 cloves garlic
> ⅔ cup (150 ml) fresh parsley
> 2 tablespoons (30 ml) olive oil
> 1 can (14 ounces/398 ml) chickpeas, drained and rinsed
> 5 cups (1.25 L) vegetable stock (see page 8)
> grated zest and juice of ½ lemon
> salt and pepper

Put the onion, garlic and parsley in a food processor or blender and process until finely chopped.

Heat the oil in a saucepan and cook the onion mixture over low heat until slightly softened. Add the chickpeas and cook gently for 1–2 minutes.

Add the stock, season well with salt and pepper and bring to a boil. Cover and cook for 20 minutes or until the chickpeas are really tender.

Allow the soup to cool for a while, then partly purée it in a food processor or blender or mash it with a fork so that it retains plenty of texture.

Pour the soup into a clean pan, add the lemon juice and adjust the seasoning if necessary. Heat through gently. Serve the soup topped with grated lemon zest and pepper.

WHY NOT TRY... FLAGEOLET, CANNELLINI & PARSLEY SOUP

Replace the chickpeas with 7 ounces (200 g) each canned flageolet and cannellini beans, and use the zest and juice of 1 lemon. Otherwise, cook as above.

FRIENDS FOR DINNER
Lamb with orange & chickpeas

Serves 8
Preparation time: 25 minutes, plus soaking
Cooking time: 2½ hours

> 1 cup (250 ml) chickpeas, soaked in cold water overnight
> 4 tablespoons (60 ml) olive oil
> 2 teaspoons (10 ml) ground cumin
> 1 teaspoon (5 ml) each ground cinnamon, ginger and turmeric
> ½ teaspoon (2 ml) saffron threads
> 3 pounds (1.5 kg) shoulder of lamb, trimmed of all fat and cut into 1-inch (2.5 cm) cubes
> 2 onions, roughly chopped
> 3 cloves garlic, finely chopped
> 2 tomatoes, skinned, seeded and chopped
> 12 pitted black olives, sliced
> grated zest of 1 unwaxed lemon
> grated zest of 1 unwaxed orange
> 6 tablespoons (90 ml) chopped fresh coriander
> salt and pepper

Drain the chickpeas and rinse. Put in a casserole dish, cover with water, bring to a boil, then simmer, covered, for about 1–1½ hours.

Combine half the olive oil with the cumin, cinnamon, ginger, turmeric and saffron in a large bowl with ½ teaspoon (2 ml) salt and ½ teaspoon (2 ml) pepper. Add the lamb, toss and set aside in a cool place for 20 minutes. Wipe the pan and then fry the lamb in the remaining oil in batches until well browned, draining to a plate.

Add the onions and cook, stirring continuously, until browned. Add the garlic and the tomatoes with 1 cup (250 ml) water, stirring and scraping the base of the pan. Return the lamb to the pan and add enough water to just cover. Bring to a boil and skim off any foam. Reduce the heat, cover and simmer for about 1 hour.

Drain the chickpeas and reserve the cooking liquid. Add the chickpeas with about 1 cup (250 ml) of the cooking liquid to the lamb. Simmer for 30 minutes.

Stir in the olives and lemon and orange zest and simmer for a final 30 minutes. Mix in half the chopped coriander, then serve garnished with the rest. When cool, this dish may be frozen.

9

WATCHING MY WEIGHT
Chickpea & tomato casserole

Serves 4
Preparation time: 10 minutes
Cooking time: about 30 minutes

3 cloves garlic, crushed
3 sprigs fresh rosemary
2 pounds (1 kg) vine tomatoes, halved
olive oil spray
1 mild onion, chopped
2 tablespoons (30 ml) fresh rosemary
1 red chili, seeded and chopped
¼ cup (60 ml) vegetable stock (see page 8)
2 cans (each 14 ounces/398 ml) chickpeas, drained and rinsed
salt and pepper

Stir the garlic and rosemary sprigs through the tomatoes. Spread them out in a roasting tin and cook in a preheated 400°F (200°C) oven for 30 minutes.

Meanwhile, lightly spray a casserole dish with oil and gently cook the onion for 10 minutes. Add the chopped rosemary, chili, stock and chickpeas, season to taste, cover and transfer to the oven for 20 minutes or the remainder of the tomato cooking time.

When the tomatoes are cooked, stir them into the chickpeas with all the juices from the roasting pan. Check the seasoning and, if desired, serve with baked potatoes and a green salad.

10

INSPIRE ME
Herby chickpea crab cakes

Serves 4
Preparation time: 10 minutes
Cooking time: 7 minutes

1 can (14 ounces/398 ml) chickpeas, rinsed and drained
2 green onions, thinly sliced
3 tablespoons (45 ml) chopped fresh parsley
2 tablespoons (30 ml) chopped chives
1 egg yolk
1 teaspoon (5 ml) piri piri sauce
1 teaspoon (5 ml) Worcestershire sauce
2 tablespoons (30 ml) mayonnaise
1–1¼ cups (250–300 ml) coarse dry breadcrumbs
10 ounces (300 g) white crab meat
2 tablespoons (30 ml) olive oil

TO SERVE
4 ounces (125 g) arugula leaves

Put the chickpeas, green onions, herbs, egg yolk, piri piri sauce, Worcestershire sauce, mayonnaise and ⅓ cup (75 ml) of the breadcrumbs in a food processor and process briefly. Add the crab meat and pulse quickly to combine, adding more breadcrumbs if the mixture is too wet.

Transfer the mixture to a bowl and form it into 4 large or 8 small patties. Press them into the remaining breadcrumbs until well coated.

Heat the oil in a large frying pan and fry the crab cakes for about 5 minutes, turning carefully once, until crisp and golden. Drain on paper towels and serve immediately with arugula leaves.

DESSERTS

Try something different with these tempting and delicious desserts using strawberries, chocolate, cream, lemons and vanilla. Go on, treat yourself!

DESSERTS

 1 BASIC

 2 GIVE IT A TWIST

 3 SAVE ME TIME

 4 SAVE ME MONEY

 5 KIDS WILL LOVE THESE

Strawberries & meringue

Shortcakes with elderflower cream

Grilled strawberry zabaglione

Scrumptious strawberry scones

Custard cream berry slices

Really moist chocolate slice

Flourless chocolate cake

Chocolate brioche sandwich

Chocolate cornflake bars

Real chocolate brownies

Pink grapefruit cream

Lime & passion fruit crunch tart

White chocolate & raspberry tiramisu

White chocolate & raspberry puffs

Honeyed banana ice cream

Lemon meringue pie

Tangy lemon cupcakes

Cheat's lemon dainties

Lemon angel food cake

Lemon puddle pudding

Vanilla cupcakes

Vanilla crème brûlée

Macadamia & vanilla tart

Vanilla & cocoa cookies

Vanilla flowers

6

 **7**

 8

 9

 **10**

LEFTOVER TO LUNCH

BUT I DON'T LIKE...

FRIENDS FOR DINNER

WATCHING MY WEIGHT

INSPIRE ME

Rhubarb & strawberry compote

Strawberry cheesecake pots

Tuile baskets & cream

Low-calorie strawberry roulade

Strawberry rose jelly & syllabub

Chocolate hazelnut spread

Mixed berry chocolate roulade

Tiramisu cheesecake

Low-fat chocolate soufflés

Chocolate sorbet

Gingered profiteroles

Neopolitan whirl ice cream

Peach & chocolate vacherin

Pavlovas with orange cream

Rosemary panna cotta

Lemon polenta cake

Lemon, pistachio & date squares

Classic lemon tart

Lemon drizzle loaf

Lemon creams with raspberries

Portuguese custard tarts

Venetian rice pudding

Vanilla soufflés & apricot coulis

Vanilla muffins

Florentine vanilla cheesecake

10 WAYS WITH STRAWBERRIES

1

BASIC
Strawberries & meringue

Serves 4
Preparation time: 15 minutes
Cooking time: 2½ hours

> **3 egg whites**
> **⅔ cup (150 ml) light brown or muscovado sugar**
> **1 tablespoon (15 ml) cornstarch**
> **1 teaspoon (5 ml) white vinegar**
> **1 teaspoon (5 ml) vanilla extract**
> **8 ounces (250 g) strawberries, hulled and sliced**

Line 4 tart tins or ramekins with parchment paper. Beat the egg whites until they form stiff peaks, then beat in the brown sugar, a spoonful at a time, making sure the sugar is incorporated between additions. Fold in the cornstarch, vinegar and vanilla extract.

Spoon the mixture into the tart tins or ramekins and bake in a preheated 250°F (120°C) oven for 2½ hours.

Place the strawberries in an ovenproof dish and bake with the meringues for the last hour of the cooking time.

Spoon the strawberries and any cooking juices over the meringues to serve.

2 ◎

GIVE IT A TWIST
Shortcakes with elderflower cream

Makes 8
Preparation time: 20 minutes
Cooking time: 10–15 minutes

> **2 cups (500 ml) self-rising flour**
> **2 teaspoons (10 ml) baking powder**
> **3 ounces (75 g) unsalted butter, diced**
> **⅓ cup (75 ml) granulated or superfine sugar**
> **1 egg, lightly beaten**
> **2–3 tablespoons (30–45 ml) 1% or 2% milk**
> **1 tablespoon (15 ml) butter, melted**
> **8 ounces (250 g) strawberries, hulled and sliced**
> **confectioners' sugar, for dusting**
>
> **FOR THE ELDERFLOWER CREAM**
> **1¼ cups (300 ml) whipping (35%) cream**
> **2 tablespoons (30 ml) elderflower syrup or undiluted cordial**

Sift the flour and baking powder into a mixing bowl or a food processor. Add the butter and rub in with your fingertips or process until the mixture resembles fine breadcrumbs. Stir in the sugar. Gradually add the egg and milk and continue mixing until the mixture just comes together to form a dough.

Roll out the dough on a lightly floured surface until ½-inch (1 cm) thick. Cut out eight 3-inch (8 cm) circles using a plain round cookie cutter. Transfer to a large, lightly oiled baking sheet and brush each round with a little melted butter.

Bake in a preheated 400°F (200°C) oven for 10–15 minutes, until risen and golden. Remove from the oven and transfer to a wire rack to cool. While they are still warm, carefully slice each cake in half horizontally and return to the wire rack to cool completely.

Make the elderflower cream. Put the cream and elderflower syrup in a mixing bowl and whip until thickened. Spread the cream over the base of each cake, top with sliced strawberries and the cake lids. Serve dusted with confectioners' sugar.

3 🕐

SAVE ME TIME

Grilled strawberry zabaglione

Serves 4
Preparation time: 10 minutes
Cooking time: 10 minutes

> 1 pound (500 g) strawberries, halved or quartered, depending on size
> 3 egg yolks
> 7 tablespoons (100 ml) granulated or superfine sugar
> 6 tablespoons (90 ml) dry or sweet sherry
> 4 teaspoons (20 ml) confectioners' sugar

Divide the strawberries among 4 shallow 1¼-cup (300 ml) ovenproof dishes, or use a large 5-cup (1.25 L) dish if preferred.

Put the egg yolks, sugar and 4 tablespoons (60 ml) of the sherry in a large bowl and set over a pan of simmering water. Cook the mixture, whisking continuously using a handheld electric beater (or rotary hand or balloon whisk), for 5 minutes, until the mixture is very thick and frothy and almost fills the bowl halfway.

Add the remaining sherry and cook for a few more minutes until thick once more. Pour the mixture over the strawberries and sift the confectioners' sugar over the top.

Cook under a preheated hot broiler for 3–4 minutes, until golden, or caramelize the sugar with a cook's blowtorch. Serve immediately.

4

SAVE ME MONEY

Scrumptious strawberry scones

Makes 8
Preparation time: 10 minutes, plus cooling
Cooking time: 12 minutes

> 1 cup (250 ml) rice flour, plus a little extra for dusting
> ½ cup (125 ml) potato flour
> 1 teaspoon (5 ml) xanthan gum
> 1 teaspoon (5 ml) baking powder
> 1 teaspoon (5 ml) baking soda
> ⅓ cup (75 ml) butter, cubed
> 3 tablespoons (45 ml) granulated or superfine sugar
> 1 large egg, beaten
> 3 tablespoons (45 ml) buttermilk, plus a little extra for brushing
> ⅔ cup (150 ml) whipping (35%) cream
> 8 ounces (250 g) strawberries, lightly crushed

Place the flours, xanthan gum, baking powder, baking soda and butter in a food processor and whiz until the mixture resembles fine breadcrumbs, or rub in by hand in a large bowl. Stir in the sugar. Using the blade of a knife, stir in the egg and buttermilk until the mixture comes together.

Tip the dough out onto a surface dusted lightly with rice flour and gently press it down to a thickness of 1 inch (2.5 cm). Using a 2-inch (5 cm) cutter, cut out 8 scones. Place on a lightly floured baking sheet, brush with a little buttermilk, then place in a preheated 425°F (220°C) oven for about 12 minutes, until golden and risen. Remove the scones from the oven and transfer to a wire rack to cool.

Meanwhile, whisk the cream until it forms fairly firm peaks and fold the strawberries into it. Slice the scones in half and fill with the strawberry cream.

5

KIDS WILL LOVE THIS
Custard cream berry slices

Makes 8
Preparation time: 40 minutes
Cooking time: 13–16 minutes

> 12-ounce (375 g) package frozen puff pastry, defrosted
> 1 cup (250 ml) whipping (35%) cream
> ⅔ cup (150 ml) ready-made custard
> 7 ounces (200 g) strawberries, sliced
> 5 ounces (150 g) raspberries
> confectioners' sugar, sifted, optional

Roll out the pastry on a lightly floured surface and cut into 2 strips, 4 x 12 inches (10 x 30 cm). Space apart on a wet baking sheet. Prick with a fork and bake in a preheated 425°F (220°C) oven for 10–12 minutes, until well risen.

Slice each strip in half horizontally, lift off the tops and place, baked side downwards, on a separate baking sheet. Bake all 4 strips for 3–4 minutes more to dry out the soft centers. Leave to cool.

Whip the cream, then fold in the custard and spoon over 3 of the pastry strips. Arrange the strawberries and raspberries on top of each strip and then assemble. Add the last pastry slice, if desired, and dust with confectioners' sugar. Transfer to a large serving plate. This is best eaten on the day it is made.

STRAWBERRIES PROBABLY MAKE US THINK OF SUMMER MORE THAN ANY OTHER FRUIT, EVEN THOUGH THEY CAN BE BOUGHT ALMOST ALL YEAR ROUND. BUT REMEMBER THAT NO STRAWBERRIES TASTE AS GOOD AS THOSE THAT YOU HAVE GROWN OR PICKED YOURSELF.

6

LEFTOVER TO LUNCH
Rhubarb & strawberry compote

Serves 4
Preparation time: 20 minutes, plus standing
Cooking time: 20 minutes

> 1 pound (500 g) rhubarb
> 1 cup (250 ml) granulated or superfine sugar
> ⅔ cup (150 ml) water
> 1 vanilla bean
> 2 teaspoons (10 ml) rose water
> 13 ounces (400 g) strawberries
>
> **TO SERVE**
> mascarpone cheese or Greek yogurt
> ⅓ cup (75 ml) roughly chopped pistachio nuts

Cut the rhubarb into 1½-inch (4 cm) lengths and put them in a shallow, non-metallic ovenproof dish.

Put the sugar and water in a small saucepan over low heat and stir until the sugar has dissolved. Add the vanilla bean and rose water. Pour the syrup over the rhubarb, cover with foil and bake in a preheated 350°F (180°C) oven for 12–15 minutes, until just soft.

Meanwhile, hull and halve the strawberries. When the rhubarb is cooked, discard the vanilla bean and add the strawberries. Cover and leave to stand for 5 minutes. Transfer the fruit to serving plates, spoon some of the cooking liquid over each one and add a dollop of mascarpone or yogurt and a sprinkling of chopped pistachios.

7

BUT I DON'T LIKE ...
STRAWBERRIES

Strawberry cheesecake pots

Serves 4
Preparation time: 15 minutes, plus cooling and chilling
Cooking time: 2–3 minutes

> 2 tablespoons (30 ml) butter
> 5 digestive cookies
> 6 ounces (175 g) strawberries
> 2 tablespoons (30 ml) granulated or superfine sugar
> 8 ounces (250 g) mascarpone cheese
> 4 tablespoons (60 ml) whipping (35%) cream
> 4 tablespoons (60 ml) confectioners' sugar
> grated zest and juice of 1 lemon

Melt the butter in a small saucepan, then transfer to a food processor with the digestive cookies and process to fine crumbs. Divide the mixture between 4 glasses and press into the base of each. Chill in the refrigerator.

Meanwhile, put the strawberries and granulated sugar in a saucepan and cook, stirring continuously, for 2–3 minutes, then leave to cool. In a bowl, mix together the mascarpone, cream, confectioners' sugar and lemon zest and juice.

Fill the glasses with the mascarpone mixture and top each with the strawberries. Chill for 2–3 hours before serving.

WHY NOT TRY... GINGER RASPBERRY CHEESECAKE POTS

Follow the recipe above, but use gingersnaps in place of the digestive cookies, raspberries instead of strawberries and Greek yogurt in place of the mascarpone. Sprinkle the top of each dessert with 1 teaspoon (5 ml) chopped candied ginger.

8

FRIENDS FOR DINNER
Tuile baskets & cream

Serves 6
Preparation time: 40 minutes
Cooking time: 15–18 minutes

> 2 egg whites
> ⅞ cup (200 ml) granulated or superfine sugar
> 4 cups (60 ml) unsalted butter, melted
> few drops vanilla extract
> ⅓ cup +1 tablespoon (90 ml) all-purpose flour

> **FOR THE STRAWBERRY CREAM**
> 1 cup (250 ml) whipping (35%) cream
> 4 tablespoons (60 ml) confectioners' sugar, plus extra for dusting
> 2 tablespoons (30 ml) chopped fresh mint, plus extra leaves to decorate
> 8 ounces (250 g) strawberries, halved or sliced, depending on size

Put the egg whites in a bowl and break up with a fork. Stir in the granulated sugar, then the butter and vanilla extract. Sift in the flour and mix until smooth.

Drop 1 heaped tablespoon (15 ml) of the mixture onto a baking sheet lined with parchment paper. Drop a second spoonful well apart from the first, then spread each into a thin circle about 5 inches (12 cm) in diameter. Bake in a preheated 375°F (190°C) oven for 5–6 minutes, until just beginning to brown around the edges.

Add 2 more spoonfuls to a second paper-lined baking sheet and spread thinly. Remove the baked tuiles from the oven and put the second tray in. Allow the cooked tuiles to firm up for 5–10 seconds, then carefully lift them off the paper one at a time and drape each over an orange. Pinch the edges into pleats and leave to harden for 2–3 minutes, then carefully ease off the oranges. Repeat until 6 tuiles have been made.

Whip the cream lightly, then fold in half of the confectioners' sugar, mint and strawberries, reserving 6 strawberry halves for decoration. Spoon into the tuiles, then top with the mint leaves and the strawberry halves. Dust with sifted confectioners' sugar.

9

WATCHING MY WEIGHT
Low-calorie strawberry roulade

Serves 8
Preparation time: 30 minutes, plus cooling
Cooking time: 8 minutes

> **3 eggs**
> **1 cup (250 ml) granulated or superfine sugar**
> **1 cup (250 ml) all-purpose flour**
> **1 tablespoon (15 ml) hot water**
> **1 pound (500 g) fresh or frozen, defrosted, drained and quartered strawberries, or 1 can (15 ounces/425 ml) strawberries in natural juice, drained and quartered**
> **¾ cup (175 ml) natural fromage frais or natural yogurt**
> **confectioners' sugar, for dusting**

Lightly grease a 13 x 9-inch (33 x 23 cm) baking or jellyroll pan. Line with a single sheet of parchment paper to come about ½ inch (1 cm) above the sides of the tin. Lightly grease the paper.

Whisk the eggs and sugar in a large bowl over a saucepan of hot water until pale and thick. Sieve the flour and fold into the egg mixture with the hot water. Pour the batter into the prepared pan and bake in a preheated 425°F (220°C) oven for 8 minutes, until golden and set.

Place a sheet of parchment paper 1 inch (2.5 cm) larger all round than the baking pan on a clean damp tea towel. Once cooked, turn out the baking pan immediately, face down, onto this second sheet of parchment paper. Carefully peel off the lining paper. Roll the sponge up tightly with the new parchment paper inside. Wrap the tea towel around the outside and place on a wire rack until cool, then unroll carefully.

Add half the strawberries to the fromage frais or yogurt and spread over the sponge. Roll the sponge up again and trim the ends. Dust with confectioners' sugar and decorate with a few strawberries. Purée the remaining strawberries in a food processor or blender and serve as a sauce with the roll.

10

INSPIRE ME
Strawberry rose jelly & syllabub

Serves 6
Preparation time: 25 minutes, plus soaking and chilling

> **4 tablespoons (60 ml) water**
> **1 envelope or 1 tablespoon (15 ml) powdered gelatine**
> **5 tablespoons (75 ml) granulated or superfine sugar**
> **2 cups (500 ml) rosé wine**
> **8 ounces (250 g) small strawberries, hulled and halved**
>
> **FOR THE SYLLABUB CREAM**
> **finely grated zest of 1 lemon**
> **2½ tablespoons (37 ml) granulated or superfine sugar**
> **6 tablespoons (90 ml) rosé wine**
> **1 cup (250 ml) whipping (35%) cream**

Spoon the water into a small ovenproof bowl or mug, then sprinkle the gelatine over the top, tilting the bowl so that the dry powder is completely absorbed by the water. Leave to soak for 5 minutes.

Heat the bowl or mug in a small pan of simmering water for 5 minutes or until a clear liquid forms. Take off the heat, then stir in the sugar until dissolved. Cool slightly, then gradually mix into the rosé wine.

Divide the strawberries between 6 tall Champagne-style glasses. Pour the rosé jelly mixture over and chill in the refrigerator until the jelly is set.

Mix the lemon zest, sugar and wine for the syllabub together and set aside. When ready to serve, whip the cream until it forms soft swirls, then gradually whisk in the lemon zest mixture. Spoon over the jellies.

10 WAYS WITH CHOCOLATE

1

BASIC
Really moist chocolate slice

Serves 12–14
Preparation time: 20 minutes, plus cooling
Cooking time: 45 minutes

8 ounces (250 g) plain dark chocolate
1 cup (250 ml) butter
5 eggs
¼ cup (60 ml) light brown or muscovado sugar
1 cup (250 ml) self-rising flour
¾ cup (175 ml) ground almonds

FOR THE CHOCOLATE CREAM
⅔ cup (150 ml) whipping (35%) cream
5 ounces (150 g) plain dark chocolate, chopped

Melt the chocolate with the butter in a bowl over a pan of barely simmering water, making sure the bowl does not touch the surface of the water.

Beat the eggs and sugar until slightly thickened. Sift the flour over the mixture, then add the almonds and chocolate mixture and fold in until evenly combined.

Grease and line a 9-inch (23-cm) square cake pan. Turn the mixture into the pan and bake in a preheated 325°F (160°C) oven for about 35 minutes, until just firm. Transfer to a wire rack to cool.

Heat the cream in a pan until almost boiling. Remove the pan from the heat and add the chocolate. Leave until the chocolate has melted, then stir until smooth. Transfer to a bowl and leave to cool until thickened.

Slice off the top of the cake if it has risen in the center. Halve the cake horizontally and sandwich the halves with one-third of the chocolate cream. Spread the remainder over the top and sides of the cake, swirling it decoratively with a palette knife.

2

GIVE IT A TWIST
Flourless chocolate cake

Serves 8
Preparation time: 15 minutes, plus cooling
Cooking time: 50 minutes

10 ounces (300 g) plain dark chocolate, broken into pieces
¾ cup (175 ml) butter
2 teaspoons (10 ml) vanilla extract
5 eggs
6 tablespoons (90 ml) whipping (35%) cream, plus extra to serve
1¾ cups (425 ml) golden granulated or superfine sugar
1 handful of blueberries
1 handful of raspberries

Melt the chocolate and butter together in a large bowl over a pan of barely simmering water, making sure the bowl does not touch the surface of the water, stirring until the mixture is smooth. Remove from the heat and add the vanilla extract.

Beat the eggs, cream and granulated or superfine sugar for 3–4 minutes (it will remain fairly runny), then fold into the chocolate mixture.

Line the base and sides of a 9-inch (23 cm) cake pan with parchment paper. Pour the mixture into the pan and bake in a preheated 350°F (180°C) oven for 45 minutes or until the top forms a crust. Allow the cake to cool and then run a knife around the edges to loosen it from the pan.

Turn out the cake on a serving plate and top with a mixture of blueberries and raspberries. Serve with extra cream, if desired.

3

SAVE ME TIME
Chocolate brioche sandwich

Serves 1
Preparation time: 1 minute
Cooking time: 4 minutes

> **2 slices brioche**
> **1 tablespoon (15 ml) ready-made chocolate spread**
> **1 tablespoon (15 ml) butter**
> **2 teaspoons (10 ml) granulated sugar**

Spread one slice of brioche with chocolate spread, then top with the other slice.

Butter the outsides of the chocolate sandwich and sprinkle with the sugar.

Heat a grill, frying pan or sandwich maker and cook the chocolate brioche for 3 minutes, turning as needed.

4

SAVE ME MONEY
Chocolate cornflake bars

Makes 12
Preparation time: 10 minutes, plus chilling
Cooking time: 5 minutes

> **7 ounces (200 g) milk chocolate, broken into pieces**
> **2 tablespoons (30 ml) corn syrup**
> **¼ cup (60 ml) olive oil margarine**
> **4 cups (1 L) cornflakes**

Melt the chocolate with the syrup and olive oil margarine in a bowl over a pan of barely simmering water, making sure the bowl does not touch the surface of the water.

Stir in the cornflakes and mix well together.

Grease an 11 x 7-inch (28 x 18 cm) pan. Turn the mixture into the pan, chill until set, then cut into 12 bars.

THE HIGHER THE PERCENTAGE OF COCOA SOLIDS IN THE CHOCOLATE YOU BUY, THE LESS SUGAR IT WILL CONTAIN AND THE MORE INTENSE ITS FLAVOR.

5

KIDS WILL LOVE THIS
Real chocolate brownies

Makes 10
Preparation time: 15 minutes, plus cooling
Cooking time: 30 minutes

> 3 ounces (75 g) plain dark chocolate
> ⅓ cup (75 ml) butter
> 2 eggs
> 1⅓ cups (325 ml) raw sugar
> ¾ cup (175 ml) all-purpose flour
> ½ teaspoon (2 ml) baking powder

Melt the chocolate with the butter in a bowl over a pan of barely simmering water, making sure the bowl does not touch the surface of the water.

Whisk the eggs and sugar together in a bowl until the mixture is pale and creamy. Stir the melted chocolate into the egg mixture. Sieve in the flour and baking powder and fold together.

Grease an 8-inch (20 cm) square pan and line the base with parchment paper. Turn the mixture into the tin and bake in a preheated 375°F (190°C) oven for 25 minutes, until the brownies are firm on top and a skewer inserted into the center comes out clean. Cool in the pan for 5 minutes, then cut into squares.

6

LEFTOVER TO LUNCH
Chocolate hazelnut spread

Makes 1 pound (500 g)
Preparation time: 10 minutes, plus cooling
Cooking time: 5 minutes

> 12 ounces (375 g) milk chocolate
> 4 ounces (125 g) hazelnuts
> 2 tablespoons (30 ml) vegetable oil
> 2 tablespoons (30 ml) raw, granulated or superfine sugar
> 1 tablespoon (15 ml) cocoa powder
> ½ teaspoon (2 ml) vanilla extract

Melt the chocolate in a bowl over a pan of barely simmering water, making sure the bowl does not touch the surface of the water.

Grind the hazelnuts into a paste in a food processor. Add the oil, sugar, cocoa powder and vanilla extract and whiz again, to combine.

Pour in the melted chocolate and blend until the mixture is very smooth, warm and runny. Pour it into a 14-ounce (400 ml) sterilized jar and cover. Leave to cool and thicken slightly before using. It will keep for up to 1 month, covered, at room temperature.

BUT I DON'T LIKE ...
CHOCOLATE

Mixed berry chocolate roulade

Serves 4
Preparation time: 20 minutes, plus cooling
Cooking time: 15 minutes

> **3 large eggs**
> **½ cup (125 ml) granulated or superfine sugar**
> **½ teaspoon (2 ml) chocolate extract**
> **⅓ cup + 1 tablespoon (90 ml) all-purpose flour**
> **3½ tablespoons (52 ml) cocoa powder, plus extra to dust**
> **⅔ cup (150 ml) low-fat crème fraîche**
> **⅔ cup (150 ml) fat-free Greek yogurt**
> **3 tablespoons (45 ml) confectioners' sugar**
> **1 tablespoon (15 ml) chocolate sauce**
> **7 ounces (200 g) mixed berries, chopped, plus extra to decorate**

Grease and line a 12 x 8-inch (30 x 20 cm) baking or jellyroll pan. Whisk together the eggs and sugar until the mixer leaves a trail over the surface. Add the chocolate extract, sift in the flour and cocoa powder and fold in carefully.

Pour the mixture into the prepared pan. Bake in a preheated 400°F (200°C) oven for 15 minutes.

Place a clean tea towel on the work surface and put a piece of parchment paper on top. When the sponge is cooked, turn it out onto the paper, roll it up carefully and leave to cool.

Mix together the crème fraîche, yogurt, confectioners' sugar and chocolate sauce.

Unroll the roulade and spread the crème fraîche mix over it. Spoon the berries over the crème fraîche and roll up the roulade again. Dust with cocoa and serve immediately, decorated with extra berries.

WHY NOT TRY... STRAWBERRY & VANILLA ROULADE

Omit the cocoa, increase the flour to ⅔ cup (150 ml) and use ½ teaspoon (2 ml) vanilla extract instead of the chocolate extract. Use 7 ounces (200 g) strawberries to fill the roulade and serve decorated with extra sliced strawberries, if desired.

FRIENDS FOR DINNER
Tiramisu cheesecake

Serves 8–10
Preparation time: 20–25 minutes, plus cooling and chilling
Cooking time: 50 minutes

> **20 sponge fingers**
> **6 ounces (175 g) plain dark chocolate**
> **1½ pound (750 g) mascarpone cheese**
> **¾ cup (175 ml) raw or granulated sugar**
> **3 eggs, separated**
> **⅓ cup (75 ml) plain white flour**
> **3 tablespoons (45 ml) grappa**
> **1 teaspoon (5 ml) vanilla extract**
> **2 tablespoons (30 ml) very strong espresso coffee**
> **2 tablespoons (30 ml) coffee liqueur**
>
> **TO DECORATE**
> **chocolate curls**
> **2 tablespoons (30 ml) golden confectioners' sugar, sifted**

Line a 9-inch (23 cm) springform pan with a greaseproof cake liner or parchment paper. Arrange the sponge fingers over the base, cutting them to fit as needed.

Melt the chocolate in a bowl over a pan of barely simmering water, making sure the bowl does not touch the surface of the water.

Blend the mascarpone, sugar and egg yolks in a food processor until smooth. Remove one-third of the mix to another bowl, add the flour, grappa and vanilla extract and mix well. Add the melted chocolate, espresso coffee and coffee liqueur to the mascarpone in the processor and blend to combine. Remove to a large bowl.

Whisk the egg whites in a grease-free bowl until they are softly peaking. Fold two-thirds into the chocolate mixture and one-third into the white mixture. Pour the chocolate mixture into the sponge finger–lined tin. Pour on the chocolate mascarpone mixture, then spoon on the white mixture to cover the chocolate layer.

Bake in a preheated 400°F (200°C) oven for 45 minutes, then turn off the oven, leave the oven door slightly ajar and leave to cool in the oven.

Chill for 3 hours when cooled. Decorate with chocolate curls, dust with confectioners' sugar and serve.

9

Low-fat chocolate soufflés

Makes 6
Preparation time: 5 minutes, plus cooling
Cooking time: 20 minutes

- 2 ounces (50 g) plain dark chocolate, broken into pieces
- 2 tablespoons (30 ml) cornstarch
- 1 tablespoon (15 ml) cocoa powder
- 1 teaspoon (5 ml) instant espresso granules
- 4 tablespoons (60 ml) raw or granulated sugar
- ⅔ cup (150 ml) skim milk
- 2 eggs, separated
- 1 egg white
- 1 tablespoon (15 ml) cocoa powder, sifted, for dusting

Heat the chocolate, cornstarch, cocoa powder and coffee granules with 1 tablespoon (15 ml) of the sugar and the milk in a pan over low heat until the chocolate has melted. Continue heating, stirring all the time, until the chocolate mixture thickens. Remove from the heat and cool slightly, then stir in the egg yolks and cover with a piece of parchment paper.

Whisk all the egg whites in a grease-free bowl until softly peaking. Gradually whisk in the rest of the sugar until the eggs are stiffly peaking. Fold one-third of the egg whites into the chocolate mixture, then fold in the rest of the egg whites.

Grease 6 heatproof cups or ramekins, each 6 ounces (150 ml), and spoon in the chocolate soufflé mixture. Bake in a preheated 375°F (190°C) oven on a hot baking sheet for 12 minutes or until the soufflés are puffed up.

Dust with cocoa powder and eat immediately.

10

Chocolate sorbet

Serves 6
Preparation time: 5 minutes, plus cooling, churning and freezing
Cooking time: 15 minutes

- 1 cup (250 ml) dark brown or muscovado sugar
- 7 tablespoons (100 ml) cocoa powder
- 1 teaspoon (5 ml) instant espresso coffee granules
- 1 cinnamon stick
- 2⅓ cups (575 ml) water
- 12 chocolate coffee matchsticks
- 2 tablespoons (30 ml) chocolate liqueur, to serve

Mix the sugar, cocoa powder, coffee and cinnamon stick in a large pan with the water. Slowly bring to a boil, stirring until the sugar has dissolved, boil for 5 minutes, then take off the heat. Leave to cool. Remove the cinnamon stick.

Pour the cooled liquid into a freezer-proof container, seal and freeze for 2–4 hours, until firm. Whiz in a food processor until smooth, then pour into a large loaf pan and freeze for 2 hours or until frozen solid. Alternatively, place in an ice cream maker and churn for 30 minutes, until frozen, then pour into a loaf pan and freeze for 2 hours.

Turn out onto a serving plate and arrange the coffee matchsticks over the top to decorate. Cut into slices to serve and drizzle 1 teaspoon (5 ml) chocolate liqueur around each portion.

10 WAYS WITH CREAM

1

BASIC

Pink grapefruit cream

Serves 4
Preparation time: 15 minutes

> **2 pink grapefruits**
> **5 tablespoons (75 ml) dark brown sugar, plus extra for sprinkling**
> **1 cup (250 ml) whipping (35%) cream**
> **⅓ cup (75 ml) Greek yogurt**
> **3 tablespoons (45 ml) concentrated elderflower cordial**
> **½ teaspoon (2 ml) ground ginger**
> **½ teaspoon (2 ml) ground cinnamon**
> **brandy snaps, to serve (optional)**

Grate the zest of 1 grapefruit finely, making sure you don't take any of the bitter white pith. Cut the skin and the white membrane off both grapefruits, and cut between the membranes to remove the segments. Place in a large dish, sprinkle with 2 tablespoons (30 ml) of the sugar and set aside.

Whisk the cream in a large bowl until thick but not stiff. Fold in the yogurt, elderflower cordial, spices, grapefruit zest and remaining sugar until smooth.

Spoon the mixture into attractive glasses, arranging the grapefruit segments between layers of grapefruit cream. Sprinkle the top with a little extra sugar, add the brandy snaps, if desired, and serve immediately.

2

GIVE IT A TWIST

Lime & passion fruit crunch tart

Serves 6–8
Preparation time: 30 minutes, plus chilling and freezing

> **7 tablespoons (100 ml) unsalted butter**
> **2 tablespoons (30 ml) corn syrup**
> **8 ounces (250 g) digestive cookies, crushed**
> **1¼ cups (300 ml) whipping (35%) cream**
> **grated zest and juice of 3 limes**
> **1 can (13 ounces/370 g) full-fat evaporated milk**
>
> **TO DECORATE**
> **3 passion fruits, halved**
> **5 ounces (150 g) blueberries**

Heat the butter and corn syrup in a saucepan, stir in the cookie crumbs and mix well. Tip into a greased 9-inch (23 cm) springform pan, and press into the base of the tin with the end of a rolling pin. Chill while making the filling.

Whip the cream in a large bowl until it forms soft swirls. Add the lime zest and condensed milk and gently fold together, then gradually mix in the lime juice. Pour over the base and freeze for 4 hours or overnight.

Loosen the edge of the tart from the pan with a round-bladed knife, remove the sides, then slide off the base onto a serving plate. Spoon the seeds from the passion fruits over the top, then scatter with the blueberries. Allow to soften for 30 minutes before cutting into slices to serve.

3 🕐

SAVE ME TIME
White chocolate & raspberry tiramisu

Serves 6
Preparation time: 20 minutes

> 3 level teaspoons (15 ml) instant coffee granules
> 7 tablespoons (100 ml) confectioners' sugar
> 1 cup (250 ml) boiling water
> 12 ladyfingers, about 3½ ounces (100 g)
> 8 ounces (250 g) mascarpone cheese
> ⅔ cup (150 ml) whipping (35%) cream
> 3 tablespoons (45 ml) kirsch (optional)
> 8 ounces (250 g) fresh raspberries
> 3 ounces (75 g) white chocolate, diced

Put the coffee and 4 tablespoons (60 ml) of the confectioners' sugar into a shallow dish, then pour on the boiling water and mix until dissolved. Dip 6 ladyfingers, one at a time, into the coffee mixture, then crumble into the bases of 6 glass tumblers.

Put the mascarpone into a bowl with the remaining confectioners' sugar, then gradually whisk in the cream until smooth. Stir in the kirsch, if using, then divide half the mixture between the glasses.

Crumble half the raspberries over the top of the mascarpone in the glasses, then sprinkle with half the chocolate. Dip the remaining biscuits in the coffee mix, crumble and add to the glasses. Then add the rest of the mascarpone and the remaining raspberries, this time left whole, finishing with a sprinkling of the chocolate. Serve immediately or chill until required.

4

SAVE ME MONEY
White chocolate & raspberry puffs

Makes 6
Preparation time: 20 minutes, plus chilling
Cooking time: 15 minutes

> 12 ounces (375 g) chilled ready-made puff pastry
> a little flour, for dusting
> ¾ cup +2 tablespoons (200 ml) whipping (35%) cream
> ½ vanilla bean
> 7 ounces (200 g) white chocolate, chopped
> 5 ounces (150 g) raspberries
> confectioners' sugar, for dusting

Roll out the pastry dough on a lightly floured surface until it is a rectangle that is ⅛ inch (3 mm) thick. Cut it into 6 rectangles, each 5 x 3 inches (12 x 7 cm), and put them on a baking sheet. Chill for 30 minutes. Bake in a preheated 400°F (200°C) oven for 15 minutes, until the pastry is puffed and golden. Transfer to a wire rack to cool.

Put the cream and vanilla bean in a saucepan and heat gently until it reaches boiling point. Remove from the heat and scrape the seeds from the vanilla bean into the cream (discard the bean). Immediately stir in the chocolate and continue stirring until it has melted. Cool, chill for 1 hour, until firm, then whisk until it is spreadable.

Split the pastries in half crosswise and fill each with white chocolate cream and raspberries. Serve dusted with confectioners' sugar.

KIDS WILL LOVE THIS
Honeyed banana ice cream

Serves 4–6
Preparation time: 15 minutes, plus churning, freezing and setting
Cooking time: 8–10 minutes

> 1 pound (500 g) bananas
> 2 tablespoons (30 ml) lemon juice
> 3 tablespoons (45 ml) thick honey
> ⅔ cup (150 ml) natural yogurt
> ⅔ cup (150 ml) chopped nuts
> ⅔ cup (150 ml) whipping (35%) cream
> 2 egg whites
>
> **FOR THE PRALINE**
> ¼ cup (60 ml) water
> ¾ cup (175 ml) granulated or superfine sugar
> 2 tablespoons (30 ml) corn syrup
> 1 cup (250 ml) toasted almonds

Put the bananas in a bowl with the lemon juice and mash until smooth. Stir in the honey, followed by the yogurt and nuts, and beat well. Place the banana mix and the cream in an ice cream machine. Churn and freeze following the manufacturer's instructions until half frozen. Alternatively, whisk the cream until it forms soft swirls, then fold into the banana mix and freeze in a plastic container for 3–4 hours, until partially frozen.

Whisk the egg whites lightly until they form soft peaks. Add to the ice cream machine and continue to churn and freeze until completely frozen. Alternatively, break up the ice cream in the plastic container with a fork, then fold in the whisked egg white and freeze until firm.

Make the praline. Pour the water into a heavy saucepan and add the sugar and corn syrup. Simmer gently until the sugar has dissolved, then cook to a caramel-colored syrup. Place the toasted almonds on a lightly greased piece of foil and pour the syrup over. Leave to set for 1 hour. Once set, break up into irregular pieces and serve with the ice cream.

LEFTOVER TO LUNCH
Gingered profiteroles

Serves 4
Preparation time: 35 minutes, plus cooling
Cooking time: 20 minutes

> ⅔ cup (150 ml) water
> ¼ cup (60 ml) unsalted butter
> 1 pinch of salt
> ½ cup (125 ml) all-purpose flour, sifted
> 2 eggs
> ½ teaspoon (2 ml) vanilla extract
> 1 cup (250 ml) whipping (35%) cream
> ¼–⅓ (60–75 ml) crystallized or glacé ginger, finely chopped
>
> **FOR THE SAUCE**
> 5 ounces (150 g) plain dark chocolate, broken into pieces
> ⅔ cup (150 ml) 1% or 2% milk
> ¼ cup (60 ml) granulated or superfine sugar
> 2 tablespoons (30 ml) brandy

Pour the water into a medium saucepan, add the butter and salt and heat until the butter has melted. Bring up to a boil, then take off the heat and stir in the flour. Put the pan back on the heat and cook briefly, stirring continuously, until the mixture makes a smooth ball. Leave to cool.

Beat the eggs and vanilla extract together, then gradually beat into the flour mixture until smooth. Spoon the mixture into a large piping bag fitted with a ¾-inch (1.5 cm) plain piping tip. Lightly grease a large baking sheet, then pipe on 20 balls, leaving space between them.

Bake in a preheated 400°F (200°C) oven for 15 minutes, until well risen. Make a slit in the side of each ball for the steam to escape, return to the turned-off oven for 5 minutes, then take out and cool.

Make the sauce by heating the chocolate, milk and sugar in a saucepan and stirring until smooth. Take off the heat and mix in the brandy.

Whip the cream until it forms soft swirls, fold in the ginger, then enlarge the slit in each profiterole and spoon in the ginger cream. Pile into serving dishes and drizzle with reheated sauce.

7

BUT I DON'T LIKE ...
CREAM

Neopolitan whirl ice cream

Serves 8
Preparation time: 20 minutes, plus cooling and freezing
Cooking time: 5 minutes

> 7½ ounces (225 g) raspberries
> ¾ cup (175 ml) granulated or superfine sugar
> ⅔ cup (150 ml) water
> 7 ounces (200 g) plain dark chocolate
> 2⅓ cups (575 ml) whipping (35%) cream

Press the raspberries through a sieve to make a purée. Heat the sugar and water in a pan until the sugar dissolves. Bring to a boil and boil for 2 minutes until syrupy. Leave to cool.

Melt the chocolate with ⅔ cup (150 ml) of the cream in a bowl over a pan of barely simmering water, making sure the bowl does not touch the surface of the water. Stir until smooth, then allow to cool slightly. Whip the remaining cream with the cooled syrup until the mixture is softly peaking.

Spoon half the cream and syrup mixture into a separate bowl and fold in the raspberry purée. Half-fold the chocolate mixture into the remaining cream and syrup mixture until marbled.

Put alternate spoonfuls of the raspberry and chocolate mixtures in a freezer container. Using a large metal spoon, fold the mixtures together two or three times until slightly mingled. Freeze overnight until firm.

Transfer the ice cream to the refrigerator about 30 minutes before serving. Serve scooped into bowls.

WHY NOT TRY...
STRAWBERRY-YOGURT ICE CREAM

Whiz 7½ ounces (225 g) strawberries in a blender until they make a smooth purée. Melt the chocolate with ⅔ cup (150 ml) whipping (35%) cream and fold it into 1¼ cups (300 ml) strained Greek yogurt. Add alternate spoonfuls of the strawberry purée and chocolate yogurt mix, fold together and freeze as above.

8

FRIENDS FOR DINNER

Peach & chocolate vacherin

Serves 6–8
Preparation time: 30 minutes, plus cooling
Cooking time: 1 hour, 30 minutes–1 hour, 45 minutes

> 4 egg whites
> ⅔ cup (150 ml) granulated or superfine sugar
> ½ cup (125 ml) light brown or muscovado sugar
> 5 ounces (150 g) plain dark chocolate, broken into pieces
>
> **FOR THE FILLING**
> ⅔ cup (150 ml) whipping (35%) cream
> ⅔ cup (150 ml) Greek yogurt
> 2 tablespoons (30 ml) granulated or superfine sugar
> 3 ripe peaches, pitted and sliced

Line 2 baking sheets with parchment paper and draw a 7-inch (18 cm) circle on each.

Using an electric hand beater, whisk the egg whites in a large bowl until stiff, moist-looking peaks form. Mix the sugars together, then whisk in the sugar, a teaspoonful (5 ml) at a time, and continue whisking for 1–2 minutes, until very thick and glossy.

Divide the mixture between the lined baking sheets and spread into circles of even thickness between the marked lines. Bake in a preheated 225°F (110°C) oven for 1½–1¾ hours or until the meringues may be easily lifted off the paper. Leave to cool in the switched-off oven.

Melt the chocolate in a bowl over a pan of barely simmering water, making sure the bowl does not touch the surface of the water, then spread over the underside of each meringue, leaving about one-third of the chocolate in the bowl for decoration. Leave the meringues to harden, chocolate side up.

Whip the cream, when ready to serve, until it forms soft swirls, then fold in the yogurt and sugar. Put one of the meringue circles on a serving plate, chocolate side up, spread with the cream, then arrange peach slices on top. Cover with the second meringue, chocolate side down. Decorate the top with the remainder of the melted chocolate, drizzled randomly.

9

WATCHING MY WEIGHT
Pavlovas
with orange cream

Serves 6
Preparation time: 25 minutes, plus cooling
Cooking time: 1 hour, 15 minutes–1 hour, 30 minutes

> 3½ ounces (100 g) plain dark chocolate, broken into pieces, plus a little extra, grated, to decorate
> 3 egg whites
> ¾ cup (175 ml) granulated or superfine sugar
> 1 teaspoon (5 ml) cornstarch
> 1 teaspoon (5 ml) white wine vinegar
> ½ teaspoon (2 ml) vanilla extract
> 1 cup (250 ml) whipping (35%) cream
> 2 oranges

Melt the chocolate in a bowl over a pan of barely simmering water, making sure the bowl does not touch the surface of the water, then leave to cool for 10 minutes. Whisk the egg whites in a large bowl until stiff, moist-looking peaks form. Gradually whisk in the sugar and continue to whisk until the meringue is thick and glossy.

Mix the cornstarch with the vinegar and vanilla extract, then fold into the meringue. Add the melted chocolate and fold together briefly for a marbled effect. Spoon the meringue into 6 mounds on a large baking sheet lined with parchment paper, then swirl into circles with the back of the spoon, making a slight indentation in the center.

Bake in a preheated 225°F (110°C) oven for 1¼–1½ hours or until the pavlovas may be easily lifted off the paper. Leave to cool.

Whip the cream, when ready to serve, until it forms soft swirls. Grate the zest of 1 orange and fold into the cream. Slice off the top and bottom of each orange, then cut away the rest of the peel. Remove the segments, add any juice to the cream, then spoon this over the pavlovas. Arrange the segments and grate a little dark chocolate on top.

10

INSPIRE ME
Rosemary panna cotta

Serves 6
Preparation time: 15 minutes, plus soaking, infusing and chilling
Cooking time: 15 minutes

> 3 tablespoons (45 ml) cold water
> 1 envelope or 1 tablespoon (15 ml) powdered gelatine
> 1¾ cups (425 ml) whipping (35%) cream
> ⅔ cup (150 ml) 1% or 2% milk
> 4 tablespoons (60 ml) thick honey
> 2 teaspoons (10 ml) very finely chopped rosemary leaves
>
> **FOR THE APRICOT COMPOTE**
> 7 ounces (200 g) ready-to-eat dried apricots, sliced
> 1¼ cups (300 ml) water
> 1 tablespoon (15 ml) thick honey
> 2 teaspoons (10 ml) very finely chopped fresh rosemary leaves
>
> **TO DECORATE**
> small sprigs fresh rosemary
> granulated or superfine sugar, for dusting

Spoon the water into a small ovenproof bowl or mug. Sprinkle the gelatine over and tilt the bowl or mug so that all the dry powder is absorbed by the water. Leave to soak for 5 minutes.

Pour the cream and milk into a saucepan, add the honey and bring to a boil. Add the soaked gelatine, take the pan off the heat and stir until completely dissolved. Add the rosemary and leave for 20 minutes for the flavors to infuse, stirring from time to time. Pour the cream mixture into 6 individual 6-ounce (150 ml) metal molds, straining if preferred. Leave to cool completely, then chill for 4–5 hours, until set.

Put all the compote ingredients into a saucepan, cover and simmer for 10 minutes, then leave to cool.

Dip the molds into hot water for 10 seconds, loosen the edges, then turn out the panna cottas onto small serving plates and spoon the compote around them. Lightly dust the rosemary sprigs with granulated sugar and use to decorate the panna cottas.

10 WAYS WITH LEMONS

1

Lemon meringue pie

Serves 6
Preparation time: 40 minutes, plus chilling and standing
Cooking time: 35–40 minutes

12 ounces (375 g) chilled ready-made sweet shortcrust pastry
  a little flour, for dusting
1 cup (250 ml) granulated or superfine sugar
3 tablespoons (45 ml) cornstarch
grated zest and juice of 2 lemons
4 eggs, separated
¾–1 cup (175–250 ml) water

Roll out the pastry thinly on a lightly floured surface and use to line an 8-inch (20 cm) diameter, 2-inch (5 cm) deep fluted tart pan with removable bottom, pressing evenly into the sides. Trim the top and prick the base. Chill for 15 minutes, then line with parchment paper, add macaroni or beans (to weigh down the pastry and prevent it from rising) and bake blind in a preheated 375°F (190°C) oven for 15 minutes. Remove the paper and macaroni or beans and bake for 5 more minutes.

Put ⅓ cup (75 ml) of the sugar in a bowl with the cornstarch and lemon zest, add the egg yolks and mix until smooth. Add the lemon juice to the water so that the total amount is no more than 1¼ cups (300 ml), pour into a saucepan and bring to a boil. Gradually mix into the yolk mixture, whisking until smooth. Pour back into the pan and bring to a boil, whisking until very thick. Pour into the pastry case and spread level.

Whisk the egg whites until they form stiff peaks. Gradually whisk in the remaining sugar, a teaspoonful, at a time, then whisk for 1–2 minutes more, until thick and glossy. Spoon over the lemon layer to cover completely and swirl with a spoon.

Reduce the oven to 350°F (180°C) and cook for 15–20 minutes, until the meringue is golden and cooked through. Leave to stand for 15 minutes, then remove the tart pan and transfer to a serving plate. Serve warm or cold with cream.

2

Tangy lemon cupcakes

Makes 12
Preparation time: 25 minutes, plus cooling
Cooking time: 15–18 minutes

½ cup (125 ml) soft margarine
⅔ cup (150 ml) granulated or superfine sugar
2 eggs, beaten
1 cup (250 ml) self-rising flour
grated zest and juice of 1 lemon
1⅓ cups (325 ml) confectioners' sugar, sifted
yellow or pink food coloring
sugar flowers, to decorate

Beat the margarine, sugar, eggs, flour and lemon zest in a mixing bowl or a food processor until smooth.

Divide the mixture evenly among foil cake cases arranged in a 12-cup deep muffin tin and spread the surfaces level. Bake in a preheated 350°F (180°C) oven for 15–18 minutes, until golden and the cakes spring back when gently pressed with a fingertip. Leave to cool in the tin.

Mix the confectioners' sugar with 4–5 teaspoons (20–25 ml) of the lemon juice to make a smooth, thick spreadable paste. Trim the tops of the cakes level if needed. Spoon half the icing over half the cakes and ease into a smooth layer with a wet round-bladed knife.

Color the remaining icing pale yellow or pink and spoon it over the remaining cakes. Decorate with homemade pastel-colored flowers cut out from ready-to-roll icing or use store-bought sugar flowers. Leave to harden for 30 minutes. Store in an airtight container for up to 3 days.

3

SAVE ME TIME
Cheat's lemon dainties

Cuts into 9
Preparation time: 25 minutes, plus chilling

> 8 trifle sponges, sliced in half horizontally to give shallower pieces
> 7 tablespoons (100 ml) butter, at room temperature
> ½ cup (125 ml) granulated or superfine sugar
> grated zest of 2 lemons
> 2 eggs, separated
> ⅔ cup (150 ml) whipping (35%) cream
> juice of 1 lemon
>
> **TO FINISH**
> 4 tablespoons (60 ml) confectioners' sugar
> 4 ounces (125 g) fresh raspberries
> 3½ ounces (100 g) blueberries
> fresh mint leaves

Line a 8-inch (20 cm) shallow square cake pan with plastic wrap. Arrange half the trifle sponges in a single layer in the base of the pan.

Beat the butter, sugar and lemon zest together until pale and creamy. Gradually whisk in the egg yolks.

Whisk the egg whites in a large clean bowl until stiff, then whip the cream in a separate bowl. Fold the whipped cream, then the egg whites into the creamed mixture. Gradually fold in the juice of ½ of a lemon.

Drizzle a little of the remaining lemon juice over the trifle sponges. Spoon the cream mixture on top and gently spread the surface level. Cover with a second layer of sponge slices, press them gently into the cream mixture and drizzle with the remaining lemon juice. Cover with an extra piece of plastic wrap and chill in the refrigerator for 4 hours or overnight.

Remove the top layer of plastic wrap, invert the cake onto a chopping board and peel off the remaining plastic wrap. Decorate with berries and mint leaves, dusting the tops with confectioners' sugar. Store in the refrigerator and eat within 2 days of making.

4

SAVE ME MONEY
Lemon angel-food cake

Cuts into 8
Preparation time: 30 minutes
Cooking time: 25–30 minutes

> ⅓ cup + 1 tablespoon (90 ml) all-purpose flour
> finely grated zest of ½ lemon
> 6 egg whites
> 1 pinch of salt
> ¾ teaspoon (3 ml) cream of tartar
> 1 cup (250 ml) granulated or superfine sugar
> crystallized rose petals or flowers, to decorate (optional)
>
> **FOR THE TOPPING**
> ⅔ cup (150 ml) lemon curd
> ½ cup (125 ml) sour cream

Sift the flour into a bowl, stir in the lemon zest and set aside. Whisk the egg whites, salt and cream of tartar in a large clean bowl until stiff but moist-looking. Gradually whisk in the sugar, a tablespoonful (15 ml) at a time, until it has all been added. Whisk for a few minutes more, until the meringue mixture is thick and glossy.

Gently fold in the flour mixture using a metal spoon and a swirling figure-of-eight action. Pour into a 8- or 9-inch (20 or 23 cm) nonstick tube pan. Bake in a preheated 375°F (190°C) oven for 25–30 minutes, until well risen, the cake is golden and it springs back when gently pressed with a fingertip.

Invert the pan onto a wire rack and leave to cool. As it cools the cake will fall out of the pan. When cold, mix the lemon curd and sour cream together and spread over the top of the cake. Sprinkle with crystallized rose petals or flowers, if using.

To crystallize flowers such as rose petals or viola, pansy or herb flowers, first make sure they are clean. Brush them with egg whites, then dust lightly with a little granulated sugar. Leave to dry for at least 30 minutes before using to decorate the cake.

5

KIDS WILL LOVE THIS

Lemon pudding cake

Serves 4
Preparation time: 20 minutes
Cooking time: 25 minutes

> ⅓ cup (75 ml) unsalted butter, at room temperature
> ¾ cup (175 ml) granulated or superfine sugar
> grated zest of 2 lemons, plus juice from 1 lemon
> 3 eggs, separated
> ⅓ cup + 1 tablespoon (90 ml) self-rising flour
> 1¼ cups (300 ml) 1% or 2% milk
> confectioners' sugar, for dusting (optional)

Grease a 5-cup (1.25 L) baking dish lightly, then stand the dish in a roasting pan. Put the rest of the butter in a mixing bowl with the sugar and lemon zest. Whisk the egg whites in a separate bowl until they are softly peaking. Using the still dirty whisk, beat the butter, sugar and lemon zest until light and fluffy, then mix in the flour and egg yolks.

Mix in the milk and lemon juice gradually until only just mixed. The mixture may appear to separate slightly, but this will disappear during baking.

Fold in the egg whites, then gently pour the mix into the greased dish. Pour hot water from the tap into the roasting pan to come halfway up the sides of the dish.

Cook in a preheated 375°F (190°C) oven for about 25 minutes, until slightly risen, golden brown and the top has begun to crack. Insert a knife into the center — the top two-thirds should be soufflé-like and the bottom third a saucy, custard-like layer. If it's very soft in the center, cook for an extra 5 minutes.

Dust the top with a little sifted confectioners' sugar, if desired, then serve immediately, spooned into shallow bowls. Don't leave the dessert to stand or the topping will absorb the sauce.

6 ⊕

LEFTOVER TO LUNCH

Lemon polenta cake

Cuts into 8–10
Preparation time: 20 minutes
Cooking time: 30 minutes

> 1 cup (250 ml) all-purpose flour
> 1½ teaspoons (7 ml) baking powder
> ¾ cup (175 ml) yellow cornmeal
> 3 eggs, plus 2 egg whites
> ¾ cup (175 ml) raw or golden granulated sugar
> grated zest and juice of 2 lemons
> 7 tablespoons (100 ml) vegetable oil
> ⅔ cup (150 ml) buttermilk
>
> **FOR THE RED WINE STRAWBERRIES**
> 1¼ cups (300 ml) red wine
> 1 vanilla bean, split
> ¾ cup (175 ml) granulated or superfine sugar
> 2 tablespoons (30 ml) balsamic vinegar
> 8 ounces (250 g) strawberries, hulled

Sift the flour and baking powder into a mixing bowl. Stir in the cornmeal and set aside.

Whisk the eggs, egg whites and sugar together in another bowl, using an electric beater, for 3–4 minutes, until pale and very thick. Fold in the cornmeal mixture, lemon zest and juice, vegetable oil and buttermilk to form a smooth batter.

Pour the mixture into a greased and lined 10-inch (25 cm) springform cake pan. Bake in a preheated 350°F (180°C) oven for 30 minutes, until risen and firm to the touch. Leave to cool in the pan for 10 minutes, then loosen the edges, turn out onto a wire rack and peel off the lining paper. Leave to cool.

Meanwhile, prepare the red wine strawberries. Put the wine, vanilla bean and sugar in a saucepan and heat gently to dissolve the sugar. Increase the heat and simmer for 10–15 minutes, until reduced and syrupy. Leave to cool, then stir in the balsamic vinegar and strawberries.

Cut the cake into slices and serve as a dessert with the strawberries and their syrup.

7

BUT I DON'T LIKE ...
LEMONS

Lemon, pistachio & date squares

Makes 15–20
Preparation time: 10 minutes, plus cooling and chilling
Cooking time: 20 minutes

> grated zest of 1 lemon
> 3 ounces (75 g) ready-to-eat dried dates, chopped
> 3 ounces (75 g) unsalted pistachios, chopped
> 3 ounces (75 g) flaked almonds, chopped
> ½ cup (125 ml) soft light brown sugar
> 1¼ cups (300 ml) millet flakes
> 1½ cups (375 ml) cornflakes, lightly crushed
> 1 can (13 ounce/370 ml) evaporated milk
> 1 ounce (25 g) mixed seeds, such as pumpkin and sunflower

Simply place all the ingredients in a large bowl and mix together. Spoon into an 11 x 7-inch (28 x 18 cm) baking dish and place in a preheated 350°F (180°C) oven for 20 minutes.

Remove from the oven, leave to cool, then mark into 15–20 squares and chill until firm. If you fancy, you could drizzle the top with some melted chocolate once the squares are cooled.

WHY NOT TRY... CHOCOLATE & ALMOND SQUARES

Make the mixture as above, omitting the pistachios and flaked almonds. Roughly chop 3½ ounces (100 g) blanched almonds and add to the mixture with 2½ cups (625 ml) bran flakes and 2 ounces (50 g) melted plain chocolate. Cook and cool, mark and chill as above, drizzling the top with melted white chocolate once cooled, if desired.

8

FRIENDS FOR DINNER
Classic lemon tart

Serves 8
Preparation time: 20 minutes, plus chilling and cooling
Cooking time: 45–50 minutes

> 14½ ounces (450 g) chilled ready-made sweet shortcrust pastry
> 3 eggs
> 1 egg yolk
> 1¾ cups (425 ml) whipping (35%) cream
> ½ cup (125 ml) granulated or superfine sugar
> ⅔ cup (150 ml) lemon juice
> confectioners' sugar, for dusting

Roll out the pastry thinly on a lightly floured surface and use it to line a 10-inch (25 cm) fluted tart pan. Prick the pastry shell with a fork and then chill for 15 minutes.

Line the pastry shell with parchment paper, add macaroni or beans (to weigh down the pastry and prevent it from rising) and bake blind in a preheated 375°F (190°C) oven for 15 minutes. Remove the paper and macaroni or beans and bake for a further 10 minutes, until crisp and golden. Remove from the oven and reduce the temperature to 300°F (150°C).

Beat together the eggs, egg yolk, whipping (35%) cream, sugar and lemon juice, then pour into the pastry shell.

Bake for 20–25 minutes or until the filling is just set. Let the tart cool completely, then dust with confectioners' sugar and serve.

LEMON DESSERTS PROVIDE A ZINGY, REFRESHING TASTE AT THE END OF A RICH MEAL. ANY SPARE LEMON JUICE OR ZEST CAN BE FROZEN FOR LATER USE.

9

WATCHING MY WEIGHT
Lemon drizzle loaf

Serves 12
Preparation time: 10 minutes
Cooking time: 35–40 minutes

> 1 cup (250 ml) butter, softened
> 1⅓ cups (325 ml) granulated or superfine sugar
> 1⅔ cups (400 ml) brown rice flour
> 2 teaspoons (10 ml) baking powder
> 4 eggs, beaten
> grated zest and juice of 1 lemon
>
> **FOR THE LEMON DRIZZLE**
> grated zest and juice of 2 lemons
> ½ cup (125 ml) granulated or superfine sugar

Grease and line a large loaf pan. Place all the cake ingredients in a food processor and whiz until smooth, or beat in a large bowl.

Pour the mixture into the prepared pan and place in a preheated 350°F (180°C) oven for 35–40 minutes, until golden and firm to the touch. Remove the cake from the oven and transfer to a wire rack.

Prick holes all over the cake with a cocktail stick. Place the drizzle ingredients in a bowl and mix together, then drizzle the liquid over the warm loaf. Leave until completely cold. Decorate with a twist of lemon zest, if desired.

10

INSPIRE ME
Lemon creams with raspberries

Serves 4
Preparation time: 5 minutes, plus chilling and standing
Cooking time: 5 minutes

> 1⅔ cups (400 ml) whipping (35%) cream
> ½ cup (125 ml) granulated or superfine sugar
> 7 tablespoons (100 ml) lemon juice
> 5 ounces (150 g) fresh raspberries
> 2 tablespoons (30 ml) confectioners' sugar

Heat the cream and granulated sugar together in a saucepan until the sugar has dissolved. Bring to a boil, then reduce the heat and simmer for 3 minutes.

Remove the pan from the heat, add the lemon juice and immediately pour into four 60-ounce (150 ml) ramekins. Set aside to cool completely, then chill overnight in the refrigerator.

Combine the raspberries and confectioners' sugar in a bowl and mash lightly. Leave to stand for 30 minutes, until really juicy. Spoon the raspberry mixture onto the lemon creams and serve.

10 WAYS WITH VANILLA

BASIC
Vanilla cupcakes

Makes 12
Preparation time: 10 minutes
Cooking time: 20 minutes

⅔ cup (150 ml) lightly salted butter, softened
¾ cup (175 ml) granulated or superfine sugar
1⅓ cup (325 ml) self-rising flour
3 eggs
1 teaspoon (5 ml) vanilla extract

Line a 12-cup muffin tin with paper or foil cake liners, or stand 12 silicone cases on a baking sheet. Put all the cake ingredients in a bowl and beat with a handheld electric beater for 1–2 minutes, until light and creamy. Divide the cake mixture between the paper, foil or silicone cups.

Bake in a preheated 350°F (180°C) oven for 20 minutes or until risen and just firm to the touch. Transfer to a wire rack to cool.

GIVE IT A TWIST
Vanilla crème brûlée

Serves 6
Preparation time: 20 minutes, plus standing and chilling
Cooking time: 25–30 minutes

1 vanilla bean
2⅓ cups (575 ml) whipping (35%) cream
8 egg yolks
⅓ cup (75 ml) granulated or superfine sugar
3 tablespoons (45 ml) confectioners' sugar

Slit the vanilla bean lengthwise and place it in a saucepan. Pour the cream into the pan, then bring almost to a boil. Take off the heat and allow to stand for 15 minutes. Lift the bean out of the cream and, holding it against the side of the saucepan, scrape the black seeds into the cream. Discard the rest of the bean.

Use a fork to mix together the egg yolks and granulated sugar in a bowl. Reheat the cream, then gradually mix it into the eggs and sugar. Strain the mixture back into the saucepan.

Place 6 ovenproof ramekins in a roasting pan, then divide the custard between them. Pour warm water around the dishes to come halfway up the sides, then bake in a preheated 350°F (180°C) oven for 20–25 minutes, until the custard is just set with a slight softness at the center.

Leave the dishes to cool in the water, then lift them out and chill in the refrigerator for 3–4 hours. About 25 minutes before serving, sprinkle with the confectioners' sugar and caramelize using a blowtorch (or under a hot broiler), then leave at room temperature.

SAVE ME TIME
Macadamia & vanilla tart

Serves 8–10
Preparation time: 30 minutes, plus cooling
Cooking time: 45 minutes

> 13 ounces (400 g) chilled ready-made sweet shortcrust pastry
> a little flour, for dusting
> ⅓ cup (75 ml) light brown sugar
> ⅔ cup (150 ml) maple syrup
> ⅓ cup (75 ml) unsalted butter
> 1 teaspoon (5 ml) vanilla extract
> 1¾ cups (425 ml) ground almonds
> 4 eggs, beaten
> 2 cups (500 ml) macadamia nuts, coarsely chopped

Roll out the pastry thinly on a lightly floured surface and line a 23-cm (9 inch) tart pan with removable bottom. Prick the base, line with parchment paper, add macaroni or beans (to weigh down the pastry and prevent it from rising) and bake blind in a preheated 375°F (190°C) oven for 15 minutes. Remove the paper and macaroni or beans and bake for 5 minutes more. Reduce the oven temperature to 325°F (160°C).

Heat the brown sugar, maple syrup and butter gently until melted. Remove from the heat and beat in the vanilla extract and ground almonds, followed by the eggs. Add half the macadamia nuts and turn the mix into the pastry shell.

Sprinkle with the remaining macadamia nuts and bake for about 25 minutes or until the filling forms a crust but remains quite soft underneath. Let the tart cool for 10 minutes, then serve with ice cream or cream.

SAVE ME MONEY
Vanilla & cocoa cookies

Makes 18
Preparation time: 15 minutes, plus chilling and cooling
Cooking time: 10–12 minutes

> ½ cup (125 ml) butter
> ⅔ cup (150 ml) granulated or light brown sugar
> 1 teaspoon (5 ml) vanilla extract
> 1⅓ cups (325 ml) all-purpose flour
> 1 tablespoon (15 ml) cocoa powder
> 1 large egg
> 1 egg yolk
>
> **FOR THE ICING**
> 1 cup (250 ml) confectioners' sugar
> 2 tablespoons (30 ml) water

Blend the butter, granulated sugar and vanilla extract in a food processor. Add the flour, cocoa powder, whole egg and yolk. Blend again until the mixture forms a ball. Knead the dough lightly until it is smooth. Wrap and chill for 30 minutes.

Roll out the dough between two sheets of parchment paper until it is ⅛ inch (3 mm) thick Cut out 15 hearts using a 2-inch (5 cm) cutter. Reroll the trimmings and cut out 3 more heart shapes. Leave the hearts on the paper and slide the paper onto 2 firm baking sheets.

Bake in a preheated 350°F (180°C) oven for 10–12 minutes, until the biscuits are firm and golden. Cool for 5 minutes, then transfer to a wire rack to cool completely.

Sift the confectioners' sugar into a bowl, add 1 tablespoon (15 ml) cold water, stir and add another 1 tablespoon (15 ml) water to make a smooth piping consistency. Put into a piping bag with a fine plain tip and pipe various designs around the edges of the cookies.

5

KIDS WILL LOVE THIS
Vanilla flowers

Makes 30
Preparation time: 30 minutes
Cooking time: 10–15 minutes

> ¾ cup + 2 tablespoons (200 ml) butter, softened
> few drops vanilla extract
> 6½ tablespoons (97 ml) confectioners' sugar
> 1⅓ cups (325 ml) all-purpose flour
> ⅓ cup (75 ml) cornstarch
> cake decorations, to decorate

Place the butter and vanilla extract in a mixing bowl and sift in the confectioners' sugar. Cream the ingredients together with a wooden spoon. Sift in the flour and the cornstarch a little at a time and fold in with a metal spoon.

Spoon the mixture into a piping bag, and pipe the mixture onto a baking sheet lined with parchment paper, making little flower shapes. To finish a flower, push the nozzle down into the piped flower as you stop squeezing. Press a decoration into the center of each one.

Bake the cookies in a preheated 375°F (190°C) oven for 10–15 minutes or until they are a pale golden color. Remove from the oven and allow to cool for a few minutes on the baking sheet before transferring to a cooling rack.

6

LEFTOVER TO LUNCH
Portuguese custard tarts

Makes 12
Preparation time: 25 minutes, plus cooling
Cooking time: 35 minutes

> 1 tablespoon (15 ml) vanilla sugar
> ½ teaspoon (2 ml) ground cinnamon
> 14 ½ ounces (450 g) chilled ready-made sweet shortcrust pastry
> a little flour, for dusting
> 3 eggs
> 2 egg yolks
> 2 tablespoons (30 ml) granulated or superfine sugar
> 1 teaspoon (5 ml) vanilla extract
> 1¼ cups (300 ml) whipping (35%) cream
> ⅔ cup (150 ml) 1% or 2% milk
> confectioners' sugar, for dusting

Mix the vanilla sugar with the cinnamon. Cut the pastry in half and roll out each piece on a lightly floured surface to a 8-inch (20 cm) square. Sprinkle one square with the spiced sugar and position the second on top. Reroll the pastry to a 16 x 12-inch (40 x 30 cm) rectangle and cut out 12 circles, each 4 inches (10 cm) across, using a large cutter or small bowl as a guide.

Press the pastry circles into the sections of a 12-cup nonstick muffin tin, pressing them firmly into the bottom and around the sides. Prick each pastry base, line with a square of foil, add macaroni or beans (to weigh down the pastry and prevent it from rising) and bake blind in a preheated 375°F (190°C) oven for 10 minutes. Remove the foil and macaroni or beans and bake for an additional 5 minutes. Reduce the oven temperature to 325°F (160°C).

Beat together the eggs, egg yolks, sugar and vanilla extract. Heat the cream and milk in a pan until bubbling around the edges and pour it over the egg mixture, stirring. Strain the custard into a jug and pour into the pastry shells.

Bake for about 20 minutes or until the custard is only just set. Let the tarts cool in the tin, then remove and serve dusted with confectioners' sugar.

7

Venetian rice pudding

Serves 4
Preparation time: 10 minutes, plus soaking
Cooking time: 20–30 minutes

- ½ cup (125 ml) sultanas
- 3 tablespoons (45 ml) medium sherry (optional)
- 2⅟₁ cups (625 ml) hot 1 % or 2 % milk
- ⅔ cup (150 ml) whipping (35%) cream
- 1 vanilla bean, split lengthwise, or 2 teaspoons (10 ml) vanilla extract
- ¼ cup (60 ml) granulated or superfine sugar
- ½ teaspoon (2 ml) pumpkin pie spice
- grated zest of 1 lemon
- ½ cup (125 ml) risotto rice
- strips of lemon zest, to decorate

Put the sultanas in a bowl with the sherry, if using, and leave to soak while you prepare the risotto.

Put milk, cream, vanilla bean or extract, sugar, pumpkin pie spice and grated lemon zest in a saucepan and bring almost to a boil.

Add the rice to the pan and cook on the lowest heat, stirring frequently, for 20–30 minutes or until the rice is creamy but the grains are still firm.

Stir in the sultanas and any sherry from the bowl and serve warm or cold, decorated with lemon zest strips.

WHY NOT TRY... COCONUT RICE PUDDING WITH MANGO

Put 5 ounces (150 g) short-grain rice, 4 cups (1 L) coconut milk and ⅔ cup (150 ml) granulated or superfine sugar in a saucepan. Bring to a boil, then reduce the heat and cook gently, stirring occasionally, for 25–30 minutes, until the milk has been absorbed and the rice is tender. Spoon into bowls and serve topped with 1 peeled, pitted and sliced mango and a drizzle of liquid honey.

VANILLA IS THE SECOND MOST EXPENSIVE SPICE AFTER SAFFRON. MOST VANILLA USED IN COOKING TODAY COMES FROM MADAGASGAR.

8

Vanilla soufflés & apricot coulis

Serves 8
Preparation time: 25 minutes
Cooking time: 25 minutes

- ⅓ cup (75 ml) granulated or superfine sugar, plus extra for dusting
- 7 ounces (200 g) ready-to-eat dried apricots, coarsely chopped
- ½ cup (125 ml) water, plus 1 tablespoon (15 ml)
- 3 tablespoons (45 ml) cornstarch
- 5 tablespoons (75 ml) Cointreau or other orange-flavoured liqueur
- ⅔ cup (150 ml) 1% or 2% milk
- 1 teaspoon (5 ml) vanilla extract
- ½ cup (125 ml) whipping (35%) cream
- 4 eggs, separated
- confectioners' sugar, for dusting

Grease 8 ramekin dishes and dust each one lightly with granulated sugar. Put the apricots in a small pan with the water and simmer gently for 3 minutes, until softened. Blend ½ teaspoon (2 ml) of the cornstarch with 1 tablespoon (15 ml) water and add it to the pan. Cook gently for 1 minute or until the sauce has thickened.

Put the mixture in a food processor or blender, add the liqueur and blend until smooth. Divide the mixture among the ramekins.

Blend the remaining cornstarch in a pan with a little of the milk. Add the remaining milk and heat gently, stirring, until thickened. Stir in ¼ cup (60 ml) of the granulated sugar, the vanilla extract, cream and egg yolks and put in a large bowl.

Beat the egg whites until peaking and gradually beat in the remaining granulated sugar. Using a large metal spoon, fold the egg whites into the custard.

Spoon the mixture into the ramekins and put them on a baking sheet. Bake in a preheated 400°F (200°C) oven for 20 minutes or until well risen. Dust with sifted confectioners' sugar and serve immediately.

9

WATCHING MY WEIGHT
Vanilla muffins

Makes 12
Preparation time: 10 minutes, plus cooling
Cooking time: 20 minutes

- **1 vanilla bean**
- **¾ cup + 2 tablespoons (200 ml) 1% or 2% milk**
- **2¾ cups (675 ml) self-rising flour**
- **1 tablespoon (15 ml) baking powder**
- **⅔ cup (150 ml) granulated or superfine sugar**
- **2 eggs**
- **4 tablespoons (60 ml) vegetable oil**
- **¾ cup + 2 tablespoons (200 ml) natural yogurt**
- **confectioners' sugar, for dusting**

Line a 12-cup muffin tin with squares of waxed or parchment paper. Split the vanilla bean lengthwise, using the tip of a sharp knife, and place in a small saucepan with half of the milk. Bring just to a boil, then remove from the heat and leave to cool slightly. Remove the vanilla bean from the pan and scoop out the seeds with a teaspoon. Stir them into the milk and discard the bean.

Sift the flour and baking powder into a large bowl, then stir in the granulated sugar. In a separate bowl, beat together the eggs, vegetable oil, yogurt, vanilla milk and remaining milk. Using a large metal spoon, gently stir the liquid into the flour until only just combined.

Divide the mixture between the muffin cuse and bake in a preheated 400°F (200°C) oven for about 20 minutes, until well risen and golden. Transfer to a wire rack and dust with confectioners' sugar. Serve slightly warm.

10

INSPIRE ME
Florentine vanilla cheesecake

Serves 8–10
Preparation time: 25 minutes, plus chilling
Cooking time: 45 minutes

- **4 ounces (125 g) plain dark chocolate**
- **½ cup (125 ml) slivered almonds, lightly toasted**
- **2½ tablespoons (37 ml) glacé citrus rind, finely chopped**
- **6 glacé cherries, finely chopped**
- **6 ounces (175 g) digestive cookies, crushed**
- **¼ cup (60 ml) unsalted butter, melted**
- **15 ounces (475 g) cream cheese**
- **1 teaspoon (5 ml) vanilla extract**
- **⅔ cup (150 ml) whipping (35%) cream**
- **⅔ cup (150 ml) Greek yogurt**
- **⅔ cup (150 ml) granulated or superfine sugar**
- **3 eggs**

Grease a 8-inch (20 cm) cake pan with removable bottom and line the sides with a strip of parchment paper. Chop half the chocolate into small pieces. Lightly crush the almonds and mix them in a bowl with the chocolate, glacé fruit, cookie crumbs and butter. Stir the mixture until well combined, then turn into the pan, packing it into the bottom and slightly up the sides to form a shell.

Beat the cream cheese and vanilla extract in a bowl until smooth. Beat in the cream, yogurt, sugar and eggs to make a smooth batter.

Pour the egg mixture over the base and bake in a preheated 325°F (160°C) oven for 45 minutes or until the surface feels just firm around the edges but is still wobbly in the center. Turn off the heat and let the cheesecake cool in the oven. Transfer to the fridge and chill well.

Transfer to a serving plate and peel away the lining paper. Melt the remaining chocolate and drizzle it around the top edges of the cheesecake. Chill until ready to serve.

INDEX

Italic pagination refers to the at-a-glance recipes

ACKNOWLEDGMENTS

Executive editor: Eleanor Maxfield
Designer: Jaz Bahra
Production: Caroline Alberti

Photography copyright © Octopus Publishing Group Limited 41 top, 56 top, 161 right, 198 bottom, 244 top, 247 top; /Frank Adam 188 left, 212 left; /Stephen Conroy 20, 26, 33, 35 left, 40 right, 41 bottom, 48, 50 top, 51 right, 52 right, 59 top, 68 top, 69 right, 72, 73, 74 bottom, 76 left, 76 right, 87 bottom, 90 bottom, 91 bottom, 97 bottom, 102 top, 103 bottom, 108 top, 109 bottom, 110 left, 118 top, 119 bottom, 122, 125 bottom, 129, 130 bottom, 130 top, 132 bottom, 136 bottom, 141, 144 right, 151, 153 bottom, 154 top, 160 left, 160 right, 186 top, 188 right, 189 top, 190, 191, 192 top, 193 bottom, 193 top, 202, 205 bottom, 210 top, 213 top, 222 bottom, 233 left, 238 top; /Vanessa Davies 245 bottom; /Will Heap 22 bottom, 24 left, 32, 60, 63 left, 66, 68 bottom, 71 bottom, 86 right, 96 bottom, 106, 131 left, 159 left, 175, 176 bottom, 184, 204 bottom, 208, 210 bottom, 211 left, 220 bottom, 231, 232 bottom, 233 right, 234 right, 235 bottom, 235 top, 237, 239 bottom, 244 bottom; /Jeremy Hopley 243; /Sandra Lane 177 right; /William Lingwood 58 right, 93 bottom, 116, 123, 155 top, 195 bottom, 196; /David Loftus 28 bottom, 87 top, 178 right, 179 top; /David Munns 15, 17 left, 17 right, 18 right, 19 top, 22 top, 23 left, 24 right, 25 bottom, 27, 28 top, 29 left, 29 right, 30 left, 30 right, 31 bottom, 31 top, 82, 83, 84 top, 85 top, 88, 89, 95, 99 top, 101, 102 bottom, 104 right, 105 bottom, 107, 108 tottom, 109 top, 138 left, 157, 201 top, 203, 206 right, 207 top, 226 top, 227 bottom, 227 top, 228 right, 229 bottom, 229 top, 242; /Sean Myers 14, 21, 23 right, 25 top, 51 left; /Emma Neish 150, 155 bottom, 220 top, 240 left, 241 bottom; /Lis Parsons 16 bottom, 16 top, 19 bottom, 34 top, 35 right, 36 left, 36 right, 37 bottom, 38, 39, 40 left, 42 top, 43 bottom, 43 top, 49, 52 left, 53 bottom, 57 bottom, 57 top, 58 left, 61, 62 bottom, 64 left, 64 right, 65 bottom, 65 top, 70 right, 71 top, 74 top, 75 top, 77 top, 84 bottom, 86 left, 90 top, 91 top, 92 left, 92 right, 98 left, 103 top, 110 right, 111 bottom, 117, 119 top, 120 left, 121 bottom, 124 bottom, 127 bottom, 137 left, 143 bottom, 145 bottom, 152 bottom, 153 top, 156, 158 bottom, 158 top, 159 right, 162, 163, 164 bottom, 164 top, 165 bottom, 165 top, 166 left, 166 right, 167 top, 168, 170 bottom, 170 top, 171 right, 172 right, 173 top, 174, 178 left, 179 bottom, 187 left, 199 left, 199 right, 200 left, 201 bottom, 211 right, 212 right, 213 bottom, 218, 221 right, 228, 230, 240 right, 245 top, 246 right; /William Reavell 18 left, 85 bottom, 121 top, 139 bottom, 142 bottom, 145 top, 161 left, 185, 192 bottom, 194 right, 195 top; /Gareth Sambidge 99 bottom, 205 top; /William Shaw 63 right, 70 left, 75 bottom, 77 bottom, 94, 97 top, 98 right, 100, 105 top, 118 bottom, 125 top, 135, 136 top, 139 top, 144 left, 167 bottom, 177 left, 187 right, 200 right, 206 left, 207 bottom, 221 left, 236, 238 bottom, 247 bottom; /Eleanor Skan 34 bottom, 54, 59 bottom, 93 top, 104 left, 176 top, 189 bottom; /Simon Smith 137 right; /Ian Wallace 37 top, 42 bottom, 50 bottom, 53 top, 55, 56 bottom, 62 top, 67, 69 left, 96 top, 111 top, 120 right, 124 top, 126 left, 126 right, 127 top, 128, 131 right, 132 top, 133 bottom, 133 top, 134, 138 right, 140, 142 top, 143 top, 152 top, 154 bottom, 169, 171 left, 172 left, 173 bottom, 186 bottom, 194 left, 197, 198 top, 204 top, 209, 219, 232 top, 234 left, 239 top, 241 top, 246 left.